ECONOMIC ISSUES, PROBLEMS AND PERSPECTIVES

ECONOMIC GROWTH IN THE 21ST CENTURY

NEW RESEARCH

ECONOMIC ISSUES, PROBLEMS AND PERSPECTIVES

Additional books in this series can be found on Nova's website under the Series tab.

Additional e-books in this series can be found on Nova's website under the e-book tab.

ECONOMIC ISSUES, PROBLEMS AND PERSPECTIVES

ECONOMIC GROWTH IN THE 21ST CENTURY

NEW RESEARCH

TARA ABRAHAMS
EDITOR

nova publishers
New York

For permission to use material from this book please contact us:
Telephone 631-231-7269; Fax 631-231-8175
Web Site: http://www.novapublishers.com

Library of Congress Cataloging-in-Publication Data

Economic growth in the 21st century : new research / editor, Tara Abrahams.
pages cm. -- (Economic issues, problems and perspectives)
Includes index.
ISBN: 978-1-63321-623-5 (hardcover)
1. Economic development. 2. Economic history--21st century. I. Abrahams, Tara.
HD82.E2852 2014
338.9--dc23 2014028263

Published by Nova Science Publishers, Inc. † New York

CONTENTS

PREFACE

Although the U.S. economic recovery seems to be on solid footing nearly five years after the official end of the Great Recession, this recovery remains slow compared with past recoveries. This book begins with a discussion on the possibility of restoring economic growth in the United States without a housing boom. It then continues to discuss the stimulating GDP growth and employment in the Euro area; Brazil after the neoliberal period; economic growth in China; cognitive human capital and economic growth; the strategic growth approach as a relevant economic growth modelling for the 21st century; economic growth, integration and research development in the European Union; and the inclusive growth impacts of fiscal policies in Asia.

Chapter 1 - This paper examines whether the U.S. economy can restore robust and sustainable growth without a housing boom. In particular, using time-series data covering the span of 1955-2008 this paper attempts to empirically test whether in the future non-residential investment and net exports can be major drivers of economic growth in the United States. A simultaneous equation model is developed to estimate the growth effects of non-residential investment and net exports. The results show that the share of non-residential investment in GDP has a significant and positive effect on economic growth. Additionally, the findings of the paper also indicate that net exports enhance economic growth.

Chapter 2 - More than five years since the onset of the global financial crisis in 2008 public debt to GDP ratios are of historical highs in advanced countries. As a consequence, fiscal retrenchment tops the agenda of ruling governments, in particular in the ailing Eurozone. Casual empirical observation shows, however, that government budgets deficits are often reduced or stabilized by cutting public investment expenditures or by postponing public investment projects. Given the growth enhancing effects of infrastructure investments, this fiscal retrenchment policy appears to be counterproductive and raises the question whether there are better alternatives available. One such an alternative, proposed by Dhont and Heylen (2009) calls for a switch in the composition of government expenditures from non-employment transfers towards more productive public investment expenditures. The potential growth and employment effects are particularly large in continental Europe (the Eurozone), since here the non-employment transfer to GDP ratio is significantly higher than that in Northern Europe or in Anglo-American countries. Thus, the question addressed in this chapter is whether, or how, a switch in the composition of public expenditures towards more productive public investment expenditures might enhance growth and employment without increasing the overall public debt to GDP ratio.

The present author finds – using an analytically tractable overlapping generations model with public capital and public debt – that, in general, while a reduction of structural non-employment transfers increases employment, it simultaneously decreases the capital-output ratio, and hence the impact on public investment expenditures and GDP growth remains ambiguous. However, in a numerically specified version of the model economy calibrated for the Eurozone, there is a clear positive impact on employment and GDP growth.

Chapter 3 - Since reforming and opening, China's economy has been maintained at double-digit rates for over twenty years, China's economy is steaming ahead at more than 7.5% even under the global lash of the international finance crisis. China has made outstanding contributions to world economic prosperity, which has been a necessary and desirable part of world economic, and affects the rest of the world economy. China's economy growth has gradually become the barometer of the world economy. While under the new trend of low carbon economy, China's economy growth is facing both opportunities and challenges. China's resource and environment have reached the highest value of the load-bearing capacity, strain in energy and sources supply, inefficient use of resources and eco–environment deterioration have become the bottleneck of economy growth. China's economy growth will be profoundly affected by other variables under the severe resource-environmental. This chapter embarks from China's basic conditions, the variables which affect economic growth are deeply explored. The nonlinear evolutionary model involving economy growth, energy-saving and emission-reduction, carbon emissions, carbon tax and new energy is built based on method of system science. The dynamic behavior of the system is analyzed, artificial neural network is used to identify the quantitative coefficients of the actual system according to the statistical data of China. By adjusting the evolution curve of economy growth when variables in the system changing, the variables which are sensitive to economy growth are found, and the potential impact of government control and other constraint conditions on economy growth are investigated further. A series of conclusions are carried out with the results in perfect agreement with actual situation.

Chapter 4 - This chapter explores the interdependency between economic growth and cognitive human capital, which is also described as cognitive skills or intelligence and is measured either as performance in scholastic achievement tests or IQ. It shows that unlike the mere amount of schooling, intelligence has been a robust predictor of economic growth in the recent past. Plausible mediators of the intelligence effect include greater labor productivity, better institutions, more competent management, lower fertility, and wider time horizons.

Based on the observation of secular gains in intelligence that have become known as Flynn effects, a theory of economic growth is developed that is based on the trans-generational reinforcement between rising intelligence and economic, technological and institutional advances. It provides a parsimonious explanation for the sustained nature of economic growth since the Industrial Revolution, and a conceptual framework for more specific theories and hypotheses.

The chapter arrives at projections of economic growth for the first half of the 21st century that are based on the empiric relationship between current prosperity, human capital, and economic growth. Longer-term predictions are based on our knowledge of the conditions that are required for continued Flynn effects, and of genetic limits to human cognitive development. The conclusion is that in most countries of Europe and North America, the limits of cognitive growth are being approached or have been reached already by the younger generation. There are ongoing Flynn effects in developing countries today. These countries are now reducing the cognitive gaps separating them from the developed countries, but most of them are expected to reach their cognitive limits before the end of the 21st century. Long-term developments after the end of the Flynn effect will be driven primarily by demographic trends. Without major changes in demographic behavior, intelligence is predicted to eventually decline slowly, ending economic growth in most parts of the world within the next 3 to 4 generations.

Chapter 5 - Globalization has highly increased the interconnection among the economies of the 21st century. A consequence is that local production plans may depend now on many international partners and providers. This, in turn, has led to the prevalence of production and complementation agreements among multinational firms acting on different countries. This mutual interdependence makes economic growth dependent of other economies' performances. For instance, a considerable part of the car production in a given economy requires importing spare parts and non-locally produced components. In this way, manufacturing processes in diverse economic sectors become internationally complemented through the interaction of local production with foreign raw and intermediate inputs. Many contributions in the literature conclude that the most of international trade is composed of intermediate and raw goods, which require local processing before reaching the final consumer. Trade agreements have fostered this process and helped firms in different economies to ground their production plans on free tariff inputs. In fact, local production and foreign inputs usually compete in the domestic market. In these highly integrated economies, the production of intermediate inputs in one economy becomes crucial for production of final or intermediate goods in associated economies. How we can model optimal economic growth in this context of interdependence?

Strategic growth models capture the mutual interdependence in economic growth assuming that the process can be conceived as a differential game. Players with conflicting interests must decide how to respond with contingency plans. The model presented here analyzes economic growth in the light of the theory of differential games to reveal new aspects of macroeconomic interrelations. This contribution presents a brief survey of the relevant literature, postulates a generic model and concludes by working out two examples in which the main features are interdependence of inputs and arms race.

Chapter 6 - In recent decades, there has been an unprecedented number of regional agreements constitute one of the crucial characteristics of international economic relations. Many developing countries and/or developed countries have begun to explore and participate in RIAs. The necessitated of regional integration has been emphasized by a combination of external and internal factors, such as the acceleration of the globalization process. In this study it is assumed that economic integration is very important, especially in strengthening and accelerating economic growth and promotes Research and Development (R&D). This work is based on two samples, the EU10 and the EU15 for the period (1981-2007) and (1995-2007) respectively.

Chapter 7 - A growing concern on widening income gap between the rich and the poor have resulted in an increasing volumes of research focusing on the nexus between equity and efficient growth. Developed countries have experienced the critical challenges and trade-off between their generous welfare provisions and economic growth. Developing countries in Asia are in the process of shifting their policy direction toward more inclusive growth. This has stimulated the need to better formulate policies of fostering inclusive growth. Asian governments used many forms of fiscal policy to mitigate income gaps because they will substantially undermine the economic growth if left unchecked. The objective of this study is to review the previous studies, particularly literatures related with inclusive growth of advanced economies, and to offer efficient policy options for Asian countries. In this study, policy measures are initiated which are based on experiences of advanced welfare economies. Lessons derived from them will be a meaningful guideline for Asian countries to achieve inclusive growth.

In: Economic Growth in the 21st Century ISBN: 978-1-63321-623-5
Editor: Tara Abrahams

Chapter 1

IS IT POSSIBLE TO RESTORE ECONOMIC GROWTH WITHOUT A HOUSING BOOM?

Atrayee Ghosh Roy*

Department of Economics, Minnesota State University, Mankato, Mankato, MN, US

ABSTRACT

This paper examines whether the U.S. economy can restore robust and sustainable growth without a housing boom. In particular, using time-series data covering the span of 1955-2008 this paper attempts to empirically test whether in the future non-residential investment and net exports can be major drivers of economic growth in the United States. A simultaneous equation model is developed to estimate the growth effects of non-residential investment and net exports. The results show that the share of non-residential investment in GDP has a significant and positive effect on economic growth. Additionally, the findings of the paper also indicate that net exports enhance economic growth.

Keywords: Economic growth, housing boom, non-residential investment, residential investment, simultaneity

* Phone: (507) 389-5328; Fax: (507) 389-6377; atrayee.ghosh-roy@mnsu.edu.

1. INTRODUCTION

Although the U.S. economic recovery seems to be on solid footing nearly five years after the official end of the Great Recession, this recovery remains slow compared with past recoveries. Federal Reserve Chair Yellen (2014) has stated in her speech "... while there has been steady progress, there is also no doubt that the economy and the job market are not back to normal health."

The recent episode of robust growth from 2002 – 2007 began with an unprecedented housing bubble. In order to help the U.S. economy climb out of the recession of 2001 the Federal Reserve lowered the federal fund rate from 6.5 percent at the end of the 4th quarter of 2000 to 1 percent in 2003. Initially, investment was very slow to respond even to this large decline in the federal fund rate. However, in the 3rd quarter of 2003 investment finally began to increase. Although the growth rate of non-residential investment was slow, residential investment started to pick up significantly from the 2nd quarter of 2003. Residential investment continued to grow until 2005 leading to an exceptional housing bubble which eventually did burst throwing the economy into the "Great Recession" of 2007.

Although housing indicators are showing signs of continuous improvement, the recovery of housing market is still weak. Federal Housing Finance Agency principal economist Leventis (2014) has made the following comments about the housing market:

> Home price appreciation in the fourth quarter was considerable, but more modest than in recent periods. It is too early to know whether the lower quarterly growth rate represents the beginning of more normalized price appreciation patterns or a more significant slowdown.

Many observers argue that the steep decline in residential investment during the Great Recession is responsible for the sluggish economic recovery. Researchers indeed find that residential investment usually plays a key role in both recessions and recoveries. Green (1997) contends that "......residential investment seems to lead the nation into and out of recession." Gjerstad and Smith (2010) argue in their paper that housing plays a key role in most recessions and recoveries because monetary policy affects the real economy through the housing sector both in recessions and recoveries. However, the expansionary monetary policy failed to stimulate residential investment in the recent recession because the "Great Recession" differs from past recessions. Gjerstad and Smith (2010) provide three main reasons for this historic anomaly. First, excessive mortgage credit resulting from a rapid inflow of foreign capital created housing bubble that primarily led the economy into this recession. Second, many households and financial firms experienced severe balance sheet problems when the housing bubble collapsed. As a result, a large number of households focused on reducing their debt rather than borrowing for new housing assets have remained unresponsive to the accommodative monetary policy. Third, in a saturated housing market monetary easing could not stimulate the new constructions that usually led most recoveries.

Yellen (2013) contends that "Before the Great Recession, housing investment added an average of 1/2 percentage point to real GDP growth in the two years after each of the previous four recessions, considerably more than its contribution to growth at other times. During this recovery, in contrast, residential investment, on net, has contributed very little to growth since the recession ended. ... I'm encouraged by recent improvement in the residential sector, but the contribution of housing investment to overall economic activity remains considerably below the average seen in past recoveries..."

Additionally, observers think that residential investment will not contribute much to economic growth in the future. Romer (2009) predicts the following about the future of US economic growth:

> ... it seems fairly clear that two of the pieces will be providing a smaller portion of demand in the future than they did in recent years. The first is housing. Housing investment as a share of GDP reached its post Korean War high in 2005, and it averaged more than 51/2% over the 2002-2006 period. We were building about 305 more housing units a year in the expansion of the 2000s than in that of the 1990s. So, a return of housing's share in GDP to close to its postwar average of 41/2 to 5% seems likely..... The second piece that will be providing a smaller portion of demand in the future is consumption. This leaves two components of output to make up the shortfall from declining housing investment and consumption: net exports and business investment.

Note that the history of the United States shows that the U.S. economy can have robust economic expansion without a housing boom. For example, during the period of 1962-1967 the U.S. economy indeed experienced one of the longest and strongest expansions with real GDP growing at an average rate of 5 percent per year and a low unemployment level shrinking from a little over 6 percent to just under 4 percent. Additionally, unlike the recent period of expansion in the 2000s, real median family income rose steadily. More importantly, economic expansion in the 1960s was not accompanied by large overvaluations of assets. Although the economic expansion ended in the 1960s largely as a result of both very large monetary and fiscal expansions that overheated the economy and overvaluations of specific companies, this episode of economic expansion was neither fueled by asset price bubbles nor produced major bubbles. Economic growth over this six-year period of expansion was mainly driven by nonresidential investment which rose at a healthy rate. The average share of nonresidential investment as a percentage of GDP was 11 percent in the 1960s. Notably, unlike the 2002-2007 expansion, during this period the economy ran trade surplus with net exports averaging close to one percent of GDP, the federal budget deficit hovered near zero and U.S. debt to GDP ratio declined from 45 to 33 percent.

The purpose of this paper is to examine whether it is possible to restore robust and sustainable economic growth in the United States without a housing boom. In particular, using time-series data covering the span of 1955-2008 this paper attempts to explore whether non-residential investment and net exports can be main drivers of future economic growth in the United States.

Model

The following regression equation is specified to estimate growth effects of non-residential investment and net exports in the United States.

$$Gr(Y) = a_o + a_1 Gr(K_r) + a_2 Gr(K_{nr}) + a_3 Gr(L) + a_4 (NX/Y) \tag{1}$$

where Gr(Y), Gr(K_r), Gr(K_{nr}) and Gr(L) are the growth rates of real GDP, residential capital stock, non-residential capital stock and labor, respectively. NX/Y is the share of net export in GDP. Model (1) indeed looks like the well known sources of growth equation derived in a conventional manner from the neoclassical production function, which takes on the familiar Cobb-Douglas form.

$$Y = AK^{\alpha}L^{1-\alpha}, \tag{2}$$

where Y, K and L are real GDP, capital stock and labor, respectively. A is a parameter which measures the total factor productivity and it is assumed to be greater than zero. Converting equation (2) into log linear form yields,

$$\dot{Y} = \dot{A} + \alpha\dot{K} + (1-\alpha)\dot{L}, \tag{3}$$

where $\dot{Y}$, $\dot{A}$, $\dot{K}$ and $\dot{L}$ are the growth rates of real GDP, total factor productivity, capital and labor, respectively. α and 1- α are the relative shares of capital and labor. In practice, researchers generally use the ratio of gross private investment to output in place of growth rate of capital. Following the common practice, this paper also substitutes the ratio of gross private residential investment to output, I_r/Y for $Gr(K_r)$ and the ratio of gross private nonresidential investment to output, I_{nr}/Y for $Gr(K_{nr})$. These substitutions are often made because researchers do not have actual capital stock data, only annual investment data. In fact, even the data on the U.S. capital stock from the U.S. Department of Commerce is estimated using the perpetual inventory method, which simply sums annual investment and applies an assumed rate of depreciation to adjust the accumulated investment over time. Reliable information on actual depreciation is not available, so an arbitrary assumption is made. This means that year-to-year variations in the time-series of capital stocks is effectively driven by annual investment from the national accounts, precisely, the numerators of I_r /Y and I_{nr}/Y, respectively. Econometrically, therefore, the use of I/Y in place of Gr(K) results in a different estimated value of the regression coefficient, but the substitution implies little if any loss of information or distortion of the significance of the relationships between the other variables.

To minimize omitted variable bias, terms of trade growth, Gr(TOT), is included in equation (1). Note that Easterly et al. (1993), Fischer (1993), Mendoza (1997), Bleaney and Greenway (2001), and Blattman et al. (2003) all confirm a strong and statistically significant relationship between growth and terms of trade growth.

The U.S. economic growth rate, however, varied substantially over the time span. Four such episodes of extended robust expansions are – 1962-1967, 1983-1989, 1992-2000, and 2002-2007. Four dummy variables for four episodes of expansions – D_{1960s} for the years 1962-1967, D_{1980s} for the years 1983-1989, D_{1990s} for the years 1992-2000, D_{2000s} for the years 2002-2007 – are included in equation (1) to allow for upsurge in growth rates during those periods of expansions.

Replacing $Gr(K_r)$ with I_r/Y and $Gr(K_{nr})$ with I_{nr}/Y, and adding Gr(TOT), D_{1960s}, D_{1980s}, D_{1990s}, D_{2000s} to equation (1) yields:

$$Gr(Y) = a_o + a_1(I_r/Y) + a_2(I_{nr}/Y) + a_3 Gr(L) + a_4(NX/Y) + a_5 Gr(TOT) + a_6 D_{1960s} + a_7 D_{1980s} + a_8 D_{1990s} + a_9 D_{2000s} \tag{4}$$

The coefficient estimates of equation (4) would most likely be biased and inconsistent due to the presence of likely simultaneity between Gr(Y) and I_{nr}/Y, and between Gr(Y) and I_r/Y. A number of researchers - Liu, Park and Zheng (2002) among them - found using time-series data that economic growth stimulates both housing and non-housing investment.

There is also a potential reverse effect running from net exports to economic growth. Both the Keynesian macroeconomic model and the more recent aggregate demand/aggregate supply macroeconomic model predict such a direct relationship because net exports are part of aggregate demand. Consequently, equation (4) is likely to generate biased and inconsistent coefficient estimates due to the possible simultaneity bias between economic growth and the current account balance. Ordinary least squares coefficient estimates will be biased and inconsistent in the presence of bi-directional relationships between dependent and independent variables.

The problem of simultaneity is, of course, best addressed using a simultaneous-equation model (SEM). Therefore, a SEM that explicitly specifies several hypothesized simultaneous relationships is constructed in this paper. Equation (4) thus becomes the first equation in the SEM, and other equations are introduced to estimate other likely bi-directional relationships between Gr(Y) and other variables.

Following Dibooglu (1997), the second equation of SEM, which explains the share of net exports in GDP, is specified in order to capture the reverse effect of economic growth on net exports.

$$NX/Y = b_o + b_1 Gr(Y) + b_2 RER + b_3 Gr(TOT) + b_4 Gr(Y_F) + b_5 D_{1960s} + b_6 D_{1980s} + b_7 D_{1990s} + b_8 D_{2000s} \tag{5}$$

where $Gr(Y_F)$ is the growth rate of trade-weighted average real per capita GDP of major US trading partners and RER is the real effective exchange rate. The share of net exports in GDP has fluctuated substantially over the time span and it has been negative since 1976. In fact, by 1987 the United States turned into a net debtor country for the first time since World War I. Out of four episodes of expansions, the share of net exports in GDP was positive during only the period of 1962-1967. Four dummy variables are included in equation (5) to allow for substantial changes in shares of net exports during those episodes of extended expansions.

There are also likely reverse effects running from economic growth to non-residential investment and from economic growth to residential investment. The following regression equation for I_{nr}/Y is specified to address the likely simultaneity between Gr(Y) and I_{nr}/Y.

$$I_{nr}/Y = c_o + c_1 Gr(Y) + c_2 Gr(K_f) + c_3 RLR + c_4 D_{1960s}, \tag{6}$$

Where $Gr(K_f)$ is the growth rate of net inflow of real foreign capital. RLR is the real long-run interest rate. D_{1960s}, the dummy variable for the years 1962-1967, is included in equation (6) since economic expansion in the 1960s was mainly driven by non-residential investment. All other variables in equation (6) are defined earlier in this paper.

In order to address the potential simultaneity between Gr(Y) and I_{nr}/Y, the following equation for the share of residential investment in GDP is specified.

$$I_r/Y = d_o + d_1 Gr(Y) + d_2 RLR + d_3 P_h/P + d_4 Gr(K_f) + d_5 D_{2000s}, \tag{7}$$

where all other variables except P_h/P are defined earlier in this paper. P_h/P is the housing price index relative to other goods. D_{2000s}, the dummy variable for the years 2002-2007, is included in equation (7) to allow for substantial overinvestment in the housing sector in the recent episode of expansion in the 2000s. Both equations (6) and (7) are based on the work of Sprout and Weaver (1993).

Equations (4) to (7) comprise the following full simultaneous equation system.

$$\begin{aligned}
Gr(Y) &= a_o + a_1 (I_r/Y) + a_2 (I_{nr}/Y) + a_3 Gr(L) + a_4 (NX/Y) + a_5 Gr(TOT) + a_6 D_{1960s} \\
&\quad + a_7 D_{1980s} + a_8 D_{1990s} + a_9 D_{2000s} + t \\
NX/Y &= b_o + b_1 Gr(Y) + b_2 RER + b_3 Gr(TOT) + b_4 Gr(Y_F) + b_5 D_{1960s} + b_6 D_{1980s} \\
&\quad + b_7 D_{1990s} + b_8 D_{2000s} + t \\
I_{nr}/Y &= c_o + c_1 Gr(Y) + c_2 Gr(K_f) + c_3 RLR + c_4 D_{1960s} + t \\
I_r/Y &= d_o + d_1 Gr(Y) + d_2 RLR + d_3 (P_h/P) + d_4 Gr(K_f) + d_5 D_{2000s} + t
\end{aligned} \tag{8}$$

2. DATA

Model (8) is estimated using annual data for the period 1955-2008. The Appendix provides a detailed description of variables and their sources. Some of the time-series variables in model (8) may be non-stationary. Granger and Newbold (1974) have pointed out that regression models containing non-stationary variables may generate spurious results, and when variables are non-stationary, conventional statistical tests are biased toward finding a significant relationship among variables in levels when none in fact exists. The standard method for testing the stationarity of a time-series is to test for the presence or absence of a unit root. Testing is normally extended to account for a deterministic trend. In this paper the well-known tests proposed by Phillips and Perron (PP) and Kwiatkowski et al. (KPSS) are applied to detect the existence of unit roots in the variables in model (8). The former test assumes the null hypothesis of a unit root, while the latter test assumes the null hypothesis of no unit root. Both tests are applied so that the model specification is not biased by which null hypothesis is chosen.

Table 1. Stationarity Tests

Variables	PP Test	KPSS Test
Gr(Y)	-6.307*	0.411E-01
I_r/Y	-3.169*	0.175*
I_{nr}/Y	-2.336	0.107
Gr(L)	-4.014*	0.206*
NX/Y	-2.358	0.133*
Gr(TOT)	-6.673*	0.118
RER	-2.619	0.687E-01
Gr(Y_F)	-4.641*	0.798E-01
Gr(K_f)	-8.651*	0.597E-01
RLR	-1.914	0.160*
Ph/P	-1.427	0.337*

Notes: * - significant at the 90 percent level. The critical value for the PP test with constant and trend at the 90 percent level is -3.132. The critical value for the KPSS test with constant and trend at the 90 percent level is .119.

Table 1 reports unit root test results. Gr(Y), I_r /Y, Gr(TOT), Gr(Y_F) and Gr(K_f) are stationary according to both the PP and KPSS tests. The PP and KPSS tests indicate unit roots in variables I_{nr}/Y, NX/Y, RLR and P_h/P. The PP test confirms the presence of unit root in RER, while the KPSS test results detect no unit root. The PP test indicates no unit root in the variable Gr(L) while the KPSS test confirms the presence of unit root. One common method of addressing the problem of unit roots in variables is to difference non-stationary variables prior to the estimation of the model. All variables that are found to have unit roots by either the PP or the KPSS test are differenced. All differenced variables are then analyzed with the PP and the KPSS tests and they are found to be stationary. All variables that are found to be non-stationary in levels are entered into the model in their first differenced forms. A time trend, t, is added to each equation to capture the effect of a potential deterministic trend in the variables estimated in levels.

3. Estimation Results

Model (8) is estimated using three stage least squares (3SLS). Table 2 reports the results. In the first equation that explains economic growth, the coefficient on the ratio of private non-residential investment to GDP is positive and significant at the 95 percent level. The positive coefficient estimate suggests that, all other things equal, an increase in the share of non-residential investment in GDP enhances economic growth. The coefficient on the share of private residential investment in GDP is positive and significant at the 95 percent level.

The coefficient on the share of net export in GDP is negative and statistically significant at the 95 percent level. The negative coefficient implies that a deterioration in net exports enhances economic growth, reflecting the effect of inflow of foreign capital on economic growth. Note that the largest component of the current account balance is net exports and the current account balance is the reverse side of the inflow of foreign capital. The coefficient estimate for Gr(TOT) is positive and significant at the 95 percent level. Hence, an improvement in terms of trade increases economic growth. Coefficient estimates of D_{1960s} and D_{1980s} are positive and significant showing that the growth rates of the U.S. economy were enhanced during both periods of expansions. The coefficient estimate of D_{1990s} is positive but insignificant. Notably, the coefficient on D_{2000s} is negative and significant. The last two episodes of extended economic expansions – one from 1992-2000 and the other from 2002-2007 - were accompanied by asset price “bubble” resulting in overinvestment in high-tech in the 1990s and housing in the 2000s. In both cases in the end the bubble did burst which led the economy into a recession –

a long and severe one in late 2007 while a mild one at the end of the 1990s expansion. The negative and significant coefficient on D_{2000s} reflects the effect of the collapse of the housing bubble and Great Recession on economic growth.

Table 2. Estimated Equations

Equation 1 **Gr(Y)**	**Equation 2** **NX/Y**	**Equation 3** **I_{nr} /Y**	**Equation 4** **I_r/Y**
1.71I_r/Y	-0.18Gr(Y)	0.13Gr(Y)	0.18Gr(Y)
(5.26)**	(-4.39)**	(3.86)**	(5.89)**
1.56I_{nr}/Y	0.20E-01RER	0.54E-03Gr(K_f)	-0.51E-01RLR
(4.44)**	(1.26)	(1.28)	(-0.93)
0.19Gr(L)	0.43E-01Gr(TOT)	0.80E-01RLR	0.16E-01P_h/P
(0.69)	(2.25)**	(1.43)	(0.41)
-1.40NX/Y	0.99E-01Gr(Y_F)	0.12E-02D1960s	-0.34E-03Gr(K_f)
(-4.52)**	(1.99)**	(0.52)	(-.80)
0.13Gr(TOT)	0.18E-02D_{1960s}	0.24E-04t	0.14E-01D_{2000s}
(2.40)**	(0.81)	(0.52)	(6.09)**
0.17E-01D_{1960s}	0.45E-03D_{1980s}	-0.47E-02	-0.19E-03t
(3.06)**	(0.20)	(-2.55)**	(-3.60)
0.12E-01D_{1980s}	-0.28E-02D_{1990s}		0.44E-01
(2.19)**	(-1.21)		(23.55)**
0.40E-02D_{1990s}	-0.46E-02D_{2000s}		
(0.63)	(-1.53)		
-0.21E-01D_{2000s}	0.68E-04t		
(-2.23)**	(0.91)		
0.23E-03t	0.12E-02		
(1.14)	(0.54)		
-0.60E-01			
(-3.37)**			

Notes: t-ratios are in parentheses; E indicates scientific notation.
**-significant at the 95 percent level.
*-significant at the 90 percent level.

In the second equation, the equation for NX/Y, the coefficient estimate for Gr(Y), is negative and significant at the 95 percent level, implying that as the U.S. economy grows the share of net exports in GDP deteriorates or inflow of foreign capital increases. The negative and significant coefficient of Gr(Y) verifies the fact that the relationship between NX/Y and Gr(Y) is bi-directional, which implies that the use of a simultaneous-equation model is justified. The largest component of the current account is net exports and evidence on current account deficit and economic growth indicates that since 1980 most episodes of downward trend in current account deficit in industrialized countries have been occurring during economic slowdown. A fair number of studies also argue that one of the key drivers of the growing U.S. current account deficit is the robust U.S. economic growth, which thus supports the finding of this study that net exports deteriorate or trade deficits rise as U.S. economic growth enhances.

The coefficient estimate for $Gr(Y_F)$ is positive and significant. All other things equal, the growth of the economies of major US trading partners improves the U.S. trade balance while the growth of the U.S. economy deteriorates the U.S. trade balance or net exports. The coefficient on Gr(TOT) is positive and significant at the 95 percent level. Hence, an improvement in terms of trade improves net exports.

In the third equation, the equation for the non-residential investment share, the coefficient estimate of Gr(Y) is positive and significant at the 95 percent level, which confirms the simultaneity between Gr(Y) and I_{nr}/Y. The positive coefficient indicates that as the economy grows, the share of non-residential investment increases. All other variables are insignificant. This equation, however, is not excluded from the model because it does capture the reverse relationship between growth and private non-residential investment, which might cause the simultaneity bias in the first equation if this equation is left out from the model.

In the last equation, which explains the private residential investment to income ratio, I_r/Y, the coefficient on the growth rate of real GDP is positive and significant at the 95 percent level. This captures the reverse relationship between growth and residential investment. As expected, the coefficient on D_{2000s} is positive and significant, reflecting overinvestment in the housing sector in the recent episode of expansion in the 2000s.

Conclusion

This paper shows that the share of non-residential investment in GDP has a significant and strong effect on economic growth. As explained earlier, in the future residential investment is not likely to play a central role in enhancing economic growth. Romer (2009) argues that "Nonhousing business investment is likely to be central to filling any demand shortfall in the long run." The results of this paper support the view that non-residential investment can be a major future driver of economic growth. Furthermore, it is also found that the relationships between economic growth and non-residential investment and between economic growth and residential investment are bi-directional. The use of a simultaneous equation model is therefore justified.

Additionally, this paper also finds that net exports increase economic growth reflecting the effect of foreign capital inflow on economic growth. The results confirm a reverse relationship between net exports and economic growth, which further justifies the use of a simultaneous equation model. However, the estimate of the growth effect of non-residential investment is significantly larger than the estimate of the growth effect of net exports. The United States has been running an exceptionally large trade deficits and concerns about the sustainability of trade deficits have been reflected in many studies. Many observers think that such large trade deficits are not sustainable in the long run. Therefore, net exports are not likely to be a significant driver of economic growth in the long run.

At the same time, it is very unlikely that the U.S. would be running trade surpluses in the near future. It is highly expected that the U.S. will continue to offer foreign investors an attractive haven because of its technological leadership and the history of its financial stability. Thus, even with the rise of national saving, it is still rational to expect domestic investment to exceed domestic savings which in turn implies a current account deficit. Additionally, returns on U.S. holdings of foreign assets have consistently been higher than returns on foreign holdings of U.S. assets, resulting in positive net investment income. Thus, many researchers predict that some trade deficit is likely to be sustainable for a considerably long time. Therefore, although net exports are not expected to enhance economic growth significantly, it is still likely that it will continue to make some contribution to economic growth in the long run.

In sum, the findings of this paper show that non-residential investment can be a key driver of economic growth. Although net exports share can contribute to economic growth to a certain extent, it will not play a very significant role in enhancing economic growth. One very important question that is beyond the scope of this study is how to stimulate business investment and innovation. Over the past five years the rate of accumulation of private capital stock has been very sluggish. Yellen (2013) has indicated in her speech that "….the slow recovery has depressed the pace of capital accumulation, and it may also have hindered new business formation and innovation, developments that would have an adverse effect on structural productivity." Hopefully, future research will address this question.

APPENDIX: VARIABLE LIST AND DATA SOURCES

Y	Real GDP – Bureau of Economic Analysis (BEA)
I_{nr}	Non-residential Investment – BEA
I_r	Residential Investment – BEA
I_{nr}/Y	Derived
I_r/Y	Derived
TOT	Terms of trade – Calculated by the ratio of export price index to import price index. Export and import price indices are from the International Financial Statistics, online version, 2011.
Gr(TOT)	Derived
RER	Trade weighted real effective exchange rate – Exchange rates of major trading partners (Canada, France, Italy, United Kingdom, Japan and Mexico) and the United States are from Penn World Data 7.0.
RLR	Real long-run interest rate (10-year government bond rate minus ation rate) – Calculated by subtracting the inflation rate from the 10-year Government bond rate. Inflation rates are based on the GDP deflator from the BEA and the data source for 10-year government bond rate is the International Financial Statistics, online version, 2011.
L	Labor force – Economic Report of the President
N	Population – Economic Report of the President
K_f	Net inflow of real foreign capital - Calculated by subtracting import from export and adding net foreign factor income from abroad. The data source for net foreign factor income abroad is the International Financial Statistics, online version, 2011. The net inflow of real foreign capital is derived by

	dividing the net inflow of nominal foreign capital by the GDP deflator.
Y_F:	Alan Heston, Robert Summers, and Bettina Aten Pen world table version 7.0 is the data source for per capita real GDP for major trading partners and U.S. Bureau of Census is the data source for the trade weights.
$Gr(Y_F)$	derived
X	Export - International Monetary Fund, *International Financial Statistics*, online version, 2011.
X/Y	Share of export in GDP – derived.
Ph	BEA
P	GDP deflator

REFERENCES

Blattman, C., Hwarn, J. & Williamson, J. G. (2003). T*he terms of trade and economic growth in the periphery* 1870-1983, NBER Working Paper No. 9940.

Bleaney, M. & Greenaway, D. (2001). The impact of terms of trade and real exchange rate volatility on investment and growth in Sub-Saharan Africa, *Journal of Development Economics,* 65: 491-500.

Dibooglu, S. (1997). Accounting for U.S. current account deficits: An empirical investigation. *Applied Economics,* 29, 787-793.

Easterly, W., Kremer, M., Pritchett, L. & Summers, L. H. (1993). Good policy or good luck? Country growth performance and temporary shocks, *Journal of Monetary Economics,* 32, 459-483.

Fischer, S. (1993). The role of macroeconomic factors in growth. *Journal of Monetary Economics,* 32, 485-512.

Green, R. K. (1997). Follow the leader: How changes in residential and non-residential investment predict changes in GDP. *Real Estate Economics,* 25, 253-70.

Gjerstad, S., & Smith, V. L. (2010). *Household expenditure cycles and economic cycles,* 1920-2010, unpublished manuscript, Chapman University.

Granger, C. W. J. & Newbold, P. (1974). Spurious regression in economics, *Journal of Econometrics,* 4, 205-210.

Kwiatkowski, D., Phillips, P. C. B. & Schmidt, P. and Shin, Y. (1992). Testing the null hypothesis of stationarity against the alternative of a unit root, *Journal of Econometrics,* 54, 159-178.

Liu, Hongyu, Yun W. Park, & Zheng Siqi (2002). The interaction between housing investment and economic growth in China, *International Real Estate Review,* 5, 40-60.

Leventis, A. (2014). *FHFA house price index rises for tenth consecutive quarter,* FHFA News Release, February 25, 2014.

Mendoza, E. G. (1997). Terms of trade uncertainty and economic growth, *Journal of Development Economics*, 54, 323-356.

Phillips, P. C. B. & Perron, P. (1988). Testing for a unit root in time series regression', Biometrika. 75, 335-346.

Romer, C. D. (2009). *Growth without bubbles,* Speech, Council on Foreign Relations.

Sprout, R. V. A. & Weaver, J. H. (1993). Exports and economic growth in a simultaneous equations model, *Journal of Developing Areas,* 28, 289-306.

Yellen, J. L. (2014). *What the Federal Reserve is doing to promote a stronger job market, Speech,* 2014 National Interagency Community Reinvestment Conference, Chicago, Illinois.

Yellen, J.L. (2013). *Challenges confronting monetary policy,* Speech, 2013 National Association for Business Economics Policy Conference, Washington, D.C.

Yellen, J. L. (2013). A painfully slow recovery for America's workers: causes, implications, and the Federal Reserve's Response, Remarks at "A Trans-Atlantic Agenda for Shared Property," *Conference Sponsored by the AFL-CIO,* Friedrich Ebert Stiftung, and the IMK Macroeconomic Policy Institute.

In: Economic Growth in the 21st Century
Editor: Tara Abrahams
ISBN: 978-1-63321-623-5

Chapter 2

STIMULATING GDP GROWTH AND EMPLOYMENT IN THE EURO AREA: FROM NON-EMPLOYMENT TRANSFERS TOWARDS PUBLIC INVESTMENT EXPENDITURES

Karl Farmer*
University of Graz, Graz, Austria

ABSTRACT

More than five years since the onset of the global financial crisis in 2008 public debt to GDP ratios are of historical highs in advanced countries. As a consequence, fiscal retrenchment tops the agenda of ruling governments, in particular in the ailing Eurozone. Casual empirical observation shows, however, that government budgets deficits are often reduced or stabilized by cutting public investment expenditures or by postponing public investment projects. Given the growth enhancing effects of infrastructure investments, this fiscal retrenchment policy appears to be counterproductive and raises the question whether there are better alternatives available. One such an alternative, proposed by Dhont and Heylen (2009) calls for a switch in the composition of government expenditures from non-employment transfers towards more productive

* Corresponding author: Karl Farmer. E-mail address: karl.farmer@uni-graz.at.

public investment expenditures. The potential growth and employment effects are particularly large in continental Europe (the Eurozone), since here the non-employment transfer to GDP ratio is significantly higher than that in Northern Europe or in Anglo-American countries. Thus, the question addressed in this chapter is whether, or how, a switch in the composition of public expenditures towards more productive public investment expenditures might enhance growth and employment without increasing the overall public debt to GDP ratio.

The present author finds – using an analytically tractable overlapping generations model with public capital and public debt – that, in general, while a reduction of structural non-employment transfers increases employment, it simultaneously decreases the capital-output ratio, and hence the impact on public investment expenditures and GDP growth remains ambiguous. However, in a numerically specified version of the model economy calibrated for the Eurozone, there is a clear positive impact on employment and GDP growth.

Keywords: Public capital, composition of government expenditures, public debt, structural non-employment transfers, overlapping generations model

INTRODUCTION

More than five years after the outbreak of the global financial crisis in 2008, public debt to GDP ratios remain are at historical highs in advanced countries. As a consequence, fiscal retrenchment tops the agenda of ruling governments, in particular in the ailing Eurozone.

Casual empirical observation and economic research show that often governments reduce budget deficits by cutting public investment expenditures or by postponing public investment projects. Given the growth enhancing effects of infrastructure investments, this fiscal retrenchment policy appears to be counterproductive and raises the question whether there are better policy alternatives available.

One such an alternative proposed by Dhont and Heylen (2009) calls for a switch in the composition of government expenditures from non-employment transfers towards productive public investment expenditures. However, such switch is easier said than done. Although the non-employment transfers are unproductive they remain (an essential) part of the national social compact, particularly in middle European countries like Austria, Germany and Italy. These countries are all plagued by a relatively high proportion of public transfers designed to subsidize structural non-employment (e.g. subsidies promoting early retirement). This can be contrasted with the situation existing in countries such as Denmark, Finland, Sweden and Norway.

Although the latter also collect high taxes and exhibit high government expenditure quotas (in contrast to the Anglo-Saxon world), the proportion of productive government expenditures (e.g. expenditures on investment in public capital) in northern European countries is significantly higher than in middle European countries (Dhont and Heylen 2009, p. 539 and p. 550). Thus, the question arises whether – commencing from both existing high public debt levels and high proportions of non-employment transfers in middle Europe – the suggested new public expenditure composition can indeed enhance growth and employment without increasing the overall public debt to GDP ratio.

To investigate this research question, an intertemporal general equilibrium model with non-neutral public debt is set up. A prime candidate for such a model is Glomm and Ravikumar's (1994) endogenous growth overlapping generations (OLG) model with public capital accumulation but without public debt. By introducing public capital (infrastructure) in Diamond's (1965) overlapping generations model the authors follow the seminal contributions of Barro (1990) and Futigami et al. (1993) in an infinitely-lived agent (ILA) intertemporal equilibrium model. However, while Glomm and Ravikumar (1994) investigate the characteristics of the balanced growth path, in particular, the growth-maximizing tax rate, they make no attempt to assess the impact of a switch in the composition of government expenditures.

In order to be able to explore the employment consequences of the proposed growth enhancing strategy we have thus to extend Glomm and Ravikumar's (1994) OLG model by introducing public debt and non-employment transfers. To this end, we follow the lead of Turnovsky (2000, 2004) and Dhont and Heylen (2009), who derive wage-elastic labor supply from intertemporal utility maximization in an infinitely-lived agent (ILA) framework. Regarding the employment and growth effects of a switch in the composition of public expenditures our OLG model is closest to Dhont and Heylen (2009). However, Dhont and Heylen (2009) neglect public debt, and while including a much richer fiscal policy package than ours, they merely offer a numerical solution for their model, thus leaving open the question of the sufficient conditions for the existence and dynamic stability of a steady-state solution. Such research lacunae set the agenda for the present work. We extend Glomm and Ravikumar's (1994) OLG model by introducing Dhont and Heylen's (2009, p. 544) unconditional or quasi-unconditional benefits for structurally non-employed people (benefits to early retirees for example). While this extension yields an endogenous labor supply, to arrive at a positive relationship between the real wage rate and labor supply we then have to assume a very special intertemporal utility function.

Given these assumptions, a specific form of intertemporal equilibrium dynamics with public capital accumulation and endogenous employment can be derived from the first-order conditions for utility and profit maximization, and from market clearing conditions. With these intertemporal equilibrium dynamics at hand, the existence and dynamic stability of steady-state growth equilibria can then be explicitly explored.

Thus, the chapter contributes to the existing literature in the following ways. First, we specify an intertemporal utility function such that in the case of structural non-employment transfers, younger households supply more labor when the real wage rate increases. Second, sufficient conditions for the existence and asymptotic stability of steady-state growth equilibria are presented. Third, the present author demonstrates analytically the steady-state impacts of a permanent reduction in unproductive government transfers on GDP growth, employment and public capital investment (hereafter, PCI) expenditures. Fourth, a numerical version of the analytical OLG model which depicts the average fiscal policy composition in middle European countries between 1995 and 2005 is used to show the quantitative effects of a reduction in the net transfer replacement rate on employment and GDP growth.

This chapter is organized as follows. In the next section, the structure of the closed-economy OLG model with public capital and public debt is described, and the related intertemporal equilibrium dynamics is derived. The following section is then devoted to the analysis of the existence and dynamic stability of the steady-state solutions. Following this, the comparative steady-state effects of a change in the composition of government expenditures towards productive public capital investment are then analyzed.

In the subsequent section, the present author then embarks on the politically more interesting question concerning the quantitative effects of a switch in the composition of government expenditures in middle European countries, i.e. the impact on employment, PCI expenditures, and GDP growth. Finally, key results are summarized and some conclusions drawn.

THE BASIC MODEL

Consider an infinite-horizon closed economy whereby $t = 1, 2, ...$ denotes discrete time periods. The model economy might be envisaged as the

Eurozone without Finland. This specification is empirically warranted since in spite of huge internal imbalances the current account of the Eurozone as a whole was roughly in balance for the period 1995-2005 (Fagan and Gaspar 2008, Farmer 2014). The model economy produces one good, a composite commodity which can be used for the purpose of consumption and for investment in private and public physical capital. The services of labor, private and public capital are combined to manufacture the composite good.

The model economy is composed of M perfectly competitive, private firms living for one period, of $2M$ private households living for two periods, and of a government living forever. The firms employ constant returns-to-scale technologies both with respect to private capital and to labor, holding public capital input fixed, and constant returns-to-scale technologies with respect to private and public capital, holding labor input fixed.

In order to preserve analytical tractability, the production technologies are specified as Cobb-Douglas production functions.

In the first period of its life cycle, the household works but does not consume, and saves the proceeds from supplying labor to firms and from receiving structural non-employment transfers from the government. In the second period, the household consumes savings and accrued interest. The then old household does not bequeath anything to its offspring. The government collects flat wage income taxes and issues debt to finance its expenditures consisting, in addition to the transfers to young households, of unproductive government consumption and productive PCI expenditures.

Since we assume a stationary population, we normalize M to 1. The labor which the younger household in period t supplies to firms is L_t where $L_t \leq 1$ denotes the hours worked in period t. Private physical capital in period t, denoted by K_t, is owned by the household entering the economy in period $t-1$. This (now old) household supplies to firms the services of the physical capital which for simplicity are equal to the capital stock.

Denoting the working hours demanded by the firm in period t by N_t, the production output in period t, Y_t, is determined by the following production function:

$$Y_t = A(G_t N_t)^{1-\alpha}(K_t)^{\alpha}, \ A > 0, 0 < \alpha < 1 , \tag{1}$$

where A denotes total factor productivity, α is the production elasticity of private capital and $0 < 1-\alpha < 1$ is the production elasticity of employees whose productivity is augmented by non-excludable public capital G_t as in Palivos et al. (2003, p. 88), in Yakita (2008, p. 899) or in Greiner (2012, pp. 231-232). The representative firm maximizes the real profit (in terms of output units):

$$\max \rightarrow A(G_t N_t)^{1-\alpha}(K_t)^{\alpha} - w_t N_t - q_t K_t \,, \tag{2}$$

with w_t denoting the real wage rate per unit of employed labor and with q_t denoting the real rental price of capital in period t.

The first-order conditions (FOCs) for profit maximization read as follows:

$$w_t = (1-\alpha)A(G_t)^{1-\alpha}(K_t)^{\alpha}(N_t)^{-\alpha} = (1-\alpha)(Y_t / N_t), \tag{3}$$

$$q_t = \alpha A(G_t N_t)^{1-\alpha}(K_t)^{\alpha-1} = \alpha(Y_t / K_t) \,. \tag{4}$$

In line with Battacharya (2014), the public capital stock at the beginning of period t is determined by public capital in period $t-1$ and by government PCI spending in period $t-1$, Γ_{t-1}.:

$$G_t = G_0 G_{t-1}{}^{\mu}(\Gamma_{t-1})^{1-\mu}, \; G_0 > 0, 0 < \mu < 1 \,, \tag{5}$$

where G_0 is a level parameter, μ represents the public capital elasticity of public capital in $t-1$, and $1-\mu$ represents the public capital elasticity of PCI spending. Note that Glomm and Ravikumar's (1994, p. 1178) accumulation equation for public capital emerges from equation (5) by setting $G_0 = 1$ and $\mu = 0$.

The economy grows, even in the absence of population growth and exogenous technological progress. The growth factor (= gross growth rate) of GDP is defined as:

$$G_t^y = Y_{t+1} / Y_t \tag{6}$$

Using equation (1), equation (6) can be rewritten as:

$$G_t^y = (G_{t+1}/G_t)(N_{t+1}/N_t)\{[(K_{t+1})/(G_{t+1}N_{t+1})]/[K_t/(G_tN_t)]\}^\alpha$$
$$= (G_{t+1}/G_t)(N_{t+1}/N_t)(k_{t+1}/k_t)^\alpha, \quad k_t \equiv K_t/(G_tN_t). \tag{7}$$

In order to determine the GDP growth factor along the intertemporal equilibrium path, the first-order conditions for intertemporal utility maximization of households are needed. The constrained maximization problem of the younger household reads as follows:

$$\text{Max} \to 1 - L_t + \beta \ln C_{t+1}^2$$
$$\text{s. t.:} \quad \text{(i) } S_t = w_t(1-\tau)L_t + \Phi_t(1-L_t), \; S_t = K_{t+1} + B_{t+1}^d,$$
$$\text{(ii) } C_{t+1}^2 = (1+i_{t+1})S_t.$$

Obviously, we assume quasi-linear utility of leisure $1-L_t$, zero utility of first-period consumption, and assume an intertemporally separable and logarithmic utility function of old-age consumption C_{t+1}^2. The subjective utility discount factor is $0<\beta<1$. Since first period-consumption is nil, all household revenues are saved, with S_t denoting young household savings in period t. The revenues of the younger household consist of net wage income $w_t(1-\tau)L_t$, with τ denoting the flat wage income tax rate, and of government transfers subsidizing non-working hours, $\Phi_t(1-L_t)$.

Notice that the subsidy per hour not worked Φ_t is considered as exogenous from the household's perspective.

Solving constraint (ii) for S_t, inserting the result into constraint (i), differentiating the Lagrangian

$$\Lambda_t = 1 - L_t + \beta \ln C_{t+1}^2 + \lambda_t[w_t(1-\tau)L_t + \Phi_t(1-L_t) - C_{t+1}^2/(1+i_{t+1})]$$

with respect to L_t, C_{t+1}^2 and with respect to the Lagrange multiplier λ_t, and setting the results equal to zero, yield the following optimal solutions for labor supply, old-age consumption and savings:

$$L_t = \beta - \Phi_t/[w_t(1-\tau) - \Phi_t], \tag{8}$$

$$C_{t+1}^2 = (1+i_{t+1})\beta[w_t(1-\tau) - \Phi_t], \tag{9}$$

$$S_t = [w_t(1-\tau) - \Phi_t]L_t + \Phi_t \quad (10)$$

Equation (8) reveals that the utility maximizing labor supply is wage-inelastic if the non-employment transfer is nil.

If, however, this transfer is larger than zero, labor supply increases with a larger net wage, and it decreases with a larger transfer per hour.

The third actor in the economy, the government, does not optimize but is nonetheless subject to the following budget constraint:

$$B_{t+1} + \tau w_t L_t = (1+i_t)B_t + \Gamma_t + \Delta_t + \Phi_t(1-L_t), \quad (11)$$

where B_t denotes the amount of outstanding government bonds at the beginning of period t, and Δ_t represents government consumption expenditures in period t.

The following clearing conditions for the labor market, the bond market and the capital market, supplement the intertemporal equilibrium conditions presented so far:

$$N_t = L_t,\ t = 0,1,2,..., \quad (12)$$

$$B_t^d = B_t,\ t = 0,1,2,... \quad (13)$$

$$S_t = K_{t+1} + B_{t+1},\quad t = 0,1,2,... \quad (14)$$

THE INTERTEMPORAL EQUILIBRIUM DYNAMICS

This section is devoted to the derivation of the intertemporal equilibrium dynamics. In order to simplify numerical specification of the main structural und policy parameters we transform all variables introduced so far into GDP ratios. To start with, the government budget constraint (11) is rewritten as follows:

$$\frac{B_{t+1}}{Y_{t+1}}\frac{Y_{t+1}}{Y_t} + \frac{\tau w_t L_t}{Y_t} = (1+i_t)\frac{B_t}{Y_t} + \frac{\Gamma_t}{Y_t} + \frac{\Delta_t}{Y_t} + \frac{\Phi_t}{Y_t}(1-L_t). \quad (11a)$$

Noting that the first-order condition for profit maximizing labor input in (3) can be rewritten as

$$w_t L_t = (1-\alpha)A(K_t)^{\alpha}(G_t L_t)^{1-a} = (1-\alpha)Y_t \, , \qquad (3a)$$

and defining the debt to GDP ratio as $b_t = B_t / Y_t$, equation (11a) can be written as follows:

$$b_{t+1}G_t^Y + \tau(1-\alpha) = (1+i_t)b_t + \gamma_t + \delta_t + (\Phi_t / Y_t)(1-L_t) \, , \qquad (11b)$$

where $\gamma_t = \Gamma_t / Y_t$ and $\delta_t = \Delta_t / Y_t$.

Following Turnovsky (2000, 2004), we assume that the government claims a given, time-stationary fraction of GDP for unproductive consumption expenditures, $\delta_t = \delta_{t+1} = \delta, \forall t$. In line with Dhont and Heylen (2009, p. 544) we also assume that the non-employment transfer Φ_t is proportional to after-tax wage income according to the replacement rate, ϕ:

$$\Phi_t = \phi(1-\tau)w_t L_t \, . \qquad (15)$$

In accordance with the empirical reality in middle European countries between 1995 and 2005 we assume time-stationary government debt to GDP ratios: $b_{t+1} = b_t = b, \forall t$ (e.g. Lane and Pels 2012).

Given the definitions and assumptions presented so far, the government budget constraint (11b) can be finally written as follows:

$$b[G_t^Y - (1+i_t)] + \tau(1-\alpha) = \gamma_t + \delta + \phi(1-\tau)(1-\alpha)(1-L_t) \, . \qquad (16)$$

Next, notice that the insertion of equation (15) into equation (8) implies the following time-stationary labor supply[1]:

$$L = [1+(1+\beta)\phi - \sqrt{[1+(1+\beta)\phi]^2 - 4\beta\phi}\,]/(2\phi) \, . \qquad (17)$$

[1] There is a second solution to the underlying quadratic equation but it does not conform to $L_t \leq 1$.

On dividing both sides of the capital market clearing condition (14) by Y_t, using the definition of the capital-output ratio $v_t = K_t / Y_t$, and considering the savings function and the specification of the non-employment transfer in (15), the capital market clearing condition can be rewritten as follows:

$$G_t^Y(v_{t+1}+b) = S_t / Y_t = \frac{L[w_t(1-\tau)-\Phi_t]+\Phi_t}{Y_t} = \frac{Lw_t(1-\tau)[1+\phi(1-L)]}{Y_t} \quad (14a)$$

Acknowledging once more (3a), equation (14a) then becomes:

$$G_t^Y(v_{t+1}+b) = (1-\alpha)(1-\tau)[1+\phi(1-L)]. \quad (18)$$

In order to derive the central equation of motion for the capital-output ratio, the public capital accumulation equation is shifted forward by one period, and $\gamma_t Y_t$ is substituted for Γ_t. The result is as follows:

$$G_{t+1} = G_0 G_t^{\mu}(\gamma_t)^{1-\mu}(Y_t)^{1-\mu} . \quad (5a)$$

Dividing equation (5a) on both sides by G_t and noting once more the production function $Y_t = AG_tL(k_t)^{\alpha}$, we obtain the following equation of motion for public capital:

$$\frac{G_{t+1}}{G_t} = G_0 G_t^{\mu-1}(\gamma_t)^{1-\mu}(A(G_tL)(k_t)^{\alpha})^{1-\mu} = G_0(\gamma_t)^{1-\mu}A^{1-\mu}L^{1-\mu}(k_t)^{\alpha(1-\mu)} . \quad (5b)$$

Since our objective is to derive the equation of motion for v_t, we use the definition of the capital-output ratio and again the production function $Y_t = A(G_tL)^{1-\alpha}(K_t)^{\alpha} = AG_tL(k_t)^{\alpha}$ in order to derive the following relationship between v_t and k_t:

$$v_t = \frac{K_t}{Y_t} = \frac{K_t}{A(K_t)^{\alpha}(G_tL)^{1-\alpha}} = \frac{(K_t)^{1-\alpha}}{A(G_tL)^{1-\alpha}} = \frac{(k_t)^{1-\alpha}}{A} . \quad (19)$$

Solving equation (19) for k_t, inserting the result into equation (5b), and rearranging finally yields:

$$\frac{G_{t+1}}{G_t} = G_0 A^{(1-\mu)/(1-\alpha)} L^{1-\mu} (\gamma_t)^{1-\mu} (v_t)^{\alpha(1-\mu)/(1-\alpha)} \quad . \qquad (20)$$

Taking account of equations (19) and (20) in equation (7), we obtain for the GDP growth factor:

$$G_t^Y = \left(\frac{G_{t+1}}{G_t}\right)\left(\frac{k_{t+1}}{k_t}\right)^{\alpha} = G_0 A^{\frac{(1-\mu)}{(1-\alpha)}} (\gamma_t)^{(1-\mu)} L^{(1-\mu)} (v_{t+1})^{\frac{\alpha}{1-\alpha}} (v_t)^{\frac{-\alpha\mu}{(1-\alpha)}}. \qquad (21)$$

Using once more the relationship between v_t and k_t in (19), we can rewrite the profit maximizing condition (4) as follows:

$$q_t = \alpha / v_t \, . \qquad (22)$$

The final steps needed to arrive at the equation of motion for the capital-output ratio entail inserting the GDP growth equation (21) into equations (16) and (18). This procedure yields:

$$b[G_0 A^{\frac{(1-\mu)}{(1-\alpha)}} L^{(1-\mu)} (\gamma_t)^{(1-\mu)} (v_{t+1})^{\frac{\alpha}{1-\alpha}} (v_t)^{\frac{-\alpha\mu}{(1-\alpha)}} - \alpha / v_t] + \tau(1-\alpha) = \gamma_t + \delta + \phi(1-\tau)(1-\alpha)(1-L) \, , \qquad (16a)$$

$$G_0 A^{\frac{(1-\mu)}{(1-\alpha)}} L^{(1-\mu)} (\gamma_t)^{(1-\mu)} (v_{t+1})^{\frac{\alpha}{1-\alpha}} (v_t)^{\frac{-\alpha\mu}{(1-\alpha)}} (v_{t+1} + b) = (1-\alpha)(1-\tau)[1+\phi(1-L)] \, . \qquad (18a)$$

Solving (18a) for γ_t, we obtain:

$$\gamma_t = \Theta(v_{t+1})^{\frac{-\alpha}{(1-\alpha)(1-\mu)}} (v_t)^{\frac{\alpha\mu}{(1-\alpha)(1-\mu)}} (v_{t+1} + b)^{\frac{1}{\mu-1}}, \; \Theta \equiv \left\{\frac{[(1-\alpha)(1-\tau)][1+\phi(1-L)]}{G_0 A^{(1-\mu)/(1-\alpha)} L^{(1-\mu)}}\right\}^{\frac{1}{(1-\mu)}}. \qquad (23)$$

Inserting the PCI expenditure to GDP ratio, γ_t, from equation (23) into equation (16a) and rearranging the result, we arrive at the fundamental equation of motion for the capital-output ratio:

$$[\varepsilon v_t + \alpha b]v_{t+1} + \Theta(v_{t+1})^{\frac{-\alpha}{(1-\alpha)(1-\mu)}}(v_{t+1}+b)^{\frac{\mu}{(\mu-1)}}(v_t)^{\frac{(1-\alpha-\mu+2\alpha\mu)}{[(1-\alpha)(1-\mu)]}} = [1-\alpha-\delta-\tau(1-\alpha)]bv_t - \alpha b^2, \quad (24)$$

where $\varepsilon \equiv \delta + \phi[(1-\alpha)(1-\tau)(1-L)] - \tau(1-\alpha)$, and represents the primary government deficit ratio (excluding PCI expenditures).

The first-order difference equation (24) represents the intertemporal equilibrium dynamics of the private capital-output ratio in our endogenous growth OLG model with PCI expenditures and unproductive non-employment transfers. The dynamics of the capital-output ratio determines the PCI expenditure ratio according to equation (23). Given the dynamics of the capital-output ratio and of the PCI expenditure ratio along the intertemporal equilibrium path, the growth factors of GDP and public capital are determined by equations (21) and (20), respectively. Finally, the real capital service price (= the real interest factor)[2] results from equation (22), and the real wage rate is determined by the following equation:

$$w_t = (1-\alpha)A^{\frac{1}{(1-\alpha)}}G_t(v_t)^{\frac{\alpha}{(1-\alpha)}}. \quad (25)$$

Obviously, with a rising capital-output ratio the real wage rate increases while the interest factor decreases, and the real wage rate increases with rising per-capita public capital along the intertemporal equilibrium path.

EXISTENCE AND DYNAMIC STABILITY OF STEADY STATES

In a steady state of intertemporal equilibrium dynamics (24), all real variables grow at a constant rate and the ratios of these variables are constant over time; that is,

$$G_{t+1}^Y = G_t^Y = G^Y, \quad v_{t+1} = v_t = v,\ g_{t+1} = g_t = g,\ \gamma_{t+1} = \gamma_t = \gamma, w_{t+1} = w_t = w,\ q_{t+1} = q_t = q.$$

The steady-state equilibrium can be characterized by the following set of equations:

[2] Since from a young household perspective real capital and government bonds are perfectly substitutable, the household holds both assets only if $q_{t+1} = 1 + i_{t+1},\ \forall t.$

$$(\varepsilon v + \alpha b)v + \Theta v^{\frac{(1-2\alpha)}{(1-\alpha)}} (v+b)^{\frac{\mu}{(\mu-1)}} = (1-\alpha-\delta)bv - \alpha b^2 , \tag{26}$$

$$\gamma = \Theta v^{\frac{-\alpha}{(1-\alpha)}} (v+b)^{\frac{1}{\mu-1}} , \tag{27}$$

$$G^Y = G_0 A^{\frac{(1-\mu)}{(1-\alpha)}} (L)^{1-\mu} (\gamma)^{1-\mu} (v)^{\frac{\alpha(1-\mu)}{1-\alpha}} , \tag{28}$$

$$q = 1 + i = \frac{\alpha}{v} , \tag{29}$$

$$w = (1-\alpha) A^{\frac{1}{(1-\alpha)}} G(v)^{\frac{\alpha}{(1-\alpha)}} . \tag{30}$$

In order to investigate the existence of a feasible steady-state solution for equations (26)-(30), we focus on the equation (26). Casual inspection of equation (26) immediately reveals that in general an explicit analytic solution is infeasible. Nonetheless, the existence of an economically feasible solution to equation (26) can still be proven. This is shown by the following proposition.

Proposition 1 (Existence of a steady-state solution).

Suppose that $\varepsilon < 0$ while $1-\alpha-\delta > 0$ and $1-2\alpha > 0$. Then, at least one solution $0 < v < \infty$ exists.

Proof. For the proof it is useful to denote the left-hand side of equation (26) as $LHS(v)$ and the right-hand side as $RHS(v)$. It is not difficult to see that $\lim_{v\to 0} LHS(v) = 0$ while $\lim_{v\to 0} RHS(v) = -ab^2$. Hence, at the lower end of the admissible range for the capital-output ratio, the left-hand side is larger than the right hand side of equation (26). On the other hand, since $1-\alpha-\delta > 0$ by assumption, it is easy to see that $\lim_{v\to\infty} RHS(v) = +\infty$.

Moreover, because by assumption $\varepsilon < 0$ and $1-2\alpha > 0$, $\lim_{v\to\infty} LHS(v) = -\infty$. Thus, near the upper end of the admissible range for the capital-output ratio the right-hand side of equation (26) is larger than the left-hand side. Both $LHS(v)$ and $RHS(v)$ are continuous functions of v. Thus, by using an intermediate value theorem we ensure that there exists at least one $0 < v < \infty$ such that $LHS(v) = RHS(v)$.■

Remark. Playing around with numerical specifications for $LHS(v)$ and $RHS(v)$ functions, the model shows that $\varepsilon < 0$ is a critical assumption. It is not difficult to find economically plausible policy parameters such that $\varepsilon \geq 0$, and $LHS(v)$ and $RHS(v)$ do not intersect upon v in the feasible interval.

Having ensured the existence of a feasible steady state, dynamic stability now remains to be shown.

For this purpose, the fundamental equation of motion of the capital-output ratio is totally differentiated with respect to v_{t+1} and v_t, and the differential quotient is evaluated at a steady-state solution. This procedure yields the following result:

$$\frac{dv_{t+1}}{dv_t} = \frac{(1-\alpha-\delta)b - \varepsilon v - (1-\alpha-\mu+2\alpha\mu)/[(1-\alpha)(1-\mu)]\Theta(v+b)^{\frac{\mu}{(\mu-1)}} v^{\frac{-\alpha}{(1-\alpha)}}}{\varepsilon v - \alpha/[(1-\alpha)(1-\mu)]\Theta(v+b)^{\frac{\mu}{(\mu-1)}} v^{\frac{-\alpha}{(1-\alpha)}} - \mu/(1-\mu)\Theta(v+b)^{\frac{1}{(\mu-1)}} v^{\frac{1-2\alpha}{(1-\alpha)}} + \alpha b}. \quad (31)$$

Using equation (31) we are now able to prove proposition 2.

Proposition 2 (Asymptotic dynamic stability of a steady-state solution).

Suppose that the assumptions of proposition 1 concerning the existence of a steady-state solution for equations (26)-(30) hold.

Moreover, assume $\varepsilon v + ab < 0$. Then, any steady-state solution for $0 < v < \infty$ is asymptotically stable, i.e. $|dv_{t+1}/dv_t| < 1$.

Proof. Since on account of the assumption $\varepsilon v + ab < 0$, the denominator of the differential quotient in (31) is smaller than zero, $|dv_{t+1}/dv_t| < 1$ is equivalent to the inequality:

$$(1-\alpha-\delta)b - \varepsilon v - (1-\alpha-\mu+2\alpha\mu)/[(1-\alpha)(1-\mu)]\Theta(v+b)^{\mu/(\mu-1)} v^{-\alpha/(1-\alpha)}$$
$$> \varepsilon v + ab - \mu/(1-\mu)\Theta(v+b)^{\frac{1}{(\mu-1)}} v^{\frac{1-2\alpha}{(1-\alpha)}} - \alpha/[(1-\alpha)(1-\mu)]\Theta(v+b)^{\frac{\mu}{(\mu-1)}} v^{\frac{-\alpha}{(1-\alpha)}},$$

which is equivalent to:

$$(1-\alpha-\delta)b - \varepsilon v > \varepsilon v + ab + \Theta[(1-2\alpha)/(1-\alpha)](v+b)^{\mu/(\mu-1)} v^{-\alpha/(1-\alpha)}$$
$$-\mu/(1-\mu) \times \times\Theta(v+b)^{\frac{1}{(\mu-1)}} v^{\frac{1-2\alpha}{(1-\alpha)}}.$$

However, this inequality holds since at the steady state

$$RHS'(v) = (1-\alpha-\delta)b > 0$$

is larger than

$$LHS'(v) = 2\varepsilon v + \alpha b + (1-2\alpha)/(1-\alpha)\Theta(v+b)^{\mu/(\mu-1)} v^{-\alpha/(1-\alpha)}$$
$$-(\mu/(1-\mu))\Theta(v+b)^{1/(\mu-1)} v^{(1-2\alpha)/(1-\alpha)},$$

and the latter must be negative since $LHS(v)$ tends towards $-\infty$.■

Remark. Note that under the existence condition $\varepsilon < 0$ the differential quotient dv_{t+1}/dv_t is larger than minus one and smaller than zero.

Thus, the equilibrium dynamics of the capital-output ratio exhibits damped oscillations in the neighborhood of a steady state.

Comparative Steady-State Analysis

Knowing that the steady-state capital-output ratio in equation (26) is dynamically stable, we are now entitled to inquire into the steady-state impacts on employment, PCI expenditures and GDP growth of a permanent marginal reduction in the replacement rate, ϕ while holding the public debt to GDP ratio, b, constant. Let us start with the employment impact of a marginal change in replacement rate. To this end, rewrite the labor supply function (17) as follows:

$$L = \{1+\phi(1+\beta) - \sqrt{1+\phi[2(1-\beta)+(1+\beta)^2\phi]}\}/(2\phi). \tag{17a}$$

This version of the labor supply function ensures that the expression under the square root is strictly larger than zero and hence the labor supply is a real number, larger than zero and smaller than one.

The marginal employment impact of a change in the replacement rate is obtained by partial differentiation of the equation (17a) with respect to the replacement rate, ϕ which yields:

$$\frac{dL}{d\phi} = \frac{1+\phi(1-\beta) - \sqrt{1+\phi[2(1-\beta)+(1+\beta)^2\phi]}}{2\phi^2\sqrt{1+\phi[2(1-\beta)+(1+\beta)^2\phi]}}. \tag{32}$$

Regarding the sign of $dL/d\phi$, it is immediate that the denominator of the fraction in (32) is larger than zero (since $\beta < 1$) and the numerator is negative which implies that $dL/d\phi < 0$.

In other words: a marginal reduction of the net replacement rate increases labor supply, and because of market clearing condition (12), employment N rises. As a next step, we have to explore the PCI expenditure and the GDP growth impacts. Not surprisingly, the impact analysis focuses first on the steady-state equation (26). This equation is totally differentiated with respect to the steady-state capital-output ratio, v, and the replacement rate, ϕ.

Hereby, we have to take into account the dependence of the parameters Θ and ε on the replacement rate ϕ. Differentiating ε with respect to ϕ yields:

$$\frac{d\varepsilon}{d\phi} = (1-\alpha)(1-\tau)(1-L) - \phi(1-\alpha)(1-\tau)\frac{dL}{d\phi}. \tag{33}$$

$d\varepsilon/d\phi > 0$ since $dL/d\phi < 0$ as shown above.

Differentiation of Θ with respect to ϕ results in the following expression:

$$\frac{d\Theta}{d\phi} = \frac{\Theta^{\mu}}{(1-\mu)G_0 A^{\frac{(1-\mu)}{(1-\alpha)}}}\left\{L^{\mu-1}\frac{d\varepsilon}{d\phi} - (1-\alpha)(1-\tau)(1-\mu)[1+\phi(1-L)]L^{\mu-2}\frac{dL}{d\phi}\right\}. \tag{34}$$

$d\Theta/d\phi$ is also larger than zero, as is implied by $d\varepsilon/d\phi > 0$ and $dL/d\phi < 0$ in (34).

With these preparations at hand, we are now in a position to calculate $dv/d\phi$ from the steady-state equation (26).

$$\frac{dv}{d\phi} = \frac{v^2\frac{d\varepsilon}{d\phi} + v^{\frac{(1-2\alpha)}{(1-\alpha)}}(v+b)^{\frac{\mu}{(\mu-1)}}\frac{d\Theta}{d\phi}}{(1-\alpha-\delta)b - 2\varepsilon v - ab - \Theta[(1-2\alpha)/(1-\alpha)](v+b)^{\frac{\mu}{(\mu-1)}}v^{\frac{-\alpha}{(1-\alpha)}} + (\mu\Theta)/(1-\mu)(v+b)^{\frac{1}{(\mu-1)}}v^{\frac{(1-2\alpha)}{(1-\alpha)}}} \tag{35}$$

Since $d\varepsilon/d\phi > 0$ and $d\Theta/d\phi > 0$, the numerator on the right-hand side of equation (35) is certainly larger than zero.

From the proof of proposition 2 we know that the denominator in (35) is larger than zero, too. Hence, $dv/d\phi > 0$, which means that a marginal reduction of the replacement rate diminishes the capital-output ratio.

Steady-state equations (29) and (30) show that, as a consequence of the decreasing capital-output ratio, the real interest factor rises and the real wage rate decreases.

With respect to the PCI to GDP ratio, γ , the response is less obvious.

However, total differentiation of steady-state equation (27) yields the following differential quotient, $d\gamma / d\phi$:

$$\frac{d\gamma}{d\phi} = v^{\frac{-\alpha}{(1-\alpha)}}(v+b)^{\frac{1}{(\mu-1)}}\frac{d\Theta}{d\phi} - \Theta[\frac{\alpha}{(1-\alpha)}v^{\frac{-1}{(1-\alpha)}}(v+b)^{\frac{1}{(\mu-1)}} + \frac{1}{(1-\mu)}v^{\frac{-\alpha}{(1-\alpha)}}(v+b)^{\frac{2-\mu}{(\mu-1)}}]\frac{dv}{d\phi}. \quad (36)$$

The differential quotient in (36) shows that the impact of a smaller replacement rate on the PCI expenditure ratio is in general ambiguous. While the negative capital-output ratio effect raises the PCI expenditure ratio, the positive effect (represented by capital theta) induces a decline in the PCI expenditure ratio. Which effect dominates depends on which numerical specifications are used in the OLG model.

The last impact concerns the GDP growth factor in steady state. Total differentiation of steady-state equation (28) yields the following differential quotient $dG^Y / d\phi$:

$$\frac{dG^Y}{d\phi} = G_0 A^{\frac{(1-\mu)}{(1-\alpha)}}[(1-\mu)L^{-\mu}\gamma^{(1-\mu)}v^{\frac{\alpha(1-\mu)}{(1-\alpha)}}\frac{dL}{d\phi} + (1-\mu)\gamma^{-\mu}L^{1-\mu}v^{\frac{\alpha(1-\mu)}{(1-\alpha)}}\frac{d\gamma}{d\phi}$$

$$+\frac{\alpha(1-\mu)}{(1-\alpha)}L^{1-\mu}\gamma^{(1-\mu)}v^{\frac{\alpha(2-\mu)-1}{(1-\alpha)}}\frac{dv}{d\phi}]. \quad (37)$$

As with the PCI expenditure ratio, the response of the GDP growth factor to a reduction in the replacement rate is, in general, ambiguous. While the labor supply response in (37) unambiguously enhances GDP growth, the response of the capital-output ratio diminishes GDP growth. PCI expenditures may increase or decrease GDP growth when the replacement rate is reduced.

Again, the overall impact can be determined only after a numerical specification of the OLG model. The next section is devoted to this question.

Core-Euro Area Benchmark Parameters and Steady-State Impacts

In order to find out which of the opposing effects of a reduced transfer replacement rate on the PCI expenditure ratio and on the GDP growth factor governs the overall effect, the structural and policy parameters of our closed-economy OLG model are now numerically specified.

The parameters are chosen such that countries of interest in middle Europe such as Austria, Germany and Italy, and other countries in west Europe such as Belgium, France and the Netherlands can be reproduced within the strictures of our simple model economy. With reference to the period between the late 1990s and the early 2000s these countries were referred to by Dhont and Heylen (2009, p. 540) as the "Core Euro Area"[3].

As mentioned in the introduction, according to Dhont and Heylen (2009, p. 550, Table 3), for the period 1995-2001 the Core Euro Area countries featured a relatively high average net transfer replacement ratio of 51.6% in contrast to the corresponding 40.8% figure for the Nordic countries Finland, Denmark, Norway and Sweden. At the same time, the Nordic countries exhibited higher productive government expenditures as a ratio of GDP, i.e. 12.5%, in contrast to 9.4% in the Core Euro Area.

Moreover, the tax rate on labor income in the Core Euro Area was on average 57.8% in contrast to 52% on average for Nordic countries[4].

As a consequence of these differences in the composition of government expenditures and in government revenues, the employment rate in hours[5] amounted to 49.9 % in the Core Euro Area in contrast to 59.2 % in Nordic countries. In addition, the average annual potential GDP growth per capita in the Core Euro Area was 1.74%, one half percentage point lower than in Nordic countries (Dhont and Heylen 2009, p. 540).

The following numerical specification of the basic OLG model is chosen such that the model is able to reproduce roughly the empirical facts for the Core Euro Area in the late 1990s and early 2000s as reported above, and such that the model accords with the assumptions in the existence proposition 1 (= benchmark case). The numerical specification of all model parameters

---

[3] From a post-crisis perspective this term now appears as somewhat of a misnomer.

[4] Dhont and Heylen (2009, p. 550) stress also the differences between core euro area and Nordic countries with respect to the tax rates on capital income. Since the capital income tax does not matter in our simple economy we do not report these differences.

[5] Employment rate in hours is the ratio of average annual hours worked per person of age 15 to 64 up to 1920 hours.

proceeds in several steps: first, the numerical values for the Core Euro Area fiscal policy parameters are those reported by Dhont and Heylen (2009) with respect to net transfer replacement rate, productive government expenditure to GDP ratio and labor income tax rate. Second, we fix the GDP growth factor at 1.539194 which corresponds to a yearly growth rate of 1.74%[6].

We set the real interest factor at 1.72295, which is equivalent to an average Core Euro Area annual real interest rate of 2.2 % for 1995-2005 (Fagan and Gaspar 2008, p. 34). The Core Euro Area public debt to GDP ratio is fixed at 0.03121. This corresponds to the yearly Core Euro Area average between 1995 and 2005 of 78% (see AMECO data basis). Third, there are some structural parameter values which we take from the relevant literature. These include the magnitude of public capital production elasticity μ which we set in line with Lin's (2000, p. 759) value for human capital production at 0.5, and the level parameter G_0 which is set at the value of 1.86[7]. Fourth, and most importantly, we calibrate the remaining structural and policy parameters β, α, A and δ, such that equation (17) and the steady-state equations (26)-(28) hold. Using equation (17), and fixing L at 0.499 and ϕ at 0.516 we get $\beta = 0.84577$. The corresponding yearly time preference rate of less than one percent is rather low but well within the range for time preference rates in other intertemporal general equilibrium models. Using all the parameter values so far obtained in the steady-state equations (26)-(28) we get the following calibration results: $\alpha = 0.33912$, $A = 10.27947$ and $\delta = 0.21$.

Both the capital production share α, and the total factor productivity A, are well within the range found for such parameter values in the literature (for the numerical value of the capital production share see Barro 1990, King and Rebelo 1990 and Mendoza et al. 1997, for a similar total factor productivity value see Auerbach and Kotlikoff 1998). Only the unproductive government expenditure to GDP ratio δ is higher than the 16.3% reported by Dhont and Heylen (2009, p. 548).

Given all parameter values reported so far we can calculate the benchmark solution for the capital-output ratio from steady-state equation (26). The calculation yields $v = 0.19682$ which corresponds to a yearly capital-output ratio of 4.92. Knowing the benchmark solution for the Core Euro Area in our simple OLG model, we are now in a position to quantify the steady-state impacts of a reduction in the transfer replacement rate and/or the wage tax

---

[6] We assume that the basic model period consists of 25 calendar years.

[7] Lin (2000, p. 759) sets the level parameter in human capital production at the value of 1.6.

rate. Let us first consider the effects of an isolated reduction in replacement rate. Suppose the net transfer replacement rate for the Core Euro Area is reduced from 51.6% to 46.6%, i.e. a reduction of 10%.

Table 1 reports the results. Comparing the benchmark case to the policy case of a reduced net replacement rate we see that the overall effects on the employment rate in hours, on the PCI expenditure ratio, and on the GDP growth factor, are unambiguously positive, although the capital-output ratio declines. The policy change also induces an increase in the real interest factor.

Finally, we want to assess the steady-state impacts of a reduction in both the Core Euro Area net replacement rate and in the wage tax rate towards the lower Nordic rates. The results of these policy shocks are reported in Table 2.

Replacing the Core Euro Area policy package of relatively high net transfer replacement rates and relatively high wage tax rates by the comparatively lower Nordic rates boosts the employment rate hours, the capital-output ratio and the real wage rate in the Core Euro Area, but impacts negatively on the GDP growth factor and the PCI expenditure ratio.

Assuming that the objective of politicians is to increase the GDP growth rate of the ailing Eurozone, this decline in the GDP growth rate has interesting policy implications. The decline in the GDP growth rate implies that ruling Core Euro Area governments may fear loss of office, and therefore not be at all inclined to reduce both the replacement rate and the wage tax rate towards the Nordic levels.

However, although this represents an interesting policy implication one has to be cautious when interpreting what the model outcome means in terms of policy advice.

Table 1. Benchmark case and the effects of a reduced replacement rate

Benchmark solution		Replacement rate reduced by 10%	
Capital output ratio	0.1968	Capital output ratio	0.1808
Employment rate hours	0.499	Employment rate hours	0.5241
PCI expenditure ratio	0.0940	PCI expenditure ratio	0.1018
GDP growth factor	1.5392	GDP growth factor	1.6061
Real interest factor	1.7229	Real interest factor	1.8755

Source: Own calculations.

Table 2. The effects of a reduced replacement rate and wage tax rate

Benchmark solution		Replacement rate 40.8%, tax rate 52%	
Capital output ratio	0.1968	Capital output ratio	0.2212
Employment rate hours	0.499	Employment rate hours	0.5538
PCI expenditure ratio	0.0940	PCI expenditure ratio	0.07427
GDP growth factor	1.5392	GDP growth factor	1.4853
Real interest factor	1.7229	Real interest factor	1.5328

Source: Own calculations.

The reason is that capital income (and consumption) taxes do not matter in our extremely simple model set-up but we know in practice that low capital income taxes are often used to induce higher GDP growth.

Indeed, capital income taxes are much lower in Nordic than in Core Euro Area countries and Dhont and Heylen (2009, p. 562) find in their analytically more complicated infinitely-lived agent, endogenous growth model "the share of productive government expenditures and the tax rate on capital income as the most effective fiscal policy variables with respect to growth." They also find – and this finding is in accordance with the results in Table 1 – that the representative individual in their alternative intertemporal general equilibrium model "may benefit most from policies that increase productive government expenditures, financed by a cut in structural non-employment transfers" (Dhont and Heylen 2009, p. 562).

CONCLUSION

This chapter reconsiders the effects of a permanent reduction in public structural non-employment benefits (non-work subsidies) on employment, on the PCI expenditure share, and on GDP growth in a closed-economy OLG model with public capital and public debt. As outlined in the introduction, our two-period OLG model extends Glomm and Ravikumar's basic OLG (1994) with public capital and balanced government budgets by introducing public debt and structural non-employment transfers to younger households in order to mimic a fiscal policy instrument widely used in middle European and other western European countries.

Assuming quasi-linear leisure utility, no young-age consumption and log-linear old-age utility, we find that the individual labor supply increases with rising real (net) wage rates and lower net replacement rates.

After deriving the intertemporal equilibrium dynamics from the first-order conditions for utility and profit maximization and market clearing conditions we prove the existence and dynamic stability of steady-state growth equilibria with time-stationary private capital-output ratios, real interest rates, and constant GDP growth rates over time. For the existence of a steady-state solution a negative primary deficit ratio (excluding the PCI expenditures), together with other mild conditions, is sufficient. Given this requirement, the steady-state solutions are asymptotically stable. However, in contrast to a comparable exogenous-growth OLG model (as in Diamond 1965), the equilibrium dynamics is not monotonous but exhibits damped oscillations.

Moving on to comparative steady-state analysis, the present author finds that a switch from unproductive to productive PCI expenditures arising from a lower net transfer replacement rate induces higher employment, but lowers the capital-output ratio and increases the real interest rate. The effects on PCI expenditures and on the GDP growth rate of a lower replacement rate are, however, analytically ambiguous.

Regarding, for example, the impact on GDP growth, larger employment increases GDP growth, while the lower capital-output ratio diminishes GDP growth. The third factor which positively influences GDP growth, the PCI expenditure ratio, can in general rise or fall in response to a lower replacement rate.

This ambiguity in the general overall impact of the replacement rate on GDP growth and the PCI share can be resolved by employing numerical specifications for structural and policy parameters in the basic OLG model. It is natural to calibrate the main model parameters so as to map those European countries in which structural non-employment benefits play a major role in the fiscal policy package: i.e. in those middle and western European countries which Dhont and Heylen (2009) call the Core Euro Area. Using this numerical specification we are able to demonstrate unambiguously the overall effects of a reduced net transfer replacement rate: i.e. both the PCI share and GDP growth rate rise.

These effects no longer occur when both Core Euro Area net replacement rate and labor income tax are reduced to the corresponding Nordic levels. This may explain why Core Euro Area politicians are not inclined to change the composition of public expenditures away from unproductive transfers towards greater use of productive public investment expenditures.

The caveats concerning political significance mentioned above clearly point to the limitations of our model set-up. In order to overcome these limitations, first and foremost, our intertemporal utility function should be generalized such that a broader set of tax instruments (including capital income taxes) can impact the general equilibrium solution.

Second, the empirically rather restrictive assumption of equal production elasticities for public capital and labor in the production function of our basic OLG model should be generalized in favor of differing elasticities in a way that preserves the analytical tractability of the model.

Third, a two-country version of our basic OLG model should be developed in order to assess the extent to which differences in national fiscal policy packages can endure at the same time when goods and/or production factors are internationally mobile.

ACKNOWLEDGMENTS

I would like to thank Laurie Conway for helpful comments which improved the style and the substance of the paper.

All remaining errors are mine.

JEL Classification: D 91, E 62

REFERENCES

Auerbach, A. J. and L. J. Kotlikoff (1998), *Macroeconomics: An integrated approach.* MIT Press: Cambridge, MA.

Barro, R. J. (1990), Government spending in a simple model of endogenous growth. *Journal of Political Economy* 98, 103-125.

Dhont, T. and F. Heylen (2009), Employment and growth in Europe and the US – the role of fiscal policy composition. *Oxford Economic Papers* 61, 538-565.

Diamond, P. A. (1965), National debt in a neoclassical growth model. *American Economic Review* 55, 1135–1150.

Fagan, G. and V. Gaspar (2008), Macroeconomic adjustment in a monetary union. *ECB Working Paper Series* No. 946.

Farmer, K. (2014), Financial integration and EMU's external imbalances in a two-country OLG model. *International Advances in Economic Research* 20 (1), 1-21.

Futagami, K., Y. Morita and A. Shibata (1993), Dynamic analysis of an endogenous growth model with public capital. *Scandinavian Journal of Economics* 95, 607-625.

Glomm, G. and B. Ravikumar (1994), Public investment in infrastructure in a simple growth model. *Journal of Economic Dynamics and Control* 18, 1173-1187.

Greiner, A. (2012), Public capital, sustainable debt and endogenous growth. *Research in Economics* 66, 230-238.

King, R. G. and S. Rebelo (1990), Public policy and economic growth: developing neoclassical implications. *Journal of Political Economy* 98, 126-150.

Lane, P. and B. Pels (2012), Current account imbalances in Europe. *CEPR Discussion Paper Series* No. 8858.

Lin, S. (2000), Government debt and economic growth in an overlapping generations model. *Southern Economic Journal* 66, 754-763.

Mendoza, E. G., G. M. Milesi-Feretti and P. Asea (1997), On the effectiveness of tax policy in altering long-run growth: Harberger's superneutrality conjecture. *Journal of Public Economics* 70, 237-254.

Palivos, T., C. K. Yip and J. Zhang (2003), Transitional dynamics and indeterminacy of equilibria in an endogenous growth model with a public input. *Review of Development Economics* 7 (1), 86-98.

Turnovsky, S. J. (2004), The transitional dynamics of fiscal policy, long-run capital accumulation, and growth. *Journal of Money, Credit and Banking* 36, 883-910.

Turnovsky, S. J. (2000), Fiscal policy, elastic labor supply, and endogenous growth. *Journal of Monetary Economics* 45, 185-210.

Yakita, A. (2008), Sustainability of public debt, public capital formation and endogenous growth in an overlapping generations setting. *Journal of Public Economics* 92, 897-914.

In: Economic Growth in the 21st Century
Editor: Tara Abrahams
ISBN: 978-1-63321-623-5

Chapter 3

ECONOMIC GROWTH IN THE 21ST CENTURY: A DYNAMIC EVOLUTION ANALYSIS ON THE CASE OF CHINA

Lixin Tian[1,*] and Guochang Fang[1,2]
[1]Center for Energy Development and Environmental Protection, Jiangsu University, Zhenjiang, Jiangsu, P.R. China
[2]Department of Basic Courses, Yancheng Institute of Technology, Yancheng, Jiangsu, P.R. China

ABSTRACT

Since reforming and opening, China's economy has been maintained at double-digit rates for over twenty years, China's economy is steaming ahead at more than 7.5% even under the global lash of the international finance crisis. China has made outstanding contributions to world economic prosperity, which has been a necessary and desirable part of world economic, and affects the rest of the world economy. China's economy growth has gradually become the barometer of the world economy. While under the new trend of low carbon economy, China's economy growth is facing both opportunities and challenges. China's resource and environment have reached the highest value of the load-bearing capacity, strain in energy and sources supply, inefficient use of

* Corresponding author. Tel.: +86 (511) 88797671; fax: +86 (511) 88791467. *E-mail addresses:* tianlx@ujs.edu.cn (L. Tian).

resources and eco–environment deterioration have become the bottleneck of economy growth. China's economy growth will be profoundly affected by other variables under the severe resource-environmental. This chapter embarks from China's basic conditions, the variables which affect economic growth are deeply explored. The nonlinear evolutionary model involving economy growth, energy-saving and emission-reduction, carbon emissions, carbon tax and new energy is built based on method of system science. The dynamic behavior of the system is analyzed, artificial neural network is used to identify the quantitative coefficients of the actual system according to the statistical data of China. By adjusting the evolution curve of economy growth when variables in the system changing, the variables which are sensitive to economy growth are found, and the potential impact of government control and other constraint conditions on economy growth are investigated further. A series of conclusions are carried out with the results in perfect agreement with actual situation.

1. INTRODUCTION

Chaos analysis and applications in dynamical systems are observed in many practical applications in engineering, biology and economics [1-3]. Energy-saving and emission-reduction system is a complex nonlinear system, which includes energy-saving and emission-reduction, carbon emissions, economic growth, energy intensity and etc.. One of the most noticeable problems is how to conduct a further research of energy-saving and emission-reduction through nonlinear dynamics, which is currently a method of rapid development.

This chapter is intended to set up a series of nonlinear dynamics models of energy-saving and emission-reduction system based on energy-saving and emission-reduction, carbon emissions and economic growth and other constraints, which have not yet been reported in existing literatures. These new systems display very complex phenomenon. The time-varying economic growth calculation formulas are first derived from the energy-saving and emission-reduction dynamic system in this research. By observing the trends of economic growth, the main variables having impact upon the energy-saving and emission-reduction are obtained.

2. THREE-DIMENSIONAL ESER DYNAMIC EVOLUTION SYSTEM

2.1. Establishment of the Model

On the basis of the previous studies, this section studies the complicated relationship between energy-saving and emission-reduction, carbon emissions and economic growth during a given period based on the existing data. The system can be described by the following differential equations:

$$\begin{cases} \dot{x} = a_1 x\left(y/M - 1\right) - a_2 y + a_3 z \\ \dot{y} = -b_1 x + b_2 y\left(1 - y/C\right) + b_3 z\left(1 - z/E\right) \\ \dot{z} = c_1 x\left(x/N - 1\right) - c_2 y - c_3 z \end{cases} \tag{1}$$

Where $x(t)$ is the time-dependent variable of energy-saving and emission-reduction, $y(t)$ is the time-dependent variable of carbon emissions, $z(t)$ is the time-dependent variable of economic growth (GDP). For the explanation of other variables, see [4].

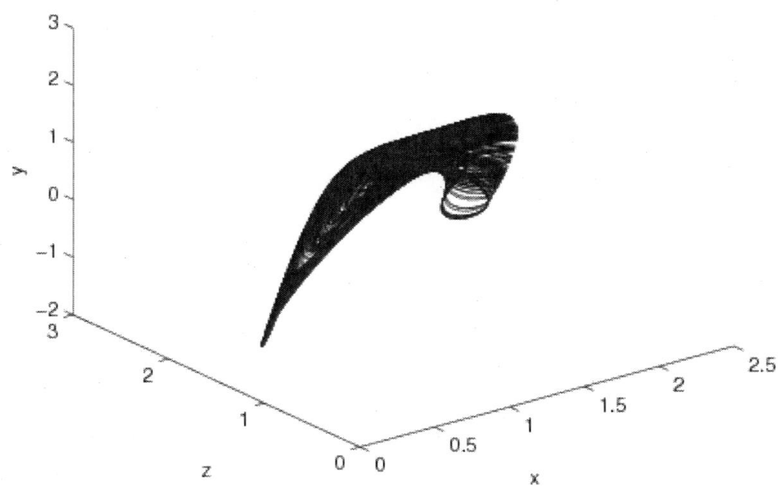

Figure 1. Energy-saving and emission-reduction attractor.

2.2. Energy-Saving and Emission-Reduction Attractor

Let initials be [0.015, 0.758, 1.83]. Fix parameters as in Eq. (7) in [4]. A chaotic attractor is observed as shown in Figure 1.

3. A NOVEL SELECTIVE-CONSTRAINED ESER DYNAMIC EVOLUTION SYSTEM

3.1. The Model

The ESER system includes carbon emissions, economic growth, energy intensity, energy efficiency and many other variables. Each variable in the actual ESER system has many restriction conditions. In the three dimensional ESER system [4], it is postulated that ESER, carbon emissions and economic growth is restrained by CCE, government control and low carbon lifestyle and investment in new technology of ESER respectively. The restriction conditions are assumed to be $F_1(x,y,z,t)$, $F_2(x,y,z,t)$ and $F_3(x,y,z,t)$. The selective-constrained ESER system can be described by the following differential equations:

$$\begin{cases} \dot{x} = a_1 x(y/M - 1) - a_2 y + a_3 z + F_1(x,y,z,t) \\ \dot{y} = -b_1 x + b_2 y(1 - y/C) + b_3 z(1 - z/E) + F_2(x,y,z,t) \\ \dot{z} = c_1 x(x/N - 1) - c_2 y - c_3 z + F_3(x,y,z,t) \end{cases} \tag{2}$$

Then Eq. (2) can be simplified as (see [5]):

$$\begin{cases} \dot{x} = a_1 x(y/M - 1) - a_2 y + a_3 z - a_4 z/y \\ \dot{y} = -b_1 x + b_2 y(1 - y/C) + b_3 z(1 - z/E) - b_4 y \\ \dot{z} = c_1 x(x/N - 1) - c_2 y - (c_3 + c_4) z \end{cases} \tag{3}$$

3.2. An Empirical Study

Figure 2 shows the effects on economic growth when a_4 changing. The brown curve corresponds to the curve when $a_4 = 0.0104$; the green curve corresponds to the curve when $a_4 = 0.0134$; the blue curve corresponds to the curve when $a_4 = 0.0164$. Comparative observations of the three curves show that when a_4 becomes bigger gradually, the effects on economic growth is big in the initial stages. The difference between peak value and stable value is bigger than the case when a_4 is small. With the development of ESER system, the effects on economic growth towards stable. The green and blue curves are higher than the red line, i.e. the stable values are greater than zero. The effect on economic growth is beneficial. The brown curve is lower than the red line after passing through the tiny yellow ring, i.e. the stable value is smaller than zero. The effect on economic growth is not beneficial. The above analyses indicate that the effect on economic growth is big in the early stages when the investment to energy-saving increases. With the development of ESER system, this practice will promote economic growth finally, and the promoting effect on economic growth increases as investment to energy-saving goes up.

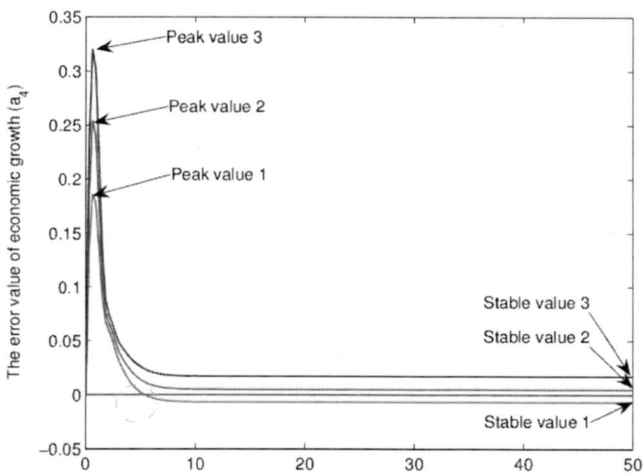

Figure 2. The error value of economic growth (a_4).

Figure 3 shows the effects on economic growth when b_4 becomes bigger gradually. The brown curve corresponds to the curve when $b_4 = 0.1225$; the green curve corresponds to the curve when $b_4 = 0.1525$; the blue curve corresponds to the curve when $b_4 = 0.1825$. Comparative observations of the three curves show when b_4 becomes bigger gradually, the effects on economic growth become bigger and bigger. The green and blue curves are under the red line after passing the small ring, i.e. these changes have inhibition effects on economic growth. The above analyses indicate that with the constraint condition $F_2(x, y, z, t)$ gradually strengthening, especially the government control, will suppress economic growth heavily. The stable value of the green and blue curves in Figure 3 has been negative. When b_4 increases with the same range, the spacing between the curves become larger and larger, i.e. the impacts of government control on economic growth enlarge.

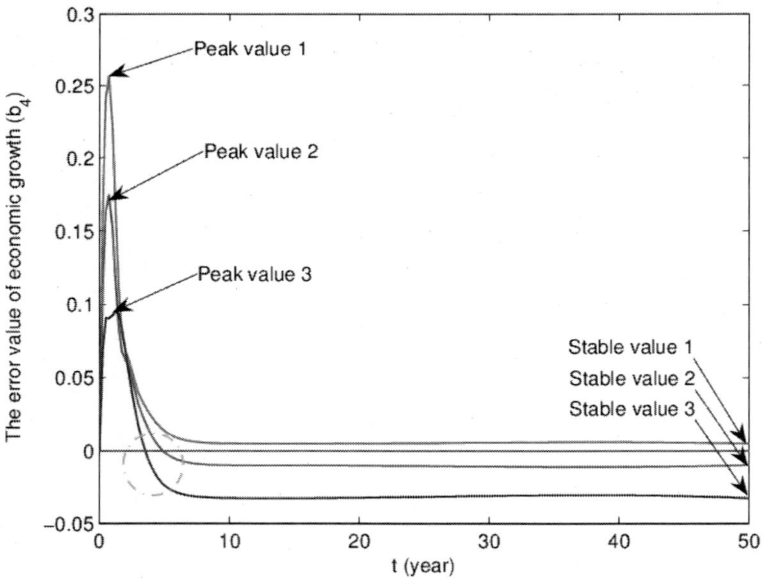

Figure 3. The error value of economic growth (b_4).

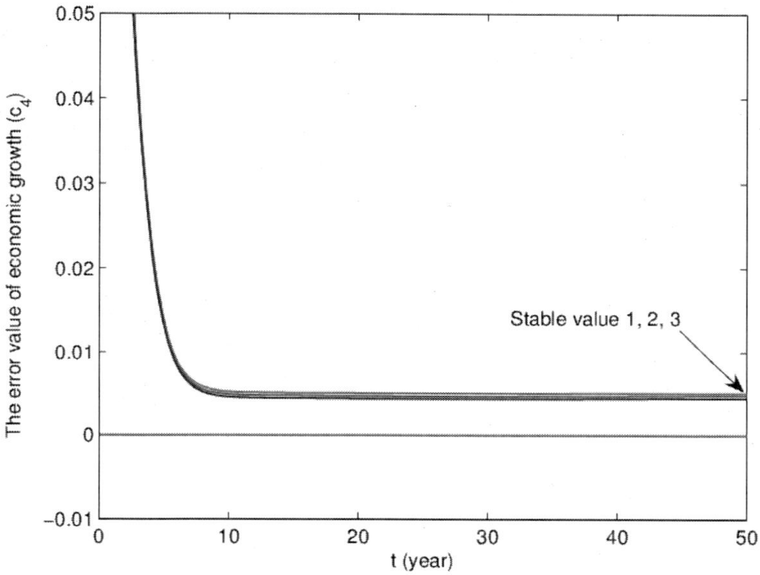

Figure 4. The error value of economic growth (c_4).

Keep the constraint intensity of $k_{21}y + k_{22}y$ changeless, i.e. keep the sum of $k_{21}y + k_{22}y$ changeless, appropriately adjust these two variables, make k_{21} decreasing and k_{22} increasing gradually, i.e. under the condition of assuring unchangeable restrained function of $F_2(x, y, z, t)$, decrease the impacts of government control on ESER, in the meantime increase the impacts of low carbon lifestyle on ESER, i.e. b_4 remains unchanged, c_4 becomes smaller, Figure 4 shows the effects on economic growth when c_4 becomes smaller gradually. The brown curve corresponds to the curve when $c_4 = 0.1002$; the green curve corresponds to the curve when $c_4 = 0.1032$; the blue curve corresponds to the curve when $c_4 = 0.1062$. In observational analyses, when c_4 becomes smaller gradually, the spacing between three curves are not immediately obvious, and the curves are always above the red line. These measures have promotion effect on economic growth. The above analyses indicate that decreasing the impacts of government control on ESER and increasing the impacts of low carbon lifestyle on ESER will have a minimal effect on economic growth, and the effect is always positive.

REFERENCES

[1] Tian LX, Jin RL. Theoretical exploration of carbon emissions dynamic evolutionary system and evolutionary scenario analysis. *Energy* 2012; 40: 376–86.

[2] Sun M, Wang XF, Chen Y, Tian LX. Energy resources demand-supply system analysis and empirical research based on non-linear approach. *Energy* 2011;36:5460–5.

[3] Fang GC, Tian LX, Fu M, Sun M. The impacts of carbon tax on energy intensity and economic growth——A dynamic evolution analysis on the case of China. *Applied Energy*. 2013 (110): 17-28.

[4] Fang GC, Tian LX, Sun M, Fu M. Analysis and application of a novel three-dimensional energy-saving and emission-reduction dynamic evolution system. *Energy* 2012; 40: 291–9.

[5] Fang GC, Tian LX, Fu M, Sun M. Government control or low carbon lifestyle?——Analysis and application of a novel selective constrained energy-saving and emission-reduction dynamic evolution system [J]. *Energy Policy* 2014 (68): 498-507.

In: Economic Growth in the 21st Century
Editor: Tara Abrahams
ISBN: 978-1-63321-623-5

Chapter 4

COGNITIVE HUMAN CAPITAL AND ECONOMIC GROWTH IN THE 21ST CENTURY

Gerhard Meisenberg*
Department of Biochemistry, Ross University School of Medicine,
Portsmouth, Dominica

Human history becomes more and more a race between education and catastrophe.

H. G. Wells: The Outline of History, 1920

ABSTRACT

This chapter explores the interdependency between economic growth and cognitive human capital, which is also described as cognitive skills or intelligence and is measured either as performance in scholastic achievement tests or IQ. It shows that unlike the mere amount of schooling, intelligence has been a robust predictor of economic growth in the recent past. Plausible mediators of the intelligence effect include greater labor productivity, better institutions, more competent management, lower fertility, and wider time horizons.

Based on the observation of secular gains in intelligence that have become known as Flynn effects, a theory of economic growth is developed that is based on the trans-generational reinforcement between

* Email: Gmeisenberg@rossu.edu.

rising intelligence and economic, technological and institutional advances. It provides a parsimonious explanation for the sustained nature of economic growth since the Industrial Revolution, and a conceptual framework for more specific theories and hypotheses.

The chapter arrives at projections of economic growth for the first half of the 21st century that are based on the empiric relationship between current prosperity, human capital, and economic growth. Longer-term predictions are based on our knowledge of the conditions that are required for continued Flynn effects, and of genetic limits to human cognitive development. The conclusion is that in most countries of Europe and North America, the limits of cognitive growth are being approached or have been reached already by the younger generation. There are ongoing Flynn effects in developing countries today. These countries are now reducing the cognitive gaps separating them from the developed countries, but most of them are expected to reach their cognitive limits before the end of the 21st century. Long-term developments after the end of the Flynn effect will be driven primarily by demographic trends. Without major changes in demographic behavior, intelligence is predicted to eventually decline slowly, ending economic growth in most parts of the world within the next 3 to 4 generations.

1. Intelligence in Space and Time

1.1. Intelligence and Human Agency

The starting point for this chapter is the obvious fact that economic change is the result of human agency. Therefore we need to seek its sources in the physical, mental and moral qualities of the economically active population. In other words, we have to seek explanations for large-scale economic developments in the human capital of the population: how it is formed, and how it is translated into economic outcomes. Cognitive human capital is the aspect of human capital that is variously described as cognitive skills, intellectual ability or intelligence, depending on personal preference, academic traditions, and conventions of political correctness.

My claim is that intelligence is the most general driving force and a major limiting factor for economic growth. It has played this role in the past, and is predicted to continue doing so in the foreseeable future. The face validity of this approach is evident when we realize that sophisticated minds are required to create and maintain complex business enterprises and government bureaucracies, make inventions, and use these inventions in the service of

Table 1. Some Flynn effect gains in Western countries

Country	Test	Age	Birth cohort	ain/decade	Source
New Zealand	Otis	10-13	1923/26 – 1955/58	2.42	Elley, 1969
USA	Army Alpha	20	1898 – 1923	7.74	Tuddenham, 1948
USA	Stanford-Binet	6-12	1920/26 – 1960/66	1.95	Flynn, 1984
USA	Stanford-Binet	13-18	1914/19 – 1954/59	2.40	Flynn, 1984
Netherlands	Raven SPM selection	18	1934 – 1964	7.03	Flynn, 1987
France	Raven	18	1931 – 1956	10.05	Flynn, 1987
France	Math/Verbal	18	1931 – 1956	3.74	Flynn, 1987
France	ECNI	10	1955 – 1978	2.61	Bradmetz and Mathy, 2006
Germany	HAWIK	7-15	1941/49 – 1968/76	7.30	Schallberger, 1991
Germany	Intelligenzstrukturtest	22	1948 – 1978	1.60	Pietschnig et al., 2011
Norway	Math/Verbal/Matrices	19	1935 – 1957	4.55	Sundet et al., 2004
Norway	Math/Verbal/Matrices	19	1957 – 1983	0.33	Sundet et al., 2004
Denmark	Børge Prien's Prøve	18	1941 – 1971	2.70	Teasdale and Owen, 2005
Denmark	Børge Prien's Prøve	18	1970 – 1980	1.65	Teasdale and Owen, 2008
Denmark	Børge Prien's Prøve	18	1980 – 1985/86	-1.49	Teasdale and Owen, 2008
Sweden	Block design/memory	35-80	1909 – 1969	2.18	Rönnlund and Nilsson, 2008
Finland	Shapes/Number/Words	19	1969 – 1977/78	4.52	Dutton and Lynn 2013
Finland	Shapes/Number/Words	19	1977/78 – 1990	-2.50	Dutton and Lynn 2013

greater efficiency. Fairly high intelligence is needed not only for innovation, but also for the maintenance of industrial and administrative structures once these have achieved high levels of complexity and efficiency.

Human capital theory explains macroeconomic developments in the recent past as outcomes of the interactions of human intelligence with the economic and social conditions that human intelligence has created. These same interactions will, in large part, determine future trend lines as well. Without a realistic understanding of human intelligence and its interactions with economic and social processes, we can neither understand the dynamic of historic change nor can we hope to predict future developments (Flynn, 2014; Meisenberg, 2014).

1.2. Temporal Trends of Intelligence: The Flynn Effect

Although subject to genetic constraints, human intelligence is malleable. This has been demonstrated beyond doubt by the Flynn effect: the rise of intelligence by approximately 30 IQ points or two standard deviations during the 20th century in the economically advanced countries (Flynn, 1987, 2012; Lynn & Hampson, 1986).[1] A person who scored at the 84th percentile of the ability distribution in 1900 would score at the 16th percentile today. It stands to reason that today's most advanced economies would not be sustainable if the intelligence of the population were nearly as low as it was in 1900. Table 1 shows examples of Flynn effects in various countries. We can note several points:

1. Flynn effects can be large, up to 10 IQ points per decade in some cases.
2. Different abilities can rise at different rates.
3. Gains were largest in Continental Europe and Japan during recovery from World War II.
4. In some countries, Flynn effects have ended or reversed in recent years.

---

[1] IQ tests are scaled to a population mean of 100 and standard deviation of 15. For international comparisons, the IQ of Britain ("Greenwich IQ") is used as a reference. For example, in a country with an average IQ of 85, the average person scores at about the 16th percentile of the British distribution.

Country	Test	Age	Birth cohort	Gain/decade	Source
Britain	Raven SPM	52	1890 – 1940	4.44	Raven et al., 1998
Britain	Raven SPM	8-12	1931/35 – 1968/72	2.48	Flynn, 2009
Britain	Raven SPM	8-12	1968/72 – 1996/00	2.00	Flynn, 2009
Britain	Raven SPM	13-15	1928/30 – 1965/67	1.66	Flynn, 2009
Britain	Raven SPM	13-15	1965/67 – 1993/95	-0.87	Flynn, 2009
Japan	Kyoto NX 9-15	10-11	1943/44 – 1961/62	9.23	Lynn and Hampson, 1986
South Korea	Several	5-16	1970 – 1990	7.70	te Nijenhuis, 2012
Sudan	WAIS-R	50 (avg.)	1937 – 1957 (avg.)	2.05	Khaleefa et al., 2009
Dominica	Raven SPM	22/56	1978/87 – 1941/54	5.14	Meisenberg et al., 2005
Saudi Arabia	Raven SPM	8-18 male	1958/68 – 1992/02	0.29	Batterjee, 2011
Saudi Arabia	Raven SPM	8-18 fem.	1958/68 – 1992/02	2.65	Batterjee, 2011
Argentina	Raven SPM	13-24	1940/51 – 1974/85	6.28	Flynn and Rossi-Casé, 2012

This rise in psychometric intelligence occurred at a time when school systems expanded massively in western countries (Benavot and Riddle, 1988; Schofer and Meyer, 2005), and longer and intensified schooling is one likely cause of the Flynn effect. The Flynn effect implies that we can treat intelligence as a fixed input only when explaining short-term economic trends on time scales of years to decades. We cannot do so when trying to explain major secular trends in society and economy that take place on time scales of generations to centuries. Intelligence is a resource that can wax and wane on this time scale, and historic changes of intelligence are plausible causes as well as consequences of social and economic change.

1.3. The Geography of Intelligence

Intelligence is distributed unequally across countries. Average IQs in Sub-Saharan Africa, although difficult to measure with confidence (Rindermann, 2013), are around 70 while IQs in East Asia average 105. With 15 IQ points defined as one standard deviation, this difference is more than 2 (within-country) standard deviations on the "global bell curve" (Lynn, 2008). One likely reason for the great magnitude of cognitive differences between countries is that Flynn effects have been small or absent in today's less developed countries at a time (roughly between the 18th century Enlightenment and today) when mental horizons and psychometric intelligence were rising in the West. The "great divergence" (Pomeranz, 2000) between the West and the rest in economic history was, to the extent that we are able to reconstruct it, accompanied by an equally great cognitive divergence.

Figure 1 shows average intelligence in different world regions, measured as a composite of IQ and school achievement as will be described in section 2. Broadly, intelligence tracks economic development. The "Confucian" countries of East Asia (China, Japan, South Korea, Taiwan, Hong Kong, Singapore) have the highest scores followed by the countries of Protestant Europe, English-speaking countries with predominantly European-origin populations, Catholic Europe, and the ex-communist countries of Eastern Europe and the former Soviet Union. The middle field is formed by the countries of Latin America, the Muslim Middle East (including North Africa), the Pacific islands, and the countries of South and South-East Asia from India to Indonesia and the Philippines. IQs are lowest in the countries of Sub-Saharan Africa.

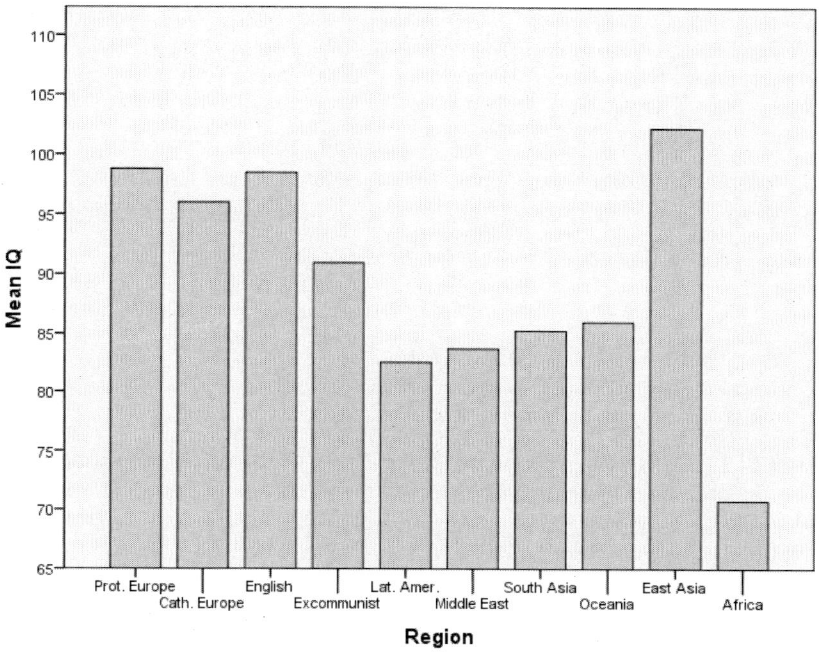

Figure 1. Average intelligence in different world regions. "Middle East" includes the predominantly Muslim countries from Morocco to Pakistan, "South Asia" reaches from India to Indonesia, and Oceania refers to the Pacific islands only, excluding Australia and New Zealand which are counted as "English". "Africa" includes only the Sub-Saharan countries.

2. Intelligence: Its Measurement and Correlates

2.1. Generality of Intelligence

The concept of intelligence would be useless if different cognitive abilities, such as short-term memory, long-term memory, speed of information processing, visuo-spatial ability, word knowledge and verbal comprehension, were statistically unrelated. But in fact, they are related. Robust positive correlations among subtests of complex IQ test batteries such as the Wechsler tests are universal (Jensen, 1998), with the partial exception of highly gifted samples that have been pre-selected rigorously for high general intelligence (Bakhiet and Ahmed, 2014). In samples representing the entire ability spectrum, between 35% and 55% of the variance in overall test performance can be attributed to the general factor *g*, with the remainder due to more specialized abilities and measurement error. Technically, *g* is defined as the unrotated first principal component of a factor analysis on the subtests of a complex test battery, whereas IQ is a simple summary score. *g* tends to correlate more highly than IQ with most outcomes, presumably because it weights those tests most heavily that are the "purest" measures of intelligence, as well as those that have the highest reliability.

2.2. Microeconomics of Intelligence

Intelligence is related with many real-world outcomes. Correlations tend to be highest with measures of scholastic achievement. The correlation of psychometric *g* with general scholastic achievement, operationalized by factor analysis of achievement tests in curricular subjects such as reading, science and mathematics, can be as high as 0.8 (Deary et al., 2007; Kaufman et al., 2012). Such high correlations require very accurate measures of *g* and scholastic achievement.

These high correlations may seem surprising because in theory, IQ tests are aptitude tests that measure pre-existing learning ability while scholastic assessments are achievement tests that measure attained knowledge and skills. In reality, however, the cognitive skills that are measured by IQ tests have to be acquired by prior learning. Much of this prior learning must occur in school, since each year of additional schooling during adolescence adds between 2 and 4 points to the IQ (e.g., Brinch and Galloway, 2012; Falch and Massih, 2011; Hansen, Heckman and Mullen, 2004). Conversely, the knowledge and skills that are tested in scholastic assessments depend on pre-existing learning ability. At the individual differences level, the two types of test are expected to be highly correlated as long as every child has the same opportunities to learn in school.

Another major use of IQ tests is for hiring decisions and the prediction of job performance or training success. Although high-confidence predictions remain elusive, the usual finding is that general mental ability is the single best predictor (e.g., Kuncel & Hezlett, 2010; Schmidt and Hunter, 2004). The effect of *g* on occupational success is mediated in part by economic preferences, strategic behavior, and job attachment (Burks et al., 2009). In prospective studies, intelligence measured in childhood or adolescence predicts occupational position and income of adults even when educational degrees and childhood socioeconomic status are controlled (Sorjonen et al., 2012; Strenze, 2007). Figure 2 shows results from the National Longitudinal Study of Youth in the United States, in which IQ measured at age 15-23 predicts log-transformed adult family income at age 28-37. In this path model, IQ predicts 15.7% of the total variance in family income directly, and 7.6% indirectly through educational attainment.

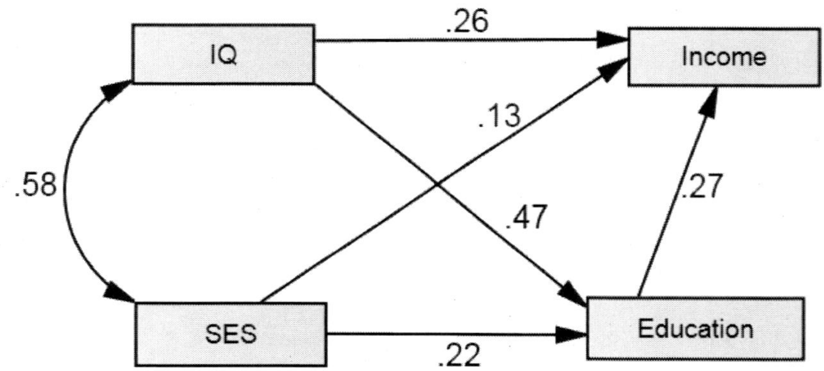

Figure 2. Log-transformed family income at age 28-37 (*Income*) is predicted for males in the NLSY79. IQ was measured with the Armed Services Vocational Aptitude Battery (ASVAB) at age 15-23. Error terms of the dependent variables (each with a regression weight fixed at 1) are omitted. SES = socioeconomic status of family of origin. N = 3525, all path coefficients are significant at p<.001.

2.2. Macroeconomics of Intelligence

If Adam Smith was right with his claim that the pursuit of personal gain translates into benefits for the entire economy, and if intelligence promotes personal economic success, it follows that everything else being equal, macroeconomic outcomes will be more favorable in a society with higher rather than lower average intelligence. This argument has been presented by Lynn and Vanhanen (2002, 2006, 2012) in their argument for a causal effect of intelligence on national wealth. This assumes that people pursue personal gain through productive work that creates valued goods and services rather than through rent seeking. Despite this limitation, correlations of average intelligence in the country with log-transformed per capita GDP are between 0.70 and 0.80 in world-wide country samples. Figure 1 gives an impression of this relationship.

3. Causes of Individual Variations in Intelligence

3.1. Quantitative Genetics: Nature and Nurture

Disregarding theories of mind-body dualism, human intelligence is a function of the human brain. As such it is the outcome of developmental processes that are guided by interactions between genetic programming and environmental inputs. Variations in both can cause individual differences in phenotypic (measured) intelligence. The relative importance of genes and environment for individual differences is studied by variance decomposition in genetically informative families, most commonly involving twins or adoptees. We still depend on these descriptive methods of quantitative genetics because only a small proportion of individual variation in general intelligence and school achievement can be explained by known genetic polymorphisms (e.g., Piffer, 2013a,b; Rietveld et al., 2013).

The most common variance decomposition in family studies partitions the phenotypic (observed or measured) variance V_P into additive genetic variance (V_G), shared environmental variance that makes family members such as twins, full siblings, half siblings and adopted children raised in the same family similar (V_C), non-shared environmental variance that makes them different (V_E), and measurement error (E):

$$V_P = V_G + V_C + V_E + E$$

In practice, E cannot be distinguished from V_E. Therefore V_G and V_C tend to be underestimated relative to V_E in heritability studies, and both tend to be higher when measurement is more accurate. Further refinements can be introduced by accounting for non-additive genetic effects (dominance and epistasis), gene-environment correlation and interaction, and assortative mating, but these need not concern us here. Heritability (V_G, also designated h^2 when only additive effects are included and H^2 when all genetic effects are included), is the proportion of the phenotypic variance that is explained by genetic factors.

Studies about the heritability of psychometric intelligence have produced broadly consistent results. Genes account for 30% to 80% of the total variance, and heritability rises with age. Based on results from 11,000 twin pairs from 4 countries, Haworth et al. (2010) calculated that broad heritability (H^2) of general intelligence increased from 41% at age 9 to 55% at age 12 and 66% at age 17. As heritability rises, shared environment becomes less important although it still has small effects on individual differences in adult intelligence (Kaplan, 2012).

The heritability of school achievement, measured by tests in curricular subjects such as reading, science and math, is about the same as the heritability of IQ (Bartels et al., 2002; Calvin et al., 2012). Therefore scholastic achievement tests measure not only the quality of schooling, but also the innate ability of the test taker. Conversely, IQ tests measure not only innate ability but also the quantity and quality of educational inputs, as shown by studies in which increased length of schooling raises the IQ (Brinch and Galloway, 2012; Falch and Massih, 2011; Hansen, Heckman and Mullen, 2004). The common practice of using scholastic achievement test scores as measures of schooling quality and IQ as a measure of innate endowments is not justified. Another observation is that in the commonly used IQ test batteries, such as the Wechsler tests, those subtests that are considered most culture-dependent (or "culturally biased") tend to have the highest *g* loadings and the highest heritabilities (Kan et al., 2013). This shows that the essence of the intelligence construct that is tapped by IQ tests is the genetically based ability to acquire culturally mediated knowledge and skills.

3.2. Limitations of Behavioral Genetics

Most heritability studies have been performed in economically advanced societies with subjects who had access to formal education and were not grossly deprived economically or intellectually. High heritabilities of adult intelligence have to be interpreted on the background of a relatively level playing field, created by modern welfare states in which environmental but not genetic inequalities have been reduced to some extent by social engineering. It does not imply that large environmental changes are unable to produce large changes in intelligence. Even in modern societies, the heritability of intelligence tends to be higher for children from higher socioeconomic status (SES) families (Turkheimer et al., 2003; *cf.* Nagoshi and Johnson, 2005; van der Sluis et al., 2008). Where this is observed, most likely environmental conditions are of similar high quality for most high-SES children but are more variable for low-SES children.

The variance decomposition shown above applies only to *individual* differences. In theory, differences in intelligence between countries and historical epochs can be decomposed into genetic and environmental components as well, but there is no established methodology to study this question. Molecular genetic studies can compare the frequencies of intelligence-related genetic variants across countries and their changes over time. First studies of this kind have been done (Piffer, 2013a,b), but conclusive results from this emerging field of IQ population genetics will have to await a better understanding of the molecular genetics of human intelligence.

3.3. The Production of Intelligence

The variance decomposition presented in subsection 3.1 is not a production function for intelligence. It does not predict the level of intellectual attainment, but describes the sources of individual differences. Production functions for intelligence or cognitive skills have been attempted by some authors. For example, Behrman et al. (2014) distinguish between pre-school, school, and post-school experiences in their analysis of a longitudinal data set from Guatemala. These factors were assumed to have additive effects.

Alternatively, inputs to human intelligence can be decomposed into genetic factors (or innate endowments), physical factors other than genes, formal education, and social-environmental factors other than formal education. Physical factors other than genes include perinatal factors (LeWinn et al., 2009; Matte et al., 2001), nutrition (Lynn, 1990), toxins (Ferrie et al., 2011), and infectious diseases (Fernando et al. 2010), but the extent to which they affect intelligence at the population level is uncertain. Most studies about the effects of nutritional deficiencies and infectious diseases on human intelligence are from developing countries, where these factors are more prevalent than in prosperous countries. The extent to which they contribute to IQ differences between countries and to Flynn effects is difficult to estimate. They can be conceptualized as largely additive with genetic factors, in that they affect physical brain development and thereby the responsiveness to educational efforts and other social-environmental factors.

Formal education is required for a level of intelligence that today is classified as non-retarded (Luria, 1976; Oesterdiekhoff, 2014). Its relationship with genetic and other biological inputs is most likely not additive but multiplicative, meaning that the return to educational efforts is proportional to the quality of the biological substrate. The same can be said of social-environmental factors other than schooling. Therefore, instead of the usual additive production function of the general form

$$IQ = \alpha + \beta_1 \text{ x Gen} + \beta_2 \text{ x Phy} + \beta_3 \text{ x Sch} + \beta_4 \text{ x Env} \qquad (1)$$

A more appropriate description would be

$$IQ = \alpha + (\beta_1 \text{ x Gen} + \beta_2 \text{ x Phy}) \text{ x } (\beta_3 \text{ x Sch} + \beta_4 \text{ x Env}) \quad (2)$$

Where Gen = genetic endowment, Phy = non-genetic physical factors, Sch = schooling, and Env = non-school social-environmental inputs.

Equation 2 is still unsatisfactory. It ignores the fact that diminishing returns to rising inputs are inevitable. Even the best school system cannot turn every child into an Einstein because not every child has the genetic potential to advance to that level—unless each child has been genetically engineered for extreme intelligence. Therefore we need to modify production function (2) to acknowledge the law of diminishing returns. One of several possibilities of doing so is:

$$IQ = \alpha + (\beta_1 \text{ x Gen} + \beta_2 \text{ x Phy}) \text{ x } \ln(\beta_3 \text{ x Sch} + \beta_4 \text{ x Env}) \quad (3)$$

The commonly cited example for the law of diminishing returns to environmental inputs is the stimulation of corn production by added fertilizer. At low levels, added fertilizer brings large returns. However, at high levels of fertilization corn yield barely responds to even more fertilizer because genetic and physical limitations, for example in the rate of photosynthesis, become prohibitive. In quantitative genetics, this ubiquitous phenomenon is known as the reaction norm of the trait (Plomin et al., 2012).

4. Measurement of Human Capital in Nations

4.1. IQ and School Achievement

There are two measures of country-level intelligence. First, we have a data set for the average IQ in more than 130 countries that has been compiled by the British scholar Richard Lynn. Data are of uneven quality. Some countries have multiple studies including high-quality standardizations of major IQ tests on representative population samples; others have only one or a few studies with convenience samples. Different stages of this data set have been presented in Lynn & Vanhanen (2001, 2002, 2006, 2012).

The second data type are scholastic assessments in curricular subjects such as mathematics, science and reading. Some large-scale international assessment programs have been performed at regular intervals, with PISA

(Programme of International Student Assessment, since 2000) and TIMSS (Trends in International Mathematics and Science Study, since 1995) being the most important. These major international testing programs are performed with representative country samples of about 5000 school children. Many of those countries that did not participate in PISA or TIMSS took part in earlier assessments that were generally of lower quality, and many countries in Africa and Latin America only have data from regional educational assessment programs that are sometimes difficult to anchor to the major international assessments. Data quality is about as variable in the scholastic data as in the IQ data (Meisenberg & Lynn, 2011).

Compared to individual differences within countries, differences between countries are approximately 30% to 40% larger for school achievement than IQ. The likely reason is that poor quality of schooling, although important for both school achievement and IQ, depresses school achievement to a greater extent than IQ. Educational quality is likely to be systematically lower in "low-IQ countries," mainly because of lower competence of teachers. For example, at the University of Khartoum (Sudan), the average IQ of students in the study program for primary education teachers was found to be 65 (Khaleefa, Amer & Lynn, 2014).

4.2. The Ecology of Country-Level Intelligence

Table 2 shows the correlations between measures of cognitive human capital, development indicators, and annual economic growth rates. The *Schooling* variable is based on average years of schooling of the adult population (1995-2010 average) from the Barro-Lee data set (hppt://www.barrolee.com), with missing data points extrapolated from World Bank and United Nations sources. *No Corruption* is a composite of Transparency International's Corruption Perception Index 1998-2003, and the Control of Corruption measure of the World Bank's Governance Indicators 1996-2005 (no earlier data available). *Political freedom* is constructed from the averaged Political Rights and Civil Liberties measures of the Freedom House Index 1975-2005 and the Voice and Accountability measure of the World Bank's Governance Indicators 1996-2005. Countries with more than 0.1 barrel/day of oil exports per capita are excluded because their economies depend heavily on the oil price, and countries with a population of less than 250,000 are excluded as well.

The first observation is that IQ and school achievement are highly correlated with each other. They also have similar correlations with other variables, including economic growth. Therefore they can be considered alternative measures of the same construct, which we can call cognitive human capital or simply intelligence.

Another observation is that these measures of human capital are closely related to the "development indicators" including log-transformed GDP (1975/2011 average). A difference of 9 IQ points between countries translates into a two-fold difference in per capita GDP. This corroborates the observations of Lynn and Vanhanen (2002, 2006, 2012) of a close relationship between IQ and GDP. We further see that economic growth is related most closely to school achievement and IQ.

Because of their conceptual and correlational similarity, IQ and school achievement were combined into a composite measure of intelligence, with weighting for data quality as described in Meisenberg & Lynn (2011).

Table 2. Correlations of economic growth (1975-2011) with IQ, school achievement, and some development indicators. Schooling is average years in school of the adult population. N = 80 countries

	Growth	IQ	School ach.	Schooling	lgGDP	No Corruption
IQ	.458	1				
School achiev.	.517	.902	1			
Schooling	.239	.770	.741	1		
lgGDP 1975/2011	.146	.817	.782	.850	1	
No Corruption	.172	.677	.659	.683	.775	1
Political Freedom	.083	.627	.537	.641	.709	.761

Because the between-country differences, relative to within-country differences, are greater for school achievement than IQ, the averaging was done by bringing the country-level school achievement scores to the same mean and standard deviation as country-level IQ for the 100 countries having both measures. The resulting *Intelligence* variable, which includes only data published before 2011, is available for 168 countries and territories. The averaging of IQ and school achievement enlarges the set of countries for which cognitive test results are available and increases accuracy by averaging out measurement error and weighting data by quality, while sacrificing little in terms of conceptual purity.

5. Determinants of Economic Growth, 1975-2011

5.1. Growth Regressions

In Table 2, log-transformed per capita GDP has high correlations with all other variables except economic growth. Because the direction of causation is indeterminate in every case, it would be futile to "predict" per capita GDP with a combination of its correlates. The endogeneity problem is mitigated when the predicted outcome is not cross-sectional per capita GDP, but change of per capita GDP over time. Although ongoing economic growth can to some extent affect other measures, such as corruption and democratization, such effects are not likely to be large.

The growth regressions of Table 3 include initial log-transformed per capita GDP based on the "advantage of backwardness": the expectation that poorer countries have more unused development potential and are therefore, ceteris paribus, likely to grow faster than countries with higher pre-existing prosperity (Weede & Kämpf, 2002). Intelligence and schooling (average years in school) are included as measures of human capital. Freedom from corruption, as an indicator of non-cognitive human capital, is predicted to promote economic growth independent of cognitive human capital, and political freedom is an indicator of general political and social conditions. A dummy for the ex-communist countries of the former Soviet bloc is included because their growth trajectories were affected by the economic dislocations after the end of communist rule. This variable is omitted for the subsample of poor countries because only one of the ex-communist countries (Mongolia) was classified as poor. The subsamples were formed by a median split, based on the average of their log-transformed per capita GDPs in 1975 and 2011. As in Table 2, small countries and oil exporting countries are excluded.

The striking result is that log-transformed per capita GDP in 1975 is a powerful negative predictor of subsequent growth, and intelligence is an equally powerful positive predictor. In the complete sample, an increase of IQ by 10 points is associated with an increase of the annual economic growth rate by 1.25%. For example, the 7 East Asian countries in the sample have an average IQ of 104.6 and an average annual growth rate of 5.10%. The 33 countries of sub-Saharan Africa have an average IQ of 70.3 and an annual growth rate of 0.59%. The effect of intelligence is virtually the same in the subsamples of rich and poor countries. This shows that the concept of intelligence has predictive validity cross-culturally, contrary to a frequent claim that intelligence tests and related assessment tools are valid only in the cultures in which they were designed (e.g., Greenfield, 1997). Schooling has only a marginal effect on growth when intelligence is included, consistent with earlier results by Weede & Kämpf (2002) and Ram (2007).

Table 3. Prediction of annual growth rates 1975-2011 for all countries and the subsets of "rich" and "poor" countries. Unstandardized B coefficients and standard errors are shown

Predictor	All countries		Poor countries		Rich countries	
	B	SE	B	SE	B	SE
Constant	-.155	1.230	-2.142	2.297	3.855	2.404
lgGDP 1975	-2.964***	.361	2.709***	.665	-3.729***	.629
Intelligence	.125***	.014	.132***	.020	.126***	.018
Schooling	.158*	.069	.067	.102	.054	.101
No corruption	.146	.074	.499**	.145	.136	.087
Political freedom	-.029	.088	.044	.135	-.040	.105
Ex-communist	-.584	.473			-.460	.467
N	120		60		60	
Adj. R2	.575		.626		.587	

* p<.05; ** p<.01; *** p<.001, two-tailed t tests.

Effects of the other predictors are smaller and more variable. Coefficients are positive for freedom from corruption and negative for (abandonment of) communism. Clearly, the transition from a communist to a capitalist system in the former Soviet bloc has not resulted in the kind of economic boom that China has experienced after the de-facto introduction of a capitalist economy. Political freedom is the only variable that stubbornly refuses to affect economic growth, consistent with the conclusions of Doucouliagos and Ulubaşoğlu (2008).

5.2. Some Caveats about Growth Regressions

The measures used in Table 3 were, as far as possible, taken for the time period between 1975 and 2011, over which growth was observed. In the case of the intelligence measures, we would ideally use a measure of cognitive ability of adolescents in the 1970s, who were economically active in the 1975-2011 period. However, the amount and quality of IQ data has increased steeply over time. The IQ measure is based on studies published from the 1930s to 2011, with a median date of 1990. Most of these studies were performed with children or adolescents. The IQ data set includes a "one size fits all" correction for the Flynn effect. Although the Flynn effect has been a tide that lifted all boats, its strength has been variable across countries and time as shown in Table 1 (see also Flynn, 1987). This invariably introduces errors when using the IQ data set as an approximation of the intelligence of the working-age population between 1975 and 2011. However, these errors are expected to be small.

The school achievement measure is derived mainly from the PISA studies of 2000-2009 and the TIMSS studies of 1995-2007, which were conducted with 15-year-olds (PISA) and 8th graders (TIMSS). Despite some differential trends (Meisenberg and Woodley, 2013), national achievement levels have been quite stable over the time periods covered by these recurrent assessment programs. Therefore it is unlikely that relative achievement has changed very much during the preceding decades. The alternative explanation, that intelligence is a consequence but not a cause of economic growth, cannot be excluded based on growth regressions alone. However, it is unlikely because the important relationship of the intelligence measure is not with cross-sectional per capita GDP, but with the *change* of per capita GDP over time. Also, earlier studies that took account of earnings and cognitive test scores of migrants in the host country or IQs in wealthy oil countries have concluded that there is a substantial causal effect of IQ on earnings and productivity (Christainsen, 2013; Jones & Schneider, 2010)

6. Mediators of the Intelligence Effect

6.1. Use of Path Models

Intelligence is predicted to favor economic growth because it improves job performance, management practices, institutional quality, technological and administrative innovation, ethical conduct, demographic behavior and/or investment decisions—in other words, most of the factors that economists have ever proposed as determinants of economic growth. Anything that is affected by intelligence net of other causes, and that itself affects economic growth, is a bona fide mediator of the intelligence effect. The method for studying mediation effects is path analysis, which models causal effects based on pre-existing theory. It includes fit indices which reject models that do not fit the empiric data.

The models in Figure 3 predict log-transformed per capita GDP in 2011. The only exogenous variables are log-transformed per capita GDP in 1975 and, except for the subsample of poor countries, a dummy for ex-communist. Schooling (average years in school) and intelligence (composite of IQ and school achievement) are assumed to mediate effects of the exogenous variables on lgGDP2011. Each endogenous variable includes an error term with regression weight fixed at 1 (omitted in the figures), to account for unmodeled influences and measurement error. *lgGDP1975* and *Excommunist* are hypothesized to influence *Schooling*, and *Schooling* and *lgGDP1975* are hypothesized to influence *Intelligence*. All variables are allowed to affect *lgGDP2011*. These models do not formally predict a growth rate, but effectively do so by determining effects on log-transformed GDP in 2011 *independent of the effects of log-transformed GDP in 1975*.

The models deal with the endogeneity problem by modeling intelligence and schooling both as effects of prosperity at an earlier time and as causes of prosperity at a later time. The models have one degree of freedom due to the omitted relationship between *Excommunist* and *Intelligence* (models 3A and 3B) or *lgGDP1975* and *Intelligence* (model 3C). Because these relationships were virtually zero, the model fit is excellent as shown by the fit indices. High p value and RMSEA<.05 indicate good model fit (Hu & Bentler, 1999).

These models replicate the results of the growth regressions in Table 3. Additional relationships are theoretically meaningful. Schooling is raised by high per capita GDP in 1975 and to a lesser extent by communism; and intelligence is raised by schooling and to a lesser extent by per capita GDP in 1975 (except in poor countries). As in the growth regressions, schooling and abandonment of communism appear to have marginal positive and negative effects, respectively.

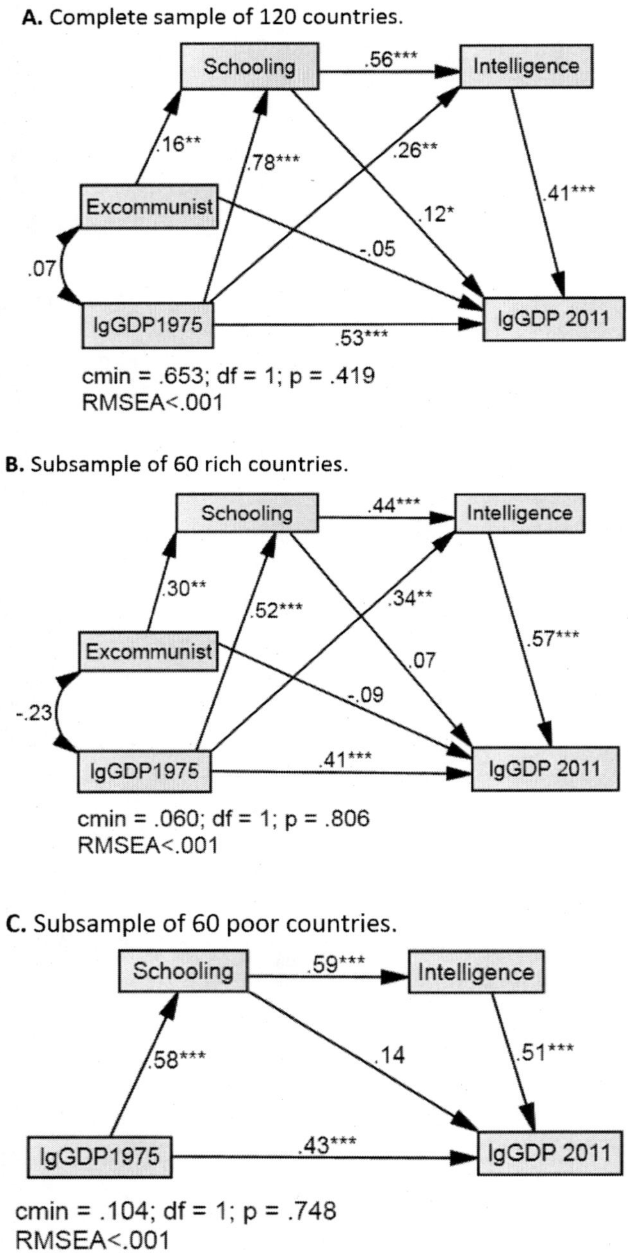

Figure 3. Path model predicting log-transformed per capita GDP in 2011. Standardized regression weights are shown. Error terms are omitted. *p<.05; **p<.01; ***p<.001.

6.2. Mediator Models

The models of Figure 3 were extended by inserting a hypothesized mediator between *Intelligence* and *lgGDP2011*. The mediator was allowed to be influenced not only by *Intelligence*, but by all variables except *lgGDP2011*. Figure 4 shows as an example the model for the complete sample of 120 countries with the total fertility rate (1975-2005 average) as a mediator. The results of this model are included in Table 4.

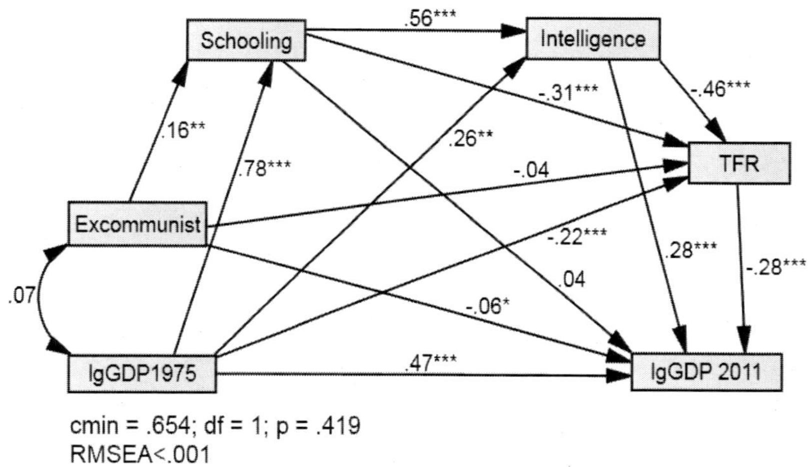

Figure 4. An example of a mediator model. The total fertility rate (TFR, 1975-2005 average) is hypothesized to mediate effects of intelligence (and other variables) on log-transformed per capita GDP in 2011. Error terms of the endogenous variables are not shown. * p<.05; ** p<.01; *** p<.001, two-tailed t tests.

A mediation effect was considered present if both the *Intelligence* → *Mediator* path and the *Mediator* → *lgGDP2011* path were significant at p<.05. For these variables, the indirect effects are highlighted in bold in Table 4. In all, 20 variables were examined as possible mediators of the intelligence effect. The results can be summarized as follows:

A. Business climate: Economic freedom is considered a condition for vigorous economic growth (e.g., Justesen, 2008; Weede & Kämpf, 2002). This concept is embodied in two major composite indices, one by the Fraser Institute (www.freetheworld.com) and the other by the Heritage Foundation (http://www.heritage.org/index/Download.aspx). Both indices combine two different kinds of measure. One type describes bureaucracy and red tape, and the other the size of government. These two components are virtually uncorrelated with each other, have different external correlates, and appear to measure different constructs. Therefore two measures were created from the relevant subindices: one for *Economic Freedom* sensu stricto (areas 2-5 of the Fraser index and domains 1, 2, and 5-8 of the Heritage index), and the other named *Big Government* (reversed area 1 of the Fraser index and domains 3-4 of the Heritage index). The correlation (Pearson's *r*) between these two measures is -.144 (N = 164 countries). Data from Fraser are for 1975-2005, and from Heritage for 1995-2005 (no earlier data available).

Table 4 shows that economic freedom does promote economic growth in the subsample of rich countries. Because intelligence favors economic freedom in rich (but not poor) countries, economic freedom qualifies as a mediator of the IQ effect in rich countries. About 17.3% of the intelligence effect in rich countries is mediated by economic freedom. Unlike economic freedom, big government has little or no adverse effect on economic growth even in rich countries, and is not much affected by intelligence either.

B. Resource allocation: Allocation of capital resources has been an element of classical growth theory (Solow, 1956). Human capital theory emphasizes that individuals with higher intelligence tend to have lower impulsivity and lower time preference (Shamosh & Gray, 2008). This is predicted to lead to higher savings rates and greater resource allocation to investment relative to consumption in countries with higher average intelligence.

Table 4 includes results for consumption, government and investment share as % of GDP (1975-2005 average) from the Penn World Tables 7.0 (Heston et al., 2011), and gross domestic savings (1975-2005 average) from the World Bank (http://data.worldbank.org/indicator/NY.GDS.TOTL.ZS?page =4). A higher investment share is related to stronger growth as expected, at least in poor countries, while the effect of consumption tends to be negative. However, the effects of intelligence on investment and consumption, although in the predicted direction, are rather weak and not always statistically significant. Therefore the investment-versus-consumption choice mediates only a small portion of the intelligence effect at best. The savings rate fares slightly better. Here, we do have a robust effect of intelligence independent of other predictors, and higher savings do have a mild association with economic growth in both rich and poor countries. However, reverse causation is possible, since rising prosperity may enable individuals and institutions to save more.

Table 4. Mediation of the effects of intelligence (*Intel*) and other variables on log-transformed per capita GDP in 2011 (*GDP11*). These are for models of the structure shown in Figure 4 except models for poor countries, which omit *Excommunist*

	Intel → M	M → GDP11	Intel → GDP11	Indirect	Other
A. Business climate					
1. Economic Freedom					
All	.171	.055	.398***	2.3%	G75++, School+, Excom--
Rich	.367**	.267***	.468***	**17.3%**	G75+, Excom-
Poor	-.203	.060	.524***	-3.2%	School+
2. Big Government					
All	-.098	-.014	.406***	0.3%	Excom+
Rich	-.244	-.064	.550***	2.8%	
Poor	.014	.000	.507***	0.0%	
B. Resource allocation					
1. Consumption share of GDP					
All	-.278*	-.052	.393***	3.5%	G75-
Rich	-.298	-.108*	.533***	5.7%	
Poor	-.313*	-.052	.491***	3.2%	G75-
2. Government share of GDP					
All	-.028	-.022	.407***	0.2%	
Rich	-.193	-.106*	.545***	3.6%	Edu+
Poor	.061	-.006	.508***	-0.1%	
3. Investment share of GDP					
All	.230	.096***	.386***	5.4%	G75-, School-
Rich	.323	.021	.559***	1.2%	
Poor	.171	.238***	.467***	8.0%	School++
4. Gross domestic savings					
All	.469***	.091**	.365***	**10.5%**	
Rich	.432**	.128*	.511***	**9.8%**	
Poor	.460***	.129	.448***	11.7%	G75+

Table 4. (Continued)

	Intel → M	M → GDP11	Intel → GDP11	Indirect	Other
C. Income (re)distribution					
1. Welfare state					
All	.306***	-.010	.411***	-0.8%	G75++, Excom+
Rich	.260*	.023	.560***	1.1%	G75++
Poor	.458***	-.033	.522***	-3.0%	
2. Gini index					
All	-.680***	-.018	.395***	3.0%	Excom-
Rich	-.447***	-.043	.547***	3.4%	G75--, School-, Excom--
Poor	-.593***	-.119	.437***	13.9%	School+
3. Social pathologies (homicide, theft, teenage pregnancy)					
All	-.822***	-.042	.373***	8.5%	
Rich	-.639***	-.213	.430***	24.0%	G75--
Poor	-.744***	-.045	.474***	6.6%	
D. Technology and trade					
1. Technological competitiveness					
All	.307***	-.049	.423***	-3.7%	G75++, School++, Excom-
Rich	.249**	-.149	.603***	-6.6%	G75++, School++
Poor	.269**	.325**	.420***	**17.2%**	School++
2. Trade openness					
All	.098	.069**	.401***	1.7%	
Rich	.244	.202***	.516***	8.7%	
Poor	-.039	.006	.508***	-0.0%	G75++
E. Good government					
1. Freedom from corruption					
All	.278**	.086*	.384***	**5.9%**	G75++, Excom-
Rich	.228*	.144	.533***	5.8%	School++, Excom-
Poor	.090	.238***	.486***	4.2%	

	Intel → M	M → GDP11	Intel → GDP11	Indirect	Other
2. Political freedom					
All	.025	.029	.407***	0.2%	G75++, School++
Rich	.117	.026	.563***	0.5%	G75++, School++
Poor	-.239	.106	.533***	-4.5%	School++
3. Political stability					
All	.239*	.075*	.390***	**4.4%**	
Rich	.363**	.122	.521***	7.8%	G75+
Poor	-.016	.141*	.510***	-0.4%	School+
4. Government effectiveness					
All	.349***	.153***	.354***	**13.1%**	G75++, School+, Exco--
Rich	.313***	.300**	.472***	**16.6%**	G75++, School++, Exco-
Poor	.186	.312***	.449***	11.4%	School++
5. Regulatory quality					
All	.281**	.127**	.372***	**8.7%**	G75++, School+
Rich	.378***	.230**	.479***	**15.4%**	G75++
Poor	-.031	.246***	.515***	-1.5%	School++
6. Rule of law					
All	.353***	.123**	.364***	**10.7%**	G75++, School+, Exco-
Rich	.371***	.250**	.473***	**16.4%**	G75++, School++
Poor	.079	.279***	.485***	4.3%	School++
F. Demography and health					
1. Total fertility rate (TFR) 1975-2005					
All	-.458***	-.275***	.282***	**30.9%**	G75--, School--
Rich	-.571***	-.304***	.392***	**30.7%**	School-
Poor	-.519***	-.323***	.340***	**33.0%**	School--
2. Life expectancy					
All	.437***	.106	.361***	11.4%	G75++, School++

Table 4. (Continued)

	Intel → M	M → GDP11	Intel → GDP11	Indirect	Other
Rich	.573***	.094	512***	9.5%	School+
Poor	.500*	.113	.451***	11.1%	School+
3. Under-5 mortality					
All	-.368***	-.138*	.357***	**12.4%**	G75--, School--
Rich	-.411***	-.217*	.476***	**15.8%**	G75-, School--
Poor	-.471***	-.128	.447***	11.9%	School--

M = hypothesized mediator. *Other* refers to significant positive (+) and negative (-) effects (+ and - p<.05, ++ and -- p<.01) of variables other than intelligence on the mediator: *G75* = log-transformed per capita GDP in 1975; *School* = schooling; *Excom* = Excommunist. Standardized regression weights are shown. N is up to 120 countries for the complete sample, and up to 60 each for the subsamples of rich and poor countries. Significant mediation effects are highlighted in bold. *p<.05; **p<.01; ***p<.001.

There are only marginal, non-significant associations of higher government expenditure with lower intelligence and slower growth in rich countries. The correlation between the *Government share of GDP* (B2 in Table 4) and *Big Government* (A2) variables is only .177 (N = 162 countries).

C. Income (re)distribution: The welfare state redistributes resources from those who work to pensioners and the unemployed, and from the healthy to the sick. Concerns about possible adverse effects of the welfare state on economic development are voiced at times, but evidence for such an effect is difficult to locate. According to Beraldo, Montolio & Turati (2009), public health expenditures actually promote economic growth.

The *Welfare state* measure used in Table 4 (variable C1) is calculated from ILO (International Labour Organisation) data available at http: //www.ilo.org/secsoc/information-resources/WCMS_146566/lang-en/ index.htm. It includes measures of pensions, unemployment benefits, health insurance, and social security benefits other than health, mainly from the 1995-2005 period. The results in Table 4 show that the welfare state is favored by high intelligence as well as high prosperity, and that it does not affect economic growth.

The Gini index of income inequality was investigated because of its inverse association with intelligence. Low intelligence and high racial diversity are considered the main predictors of a high Gini index in country-level comparisons (Meisenberg, 2007a, 2008a). The impact of income inequality on economic growth is uncertain, with some studies reporting positive and others reporting negative effects (Forbes, 2000). The Gini index used in Table 4 is based on net income or disposable income, derived mainly from the World Income Inequality Database (WIID2a) of the United Nations University. Results confirm the inverse relationship between Gini index and intelligence, but a high Gini index reduces economic growth only mildly or not at all.

High income inequality is associated with social pathologies in the form of crime, single motherhood and teenage pregnancy (Wilkinson & Pickett, 2009). Therefore a composite measure of social pathologies was created from homicide rate in 2008 (UN Office of Drugs and Crime, http://www.unodc.org/unodc/en/data-and-analysis/homicide.html), crime victimization (stealing, mugging, Gallup World Poll at http://www.gallup.com/poll/world.aspx), and adolescent fertility rate from the Demographic Yearbook of the United Nations 2009/10 (UN, 2010). These three measures are highly correlated both with each other and the Gini index.

Table 4 shows that social pathologies are indeed powerfully suppressed by higher intelligence, but negative effects on economic growth approach statistical significance only in the subsample of rich countries.

D. Technology and trade: A composite measure of technological competitiveness (variable D1 in Table 4) was computed from (1) 8 topics of the Global Competitiveness Report 2001/02 (World Economic Forum, http://www.cid.harvard.edu/archive/cr/): unique products, sophisticated production processes, sophisticated marketing, quality of research institutions, buyer sophistication, log-transformed patents/capita, company innovation, and company R&D spending; (2) Average of log-transformed royalties/capita, patents/capita, scientific articles/capita, and books published/capita, obtained from the World Development Indicators of the World Bank and the Human Development Reports of the United Nations; and (3) the Arco technology index 1990 (Archibugi & Coco, 2004).

Table 4 shows that technological competitiveness is indeed higher in countries with higher average intelligence, confirming an earlier report by Gelade (2008). However, a positive effect of technology on economic growth can be demonstrated only for poor but not rich countries. This indicates that diffusion of know-how from the technological frontier to less developed countries is beneficial for these countries. The failure of innovation to stimulate growth in rich countries might be related to the ease with which foreign innovations can be bought or copied, with the result that the countries in which the innovations originate are not always those that profit from them the most. Also, per capita rates of major innovations appear to have been declining throughout the last century (Woodley, 2012), possibly to a point where they are becoming less important for continued economic growth.

The measure of trade openness (1975-2005 average) is from the Penn World Tables 7.0 (Heston et al., 2011). The results show that trade is favored only marginally if at all by higher intelligence, and that its economic benefits can be demonstrated only for rich but not poor countries. Quite possibly, the terms of trade favor the more advanced economies, such that net benefits for less affluent countries are nil.

E. Good government: Most indicators in this category, including *Government Effectiveness*, *Regulatory Quality*, *Rule of Law*, and *Political Stability*, are from the Governance Indicators of the World Bank (www.govindicators.org), each averaged over the 1996-2005 time period. *Political Freedom* and *No Corruption* are the same variables as in Tables 2 and 3.

The only measure in this group that is consistently unrelated with intelligence and economic growth is political freedom, confirming the results of the regression models in Table 3. The others are potent promoters of economic growth in both rich and poor countries. Most of these indicators of "good government" have previously been found to be associated with intelligence (Kalonda Kanyama, 2014). The present results confirm this association for rich countries but not poor countries. The reasons for the latter observation are unknown. Uncertain quality of governance data from some of the poorer countries may be one reason. Another possibility is that higher intelligence in poor countries leads to rent seeking instead of institution building. However, good government promotes economic growth equally in poor and rich countries. The five governance indicators (excluding political freedom) are highly correlated with each other for the 120 countries in the complete sample, with Pearson's *r*'s between .770 (freedom from corruption and political stability) and .965 (government effectiveness and rule of law). Unlike big government, good government is consistently related to intelligence and economic growth in the expected direction and is an important mediator of intelligence effects on growth, at least in the more developed countries.

F. Demography and health: Rampant population growth in developing countries has been a major concern in development economics since the mid-20th century, when populations seemed to grow exponentially in the developing world. Fast population growth, it was assumed, would prevent economic growth by reducing the amount of land and capital per capita. Developing countries were seen as moving into a Malthusian trap (e.g., Ehrlich, 1968). This received wisdom was challenged by the late Julian Simon (1996, 2000), who maintained that growing populations are the most important resource for economic growth (Fitzpatrick & Spohn, 2009; see also Headey & Hodge, 2009). Table 4 and Figure 4 give a decisive answer: High fertility is a powerful correlate of slow growth, even in prosperous countries. It is also evident that high average intelligence in the country, together with extensive schooling and to some extent high prosperity, is a major predictor of low fertility, confirming earlier results (Meisenberg, 2009). Reduced fertility accounts for approximately 30% of the intelligence effect on economic growth, as well as for most or all of the effect of prolonged schooling.

The reason for this is not necessarily a mismatch between population and physical resources, since even the poorest countries today show little signs of being caught in a Malthusian trap (Kenny, 2010). Also, Asian countries with their high population densities and scarcities of land and natural resources have done far better than the sparsely populated, resource-rich Sub-Saharan African countries. A more likely reason is that in both rich and poor countries, excess fertility is contributed mainly by the least educated sections of the population (Meisenberg, 2008b). The challenge of educating large numbers of children from poor family backgrounds and integrating them into the work force is one likely contributor to the adverse effect of high fertility on growth. It is unlikely that high fertility would be an economic liability if the excess births were contributed by the most educated and productive sections of the population. The importance of the quality rather than the quantity of the human population has been emphasized, for example, by Lutz (2009).

Health and longevity are correlates of high intelligence at the individual level (e.g., Wrulich et al., 2013), most likely because more intelligent people tend to have healthier lifestyles and are better able to manage their health problems. At the country level, better health of the working-age population is a plausible contributor to labor productivity (Beraldo, Montolio & Turati, 2009). The last two variables in Table 4 show that better health, indexed by life expectancy and under-5 mortality, is indeed related to higher average intelligence in the country. Better health, in turn, is associated with economic growth, although this effect is statistically significant only for under-5 mortality.

In summary, Table 4 shows that intelligence promotes economic growth through multiple channels. Reduced fertility is a major mechanism, and it appears to mediate the effect of education as well (see Figure 4). "Good government" is another important mediator of the intelligence effect although "small government" is not. Good business management, or "managerial capital" (Bloom et al., 2010; Bruhn, Karlan & Schoar, 2010), may be important as well, but no good indicators of managerial capital are available at the country level. It is reasonable to expect that the quality of business management tends to be high in countries with effective government institutions, because both depend on the competence of managerial personnel. Therefore the governance indicators may, in part, be proxies for good business practices as well.

Another possible mediator of intelligence effects that is difficult to measure at the country level is the willingness and ability to cooperate. A review by Jones (2008) shows that cooperativeness, measured in the Prisoner's dilemma game, is positively related to intelligence. This correlate of intelligence may explain some of the relationship of intelligence with governance. Other likely mediators of the intelligence effect include less red tape and restrictions on economic activities ("economic freedom"), higher savings and/or investment, and technology adoption in developing countries.

7. A General Theory of Economic Growth, 1700-2000

7.1. The Anomaly of Economic Growth

Since the Industrial Revolution of the 18th and 19th centuries, Europe and its overseas clones have experienced more than two centuries of bumpy but sustained economic growth driven by a seemingly inexhaustible stream of innovations. That sustained economic growth is an anomaly that occurred only once in human history is obvious. Through many millennia before the Industrial Revolution, rates of economic growth and contraction were minimal by today's standards, with little change in per capita production and consumption. It is also obvious that the beginning of sustained economic growth was accompanied by rising literacy and the development of a scientifically founded world view. Thus we observe, at the same time or in short succession, phenomena as diverse as the rise of science, the Enlightenment, technological innovations, the Industrial Revolution, humanism, democracy, secularization, birth control and economic growth (Oesterdiekhoff, 2014). The co-occurrence of these disparate phenomena in the same place (northern and western Europe) at the same time (17th to 20th centuries) is unlikely to be the result of chance. Therefore the question: What is their common denominator?

7.2. The Anomaly of the Flynn Effect

The only sensible answer to the riddle of behavioral and economic modernity is that the people changed. They became more intelligent and more rational. For the 20th century, this statement is not mere conjecture but has been proven beyond doubt by psychometric intelligence research. The pervasiveness of rising intelligence in modern societies had not been appreciated until James Flynn's studies in the 1980s (Flynn, 1987), but we do have firm evidence for Flynn effects from the beginning of the 20th century. Tuddenham (1948) compared the IQ test results of white conscripts in the American army during World Wars I and II, finding a difference of 12.9 IQ points favoring the World War II draft (see Table 1). In Britain, standardizations of Raven's Standard Progressive Matrices, the most widely used "culture-reduced" non-verbal intelligence test, in 1942 and 1992 showed an IQ gain of 22 points between the 1890 and 1940 birth cohorts (Raven, Raven & Court, 1998; see Table 1). Thus there is evidence that cohorts born around 1900 were experiencing Flynn effects already.

There is no psychometric evidence for rising intelligence before that time because IQ tests were introduced only during the first decade of the 20th century, but literacy rates were rising steadily after the end of the Middle Age in all European countries for which we have evidence (Mitch, 1992; Stone, 1969), and the number of books printed per capita kept rising (Baten & van Zanden, 2008). These developments indicate that intelligence and intellectual curiosity—an almost inevitable consequence of high intelligence—were rising during these centuries. Mokyr (2005) argues that because rising intellectual development was very much in evidence before the beginnings of the Industrial Revolution, it should be considered a cause or precondition of modern economic growth, rather than only its consequence. Mokyr (2009) also argues that without effective enforcement of intellectual property rights, the technological innovations of the Industrial Revolution were not caused primarily by material incentives. What was rising at that time was the supply of creative individuals, not the demand or incentives for innovation. We also know that two negative correlates of high intelligence, income inequality and violent crime (variables C2 and C3 in Table 4), were declining in Europe since the Middle Age (Eisner, 2003; van Zanden, 2009). Thus we have at least indirect evidence for rising intelligence before, during, and after the Industrial Revolution.

The late phase of this process is the Flynn effect. Its causes have been much debated, but its sheer magnitude – approximately 30 IQ points (2 present-day standard deviations) during the 20th century – virtually excludes genetic changes, which have a major impact only on longer time scales of several centuries to millennia (Meisenberg, 2008c). Therefore massive improvements must have taken place in the environmental determinants of intelligence. Improved nutrition is one candidate (Lynn, 1990), but the extent to which it contributed to the Flynn effect is impossible to estimate. Brain size increased to some extent along with body size during the last century (Miller & Corsellis, 1977), and given the known correlation of about 0.4 between brain size and intelligence (Rushton & Ankney, 2009), this may have made a modest contribution.

More important was almost certainly the massive expansion of educational systems during the 20th century (Schofer & Meyer, 2005). Compulsory public school systems had been introduced during the 19th century in most European countries. Before that time, rising literacy and more extensive schooling had been driven more by rising demand than by rising supply (Mitch, 1992). Today, one stylized fact about formal education is that it raises IQ by 2 to 4 points per year in adolescence (Brinch & Galloway, 2012; Falch & Massih, 2011; Hansen, Heckman & Mullen, 2004). In the United States, for example, the average length of schooling rose from 7.6 years for the 1890 birth cohort to 12.9 years for the 1950 birth cohort (Goldin, 1998). This alone is expected to translate into an IQ gain of 10.5 to 21 points during this 60-year period. Other factors that most likely have contributed to the Flynn effect include better quality of education, urbanization, mass media, and generally the rising complexity of everyday life.

7.3. Feedback between Intelligence and Economic Growth

Whatever the precise causes of the Flynn effect may have been, rising intelligence solves the puzzle of sustained economic growth in the recent past. We only need to accept two propositions: (1) environmental improvements, including a more effective school system and more cognitively stimulating environments outside of school, raise children's intelligence; and (2) intelligent people are more likely than less intelligent people to provide good schools and stimulating environments for their children's intellectual growth.

In this general form, neither of these propositions is controversial. If we accept both, the following prediction emerges: Once the intelligence of a population rises beyond a certain threshold, people will begin raising their living standards through technological and institutional improvements that lead to economic growth. They will also increasingly appreciate the value of intellectual development. Aided by greater prosperity, they will provide a better education for their children, both in and outside of school. In consequence the next generation will grow up to be, on average, more intelligent than their parents. This enables them to innovate even more, raise living standards even more, provide even better education for *their* children, and thereby raise the next generation's intelligence even more. This trans-generational feedback between economic growth and rising intelligence summarizes the dynamic of modern civilization (Meisenberg, 2007b, p. 273-278). It is possible only because of the high (but not infinite) malleability of human intelligence.

7.4. Why Europe?

Why did this spiral of economic and cognitive growth take off in Europe rather than somewhere else, and why did it not happen earlier, for example in classical Athens or the Roman Empire? One part of the answer is that this process can start only when technologies are already in place to translate rising economic output into rising intelligence. The minimal requirements are a writing system that is simple enough to be learned by everyone without undue effort, and a means to produce and disseminate written materials: paper, and the printing press. The first requirement had been present in Europe and the Middle East (but not China) since antiquity, and the second was in place in Europe from the 15th century. The Arabs had learned both paper-making and printing from the Chinese in the 13th century (Carter, 1955), but showed little interest in books. Their civilization was entering into terminal decline at about that time (Huff, 1993).

A second requirement is the desire of the cognitive elite to use their abilities for technological and institutional improvements rather than philosophical musings or theological debate. This precondition was present in the educated middle classes of early modern Europe, but possibly not in classical antiquity, when many members of the educated classes expressed their disdain for physical labor and the craftsman's work (Mokyr, 1990, pp. 193-208).

Perhaps the most general condition is what we may call aggregate brainpower. A solitary genius is not sufficient to start a scientific or industrial revolution, or a major philosophical movement such as the Enlightenment. Major historical developments like these require a critical mass of interacting minds. The ability to reach this critical mass depends on two factors: the size of the population, and its level of innate talent, or "genotypic intelligence." Classical Athens may have had high genotypic intelligence and a high rate of geniuses per capita, but population size was insufficient for the transition to sustained economic and intellectual growth. Also the 17th and 18th century British had high genotypic intelligence, but they also had a sufficiently large population to bring forth the number of great minds required for the scientific and industrial revolutions.

Demographic behavior was a critical factor for the production of this aggregate brainpower in early modern Europe. In the Malthusian economies of the pre-industrial civilizations, usually greater wealth resulted in a greater number of surviving children. This has been demonstrated for medieval (Razi, 1980) and early modern England (Boberg-Fazlic, Sharp & Weisdorf, 2011; Clark & Hamilton, 2006), where the phenomenon has been dubbed the "survival of the richest." If, as is likely, higher intelligence favored upward social mobility while the excess children of the upper classes moved down the social hierarchy, cultural and genetic selection for higher intelligence was inevitable. Gregory Clark (2007, p. 112-132) proposed precisely this as the reason for the rise of England during the run-up to the Industrial Revolution. Genetic selection for a socially desirable trait such as intelligence is called eugenic fertility, while selection for undesirable traits is called dysgenic fertility.

The survival of the richest persisted into the 19th century in most European countries (Skirbekk, 2008) and to the mid-20th century in China (Lamson, 1935; Moise, 1977; Notestein, 1938; Wolf, 1984), but ended abruptly with the early stages of the demographic transition. Whenever intelligence rises and people become more rational, one invariable consequence is that birth control spreads among the more educated and intelligent sections of the population (Livi-Bacci, 1986). Fertility differentials reverse in favor of the less educated and intelligent (Skirbekk, 2008), and eugenic fertility gives way to dysgenic fertility.

One detailed study, for example, found that at the time of the French Revolution, the wealthy had more children than the poor in those French townships in which fertility was still high; but the poor had more children than the wealthy in those that were experiencing significant fertility decline already

(Cummins, 2013). Importantly, post-transitional fertility differentials are not primarily by wealth, but by education and intelligence: the survival of the richest is replaced not by the survival of the poorest, but the survival of the dumbest. Figure 4 shows that this applies not only to fertility differentials within countries, but also between countries. The reversal of fertility differentials during fertility decline can be considered a general law of demography, since exceptions are extremely rare. A survey of 77 countries showed that at the end of the 20th century, the relationship of educational attainment (years in school and highest degree) with fertility was negative in *all* of them (Meisenberg, 2008b).

This general law of demography explains why the self-reinforcing spiral of Flynn effect and economic growth could take off in Europe but not in classical antiquity or the Muslim Middle East. Usually, the adoption of contraceptive practices by the cognitive elite during the earliest stage of the demographic transition will curtail the supply of highly gifted individuals and thereby prevent further advances that could trigger sustained economic growth. In the Muslim Middle East, in particular, where contraception (mainly by withdrawal) was tolerated by religion and was practiced widely during the heyday of Muslim civilization (Musallam, 1983), we can diagnose protracted cultural and economic decline over the last millennium.

In Europe, by contrast, religious condemnation of contraception was so virulent that much of the earlier knowledge was lost by the time of the Renaissance (McLaren, 1990; Noonan, 1986; Riddle, 1992). In consequence, demographic transition and dysgenic fertility were delayed to a time *after* the Industrial Revolution and the beginnings of the Flynn effect. As late as 1848, John Stuart Mill observed: "That it is possible to delay marriage, and to live in abstinence while unmarried, most people are willing to allow; but when people are once married, the idea, in this country, never seems to enter anyone's mind that having or not having a family, or the number of which it shall consist, is amenable to their own control. One would imagine that children were rained down on married people, direct from heaven, without their being art or part in the matter, that it was really, as the common phrases have it, God's will and not their own, which decided the number of their offspring." (Mill, 1976 [1848], p. 155) Because the trans-generational feedback between Flynn effect and economic growth had started already when attitudes to birth control finally changed and fertility differentials became dysgenic in Europe, the Flynn effect could mask the slow genetic decline that resulted from the new demographic regime.

8. PROJECTIONS AND PREDICTIONS OF ECONOMIC GROWTH

8.1. Short-term Projection, 2011-2050

Turning our attention from the past to the future, we must distinguish between short-term *projections* for the next few decades, which directly apply the relationships that were observed in the recent past to the near future, and *predictions* for the more distant future, which are based on the underlying dynamic of long-term economic growth and human development. The projection of short-term economic growth can be achieved with regression equations similar to those in Table 3. Simplifying the model for all countries in Table 3 to include log-transformed initial per capita GDP and intelligence as the only predictors, we obtain the following:

% annual growth = -2.876 – 2.189 x lgGDP 1975 + 0.146 x IQ

If schooling is included, we obtain:

% annual growth = -1.299 - 2.593 x lgGDP 1975 + 0.132 x IQ + 0.144 x Schooling

Substituting lgGDP 2011 for lgGDP 1975, and average length of schooling for 20- to 24-year-olds in 2010 for the earlier schooling variable (based on all adults aged 15+, 1995-2010 average), we obtain the projected annual growth rates of per capita GDP for the near future. We call the projections that are based only on lgGDP 2011 and intelligence version 1, and those based on lgGDP 2011, intelligence and schooling version 2. As expected, growth rates in versions 1 and 2 are highly correlated, with Pearson's *r* of .974 (N = 134 countries). There is moderate continuity between observed past and projected future growth rates, with Pearson's *r* of .496 (version 1) and .484 (version 2), based on 117 countries.

Average annual growth rates are projected to decline from 3.77% in the 1975-2011 period to 1.91% (version 1) or 2.03% (version 2), based on 117 countries for which all three growth rates are available. These averages are weighted for the size of the population in 2010, and cover a total population of nearly 6.01 billion (Table 5). The projected growth rates are lower than the observed past growth rates because one of the main predictor variables, log-transformed per capita GDP, was generally higher in 2011 than in 1975, while intelligence has been assumed to be unchanging. In essence, the projections assume that countries evolve toward a level of prosperity that is commensurate with their level of intelligence. The reason for the slightly higher growth rates in version 2 is that in most countries educational exposure (years in school) is higher for the measure used in the projection (20-24 year olds in 2010) than for the measure used in the 1975-2011 growth regressions. Table 5 shows the past and projected future growth rates for the major world regions, based on the 117 countries for which complete information is available. Table 6 shows growth rates for a selection of individual countries, including most of the successor states of the former Soviet Union and Yugoslavia, which are not represented in Table 5.

Table 5. Short-term projection of economic growth for different world regions[1]

Region	Growth rates			N	
	1975-2011	2011-50 v. 1	2011-50 v. 2	Countries	Population
Prot. Europe	1.77	1.57	1.57	8	132.1
Cath. Europe	1.57	1.51	1.67	11	220.0
English	1.78	1.39	1.52	6	437.5
Excommunist	2.16	1.84	2.08	6	83.2
Latin America	1.34	1.03	1.29	23	572.6
Middle East	1.87	1.21	1.30	15	614.4
South/SE Asia	3.69	1.48	1.59	11	1950.1
Oceania	0.60	1.87	1.79	3	7.8
East Asia	7.81	3.71	3.77	7	1528.7
Africa	0.13	0.63	0.86	27	458.9
World	3.77	1.91	2.03	117	6005.1

[1] Version 1 of the projected growth rate (2011-50 v. 1) is based only on lgGDP 2011 and IQ; version 2 (2011-50 v. 2) is based on lgGDP 2011, IQ, and average length of schooling. Population is in millions (2010). For definition of the world regions, see legend of Figure 1.

Differences in growth rates between countries are projected to narrow, with a decline in the standard deviation of annual growth rates from 2.86 in the 1975-2011 period to 1.18 (version 1) or 1.15 (version 2) in the 2011-2050 period (all weighted for population size). For example, Table 5 shows that growth rates in Sub-Saharan Africa, which had been the lowest of any major world region, are projected to be somewhat higher in the near future, although still quite low. Conversely, growth in East Asia, which was the world's highest in the 1975-2011 period, is projected to decline to about half of its former value.

Table 6. Short-term projection of economic growth for selected countries[1]

			Version 1		Version 2	
Country	% Growth 1975-2011	GDP 2011	% Growth 2011-2050	GDP 2050	% Growth 2011-2050	GDP 2050
Protestant Europe						
Finland	2.05	32345	1.97	69220	1.93	68169
Germany	1.83	35071	1.57	64387	1.55	63895
Sweden	1.69	34707	1.58	63964	1.74	68013
Catholic Europe & Mediterranean						
France	1.44	29477	1.64	55591	1.80	59108
Greece	1.15	21096	1.25	34246	1.66	40092
Italy	1.47	27239	1.42	47208	1.70	52566
Spain	1.67	25694	1.54	46632	1.57	47172
English-speaking countries						
Australia	1.80	38042	1.58	70111	1.80	76283
Canada	1.54	36335	1.80	72860	1.80	72860
UK	1.89	32080	1.73	62625	1.85	65571
USA	1.77	42244	1.26	68841	1.39	72373
Ex-communist countries						
Armenia		5667	2.55	15130	2.73	16201
Azerbaijan		8801	0.87	12338		
Bosnia		7176	2.28	17287		
Bulgaria	2.66	11738	1.83	23809	2.08	26199
Croatia		15080	2.21	35371	2.37	37596
Czech Rep.		22894	2.01	49750	2.23	54110
Estonia		16741	2.45	43028	2.67	46782
Georgia		6303	1.07	9546		
Hungary	1.60	16315	2.24	38708	2.63	44904
Kazakhstan		11945	0.57	14909	0.90	16941
Kyrgyzstan		2723	0.98	3983	1.36	4612
Latvia		12859	2.15	29478	2.55	34332
Lithuania		15811	1.74	30984	2.18	36663
Romania	1.96	10844	1.55	19756	1.81	21828
Russia		14662	2.09	32850	1.95	31138
Serbia		9323	1.64	17582	1.63	17515
Ukraine		6951	2.48	18071	2.84	20719
Latin America						
Argentina	1.32	13882	1.54	25194	1.78	27624
Bolivia	0.48	3746	2.00	8109	2.74	10750
Brazil	1.46	8911	1.03	13289	1.27	14577
Chile	3.31	13519	1.15	21116	1.62	25301
Colombia	1.78	7765	0.80	10595	0.99	11402

			Version 1		Version 2	
Country	% Growth 1975-2011	GDP 2011	% Growth 2011-2050	GDP 2050	% Growth 2011-2050	GDP 2050
Mexico	1.17	12516	0.96	18167	1.28	20554
Peru	1.01	7891	0.88	11105	1.06	11905
Venezuela	-0.20	9990	0.73	13267	0.75	13370
Muslim Middle East & North Africa						
Egypt	3.98	5171	1.07	7831	1.26	8427
Iran	0.38	12269	0.67	15919	0.95	17740
Iraq	0.59	4160	1.90	8667	1.65	7876
Jordan	2.06	5199	1.65	9843	2.11	11738
Morocco	2.16	3648	1.18	5764	1.17	5742
Pakistan	2.24	2535	1.94	5363	2.06	5615
Sudan	1.86	2253	1.10	3452	0.81	3086
Tunisia	2.57	6808	1.13	10552	1.49	12121
Turkey	2.29	13058	1.12	20161	1.15	20396
South and South-East Asia						
Bangladesh	2.49	1646	1.91	3443	2.29	3980
India	3.91	3598	1.23	5796	1.26	5863
Indonesia	3.91	4208	1.72	8183	1.89	8734
Malaysia	3.62	12268	1.51	22010	1.88	25365
Philippines	1.10	3634	1.68	6959	2.08	8111
Thailand	4.30	8425	1.68	16135	1.93	17756
East Asia						
China	8.46	9486	3.87	41706	3.91	42337
Japan	1.99	31587	2.48	82117	2.75	90991
Korea, South	5.85	29618	2.64	81829	2.90	90314
Singapore	4.55	43562	2.58	117639	2.47	112819
Taiwan	5.33	34123	2.48	88710	2.75	98297
Sub-Saharan Africa						
Cameroon	0.26	1829	-0.05	1794	0.24	2008
Cote d'Ivoire	-1.22	1338	0.29	1498	0.21	1452
Ghana	1.17	2349	0.03	2377	0.49	2842
Kenya	0.61	1308	1.25	2123	1.75	2573
Mozambique	2.00	782	1.07	1184	0.80	1067
Nigeria	0.69	2014	0.66	2603		
South Africa	0.50	7918	-0.96	5435	-0.48	6563
Tanzania	1.37	1217	1.15	1901	1.38	2077
Uganda	1.30	1267	0.90	1797	1.22	2033
Zambia	-0.71	1355	0.66	1751	0.95	1959
Zimbabwe	-0.52	4306	-0.15	4061	0.21	4673

[1] Shown are projected % annual growth and per capita GDP in 2050, based either on per capita GDP 2011 and intelligence alone (version 1) or on per capita GDP 2011, intelligence, and years in school (version 2).

8.2. Limitations of short-term growth projections

The projection of economic growth rates based on current prosperity and human capital assumes that the macroeconomic returns to human capital will be the same in the near future as in the recent past. This assumption is reasonable because the strength of the relationship between intelligence and growth rates is similar in rich and poor countries today (Table 3). As many of today's poor countries become more prosperous and more intelligent, they will in all likelihood maintain the intelligence-growth relationship that is seen in rich countries today.

However, the projections ignore country-specific factors. For example, projected growth rates in Table 6 are lower for Iran and Iraq than for other Middle Eastern countries. The reason is that these countries are relatively prosperous already because of their oil wealth, and slow growth is expected because of their combination of relatively high per capita GDP with mediocre IQ. The projections do not take into account that the presence of natural resources adds to the wealth of the country. These countries evolve to a level of prosperity that is commensurate not only with their intelligence, but also with the profits they obtain from their oil exports.

Another factor is the dispersion of intelligence in the country. For example, South Africa is projected to have negative growth during the coming decades, based on its relatively high prosperity combined with low *average* IQ. One reason is again that South Africa is resource-rich. More important, however, is the strongly skewed distribution of intelligence in the country, with a white minority of approximately 15% that has a European-like IQ average in the 90s, and a large African majority with a typical African IQ near 70 (Lynn, 2006). Unbeknownst to the regression equations, this gives South Africa a higher "equilibrium GDP" because the IQ of individuals at the upper end of the distribution tends to be more important than the IQ in the middle and lower reaches of the distribution for the economic success of countries (Rindermann, Sailer and Thompson, 2009).

8.3. The Future of the Flynn Effect

However, the most important observation is that the projections offer little comfort for developing countries. Although growth in Sub-Saharan Africa is projected to pick up, the regions with the lowest growth rates will still be Africa, Latin America and the Middle East. The reason is that the projections assume unchanging intelligence differentials between countries. Therefore less developed countries are close to the level of prosperity already that matches their generally low IQs.

The assumption of unchanging intelligence differences between countries, or equal Flynn effects everywhere, is a reasonable approximation to reality on time scales of 2, 3, or even 4 decades. Therefore it is justifiable to use the same IQ data set to estimate prevailing IQs during the 1975-2011 and the 2011-2050 periods. However, we cannot realistically predict longer-term trends without making assumptions about the strengths of anticipated Flynn effects in different countries and the resulting changes in average intelligence. For example, the growth trajectories for Sub-Saharan Africa in Tables 5 and 6 are likely to rise above the projection even before 2050 if, as claimed by Wicherts et al. (2010), strong Flynn effects are beginning already to raise the average African IQ in the younger generation.

Table 1 shows that Flynn effects on IQ tests averaged about 2 or 3 points per decade during the 20th century, for example in Britain and the United States. Periods with far larger gains invariably coincided with brief periods of rapid economic growth and expanding educational systems. Gains were frequently larger for younger than older ages, as shown in Table 1 for performance on the non-verbal Raven's Progressive Matrices test in Britain: Cohorts born between the late 1960s and the 1990s were gaining 2 points/decade at age 8-12, but lost 0.8 points/decade at ages 13-15. Also, in most cases gains in reasoning ability have been larger than gains in school-related knowledge and skills. In the United States, all age groups have gained about 3 points/decade on the Wechsler tests (Flynn, 2012). However, on the National Assessment of Educational Progress (NAEP, "the nation's report card"), which tests mastery of curricular contents, gains per decade between 1971 and 2008 were the IQ equivalent of 2.02 points at age 9, 1.20 points at age 13, and 0.30 points at age 17 (Rindermann & Thompson, 2013).

Most important is that Flynn effect gains have been decelerating in recent years. Recent losses (anti-Flynn effects) were noted in Britain, Denmark, Norway and Finland. Results for the Scandinavian countries are based on comprehensive IQ testing of military conscripts aged 18-19. Evidence for losses among British teenagers is derived from the Raven test (Flynn, 2009) and Piagetian tests (Shayer & Ginsburg, 2009). These observations suggest that for cohorts born after about 1980, the Flynn effect is ending or has ended in many and perhaps most of the economically most advanced countries. Messages from the United States are mixed, with some studies reporting continuing gains (Flynn, 2012) and others no change (Beaujean & Osterlind, 2008).

Table 1 also shows that reports of Flynn effects in developing countries are becoming more frequent. Studies of international scholastic assessments (TIMSS, PISA) between 1995 and 2011 show a similar picture: little change in the high-scoring, economically developed countries, and gains in lower-scoring, less developed countries (Meisenberg & Woodley, 2013). These assessments are done at age 15 (PISA) or in grade 8 (TIMSS).

Most likely, Flynn effects are ending in the high-IQ countries because we cannot raise intelligence indefinitely with better education for the same reason that we cannot raise height indefinitely with better nutrition, longevity with healthier lifestyles, and corn yields with more fertilizer. The observations suggest that genetic limits to human intelligence are being approached in the most advanced nations, resulting in diminishing returns to additional educational inputs.

In less developed countries, however, educational systems and other aspects of children's intellectual environment are still suboptimal and sometimes awful, and nutritional deficiencies and chronic parasitic diseases are still prevalent in many places. Therefore continued environmental improvements can achieve large intelligence gains until the populations of these countries reach their genetic limits as well. The efforts being invested in the educational systems of developing countries today (Kremer, Brannen & Glennerster, 2013) make it likely that this will be achieved well before the end of the 21st century in virtually all countries, and by about 2050 in most.

We do not know where the genetic limits of cognitive development are for different countries. If each nation has the same genetic capacity for higher intelligence, world-wide differences in intelligence and prosperity will diminish or disappear within two or three generations, much as the gaps between East Asian countries and the West have diminished or disappeared in the last two or three generations. However, there is no theoretical reason to expect equal potential for high intelligence in each nation, and no empiric evidence in its favor. The only molecular genetic studies that speak to this question show that allele frequencies for genetic variants influencing educational attainment and intelligence differ between human populations, and that many of the reported "high-IQ" variants are indeed more common in countries with higher IQ and educational attainment (Piffer, 2013a,b).

8.4. Consequences of Vanishing Flynn Effects

Continuing Flynn effects in less developed countries combined with cognitive stagnation or slow decline in the more developed countries will have important economic consequences. The projected growth rates in Tables 5 and 6 will have to be adjusted downward for high-income, high-IQ countries, and upward for low-income, low-IQ countries. Eventually the empiric relationship between intelligence and economic growth, which has been positive in the recent past (see Table 2), may even reverse. In the long run, it is not high intelligence but *rising* intelligence that leads to economic growth.

Genetic endowments for high intelligence can be described as innate responsiveness to educational efforts and other environmental enhancements. Therefore the two-way interaction between improving environments and rising intelligence outlined in section 7.3 implies that even small differences in genetic endowments can become amplified into far larger actual (phenotypic) differences. At the end of the Flynn effect, nations with lower "genotypic intelligence" will have achieved lower phenotypic intelligence, which leads to lower-quality school systems compared with nations that have slightly higher genotypic intelligence. Therefore phenotypic IQ differences between nations will remain larger than genotypic differences. They may never become quite as small as the differences that we observe today, for example, between racial and ethnic groups in the United States. A single country can maintain equal standards for everyone in its educational system, and socio-economic disparities can be buffered through the welfare state. Such measures are not available to diminish achievement gaps between countries.

9. THE END OF ECONOMIC GROWTH

9.1. Interactions between History and Biological Evolution

Developments on a time scale of centuries are affected not only by Flynn effects and anti-Flynn effects, but also by ongoing genetic changes. Evidence is overwhelming that *within* virtually all countries, fertility differentials have been dysgenic for educational attainment or intelligence since the demographic transition (Meisenberg, 2008b; Skirbekk, 2008). Conservative estimates for the "genotypic" decline that this has caused in western countries since the 19th century have ranged from 0.3 to slightly more than 1 IQ point per generation (reviewed in Lynn, 2011), although higher estimates of up to

1.23 points per decade have been proposed (Woodley, te Nijenhuis & Murphy, 2013). The conservative estimates are only about one tenth as large as the environmentally caused Flynn effect gains that were observed at the same time (see Table 1). Thus the small genetic losses have been swamped by far larger environmentally caused gains.

In addition, nations with lower levels of education and intelligence are growing rapidly while those with higher intelligence are contracting (see Figure 4 and Table 4, variable F1). Differential fertility between countries has been calculated to reduce (phenotypic) intelligence by approximately 0.73 points/decade for the world population between 2000 and 2050 (Lynn & Harvey, 2008) or by 1.34 points/decade for younger cohorts (Meisenberg, 2009), assuming that average intelligence within countries does not change. We do not know what proportion of this decline is genetic, but it implies that Flynn effects of this magnitude are required to offset the predicted decline of the world's IQ that results from fertility differentials between countries.

9.2. "Peak IQ" and the Question of Sustainability

The unsustainability of this situation is obvious. Estimating that one third of the present IQ differences between countries can be attributed to genetics, and adding this to the consequences of dysgenic fertility within countries, leaves us with a *genetic* decline of between 1 and 2 IQ points per generation for the entire world population. This decline is still more than offset by Flynn effects in less developed countries, and the average IQ of the world's population is still rising. This phase of history will end when today's developing countries reach the end of the Flynn effect. "Peak IQ" can reasonably be expected in cohorts born around the mid-21st century. The assumptions of the peak IQ prediction are that (1) Flynn effects are limited by genetic endowments, (2) some countries are approaching their genetic limits already, and others will follow, and (3) today's patterns of differential fertility favoring the less intelligent will persist into the foreseeable future.

Exceptionally high intelligence will become less common *before* the average intelligence of the world population begins declining, mainly because the nations that are producing most of the exceptional talent today are contracting. At today's cohort fertility rates, the decline per generation of the young adult population is 20% in Russia, 25% in Germany, and 30% in Italy and Japan (Myrskylä, Goldstein and Cheng, 2013). A similar effect has been achieved by the one-child policy in China. There is no indication that sub-replacement fertility in the economically advanced nations is abating. The intelligence of the "cognitive elite" tends to be more important than average intelligence for patentable inventions, Nobel Prizes, and good government (Rindermann, Sailer & Thompson, 2009). A world-wide depletion of exceptional ability may be occurring already, if the reported decline in the per capita rate of major innovations since the late 19th century (Woodley, 2012) is real. Thus a dearth of innovations in society and technology, leading to a recycling of old ideas and practices, is expected to be the first sign of impending stagnation and terminal decline. The true sustainability issue of the modern world economy is not the depletion of non-renewable resources such as fossil fuels, but the depletion of the mental powers that are required for the maintenance of a functioning economy.

9.3. Brain Drain, Brain Gain and Replacement Migration

Fertility differentials between countries lead to replacement migration: the movement of people from high-fertility countries to low-fertility countries, with gradual replacement of the native populations in the low-fertility countries (Coleman, 2002). The economic consequences depend on the quality of the migrants and their descendants. Educational, cognitive and economic outcomes of migrants are influenced heavily by prevailing educational, cognitive and economic levels in the country of origin (Carabaña, 2011; Kirkegaard, 2013; Levels & Dronkers, 2008), and by the selectivity of migration. Brain drain from poor to prosperous countries is extensive already, for example among scientists (Franzoni, Scellato & Stephan, 2012; Hunter, Oswald & Charlton, 2009).

In the second half of the 21st century, when Flynn effects have ended and dysgenic IQ declines become more visible, in theory the world's most attractive countries can maintain their economic lead by attracting highly intelligent migrants from abroad. However, this parasitic existence may never be realized in most of these countries because native elites may be unwilling to compete with highly capable immigrants. Thus immigration policies may end up favoring low-skilled immigration.

9.4. The Dysgenic Meltdown

Brain drain is one reason why most of the less developed countries will never become nearly as prosperous as the more developed ones. But even the most prosperous and attractive countries will eventually become depleted of the talent that is required to maintain their economic vitality and their institutions. In the educational system, slowly declining intelligence of teachers and school administrators is predicted to reduce the quality of instruction and lead to poorer student outcomes, resulting in even greater deterioration in the following generation. The trans-generational spiral of Flynn effect and economic growth described in section 7.3 will go in reverse, with declining intelligence and deteriorating environments reinforcing each other.

How fast this dysgenic meltdown will unfold and the form it will take are difficult to predict because we have no close historic precedent. There have been "dark ages" of collapse and of cultural and technological regress in the past (Aiyar, Dalgaard & Moav, 2008; Wilkinson, 1995), but never from a level nearly as high as that achieved by the present civilization. It will most likely occur at different times in different countries and world regions. The decline may be slower than the ascent from the 17th to the early 21st centuries because people may be able for a long time to maintain technologies and practices that they no longer fully understand, or it may be faster because the effects of economic and educational deterioration are reinforced by continued dysgenic fertility.

9.5. Alternatives

Can the dysgenic meltdown be prevented with technologies that are under development today or are likely to be developed in the near future? We still experience technological advances that seem to track the Flynn effect, although by most counts (summarized in Woodley, 2012), the per capita rate of *major* innovations has been declining since the late 19th century. Incremental improvements can be achieved by well-trained people with unexceptional native talent, although extraordinary achievement requires high innate ability combined with favorable external conditions. Thus incremental improvements of technologies such as computer science and molecular genetics are likely to continue through the 21st century, although at a slowly decelerating rate.

Using methods of molecular genetics to produce highly talented people is, in theory, possible even with methods that are known today. Knowledge about the genes that contribute to intelligence and educational achievement is accumulating slowly (e.g., Rietveld et al., 2013). We can sequence the genomes of pre-implantation embryos and estimate their developmental potential and disease risks (Hens et al., 2013). In theory, the combination of in vitro fertilization, genome sequencing, and the selective use of embryos with promising genes can raise the prospects for health and intelligence of newborns even today, with potentially profound implications not only for the genetically selected children, but also for future social and economic developments if such techniques come to be employed widely.

Even methods for targeted genome editing are being developed (Gaj, Gersbach & Barbas, 2013). In addition to their medical uses, they can be used to replace genetic variants that lead to lower intelligence with alternative variants that lead to higher intelligence—in the zygote, but not in an adult person. Such methods are likely to become more widely available and even affordable (for some) by the mid-21st century.

Although the 21st century offers a window of opportunity for the use of gene technologies to solve the sustainability problem of human intelligence and civilization, ethical concerns will most likely prevent their use. The major ethical problem is obvious: With the rarest exceptions, people are indifferent about the welfare of future generations. Trans-generational altruism is not part of the innate behavioral repertoire of our species (Meisenberg, 2007b). Being not sufficiently motivated to use genetic selection or engineering even for the benefit of their own children, people are unlikely to tolerate their use by others, whose genetically enhanced children might outcompete their own in the rat race for status and money. Some bioethicists maintain that embryos should be selected for ethical qualities rather than intelligence because higher intelligence without better ethics could be dangerous (Persson & Savulescu, 2013). Today, however, even the use of preimplantation genetic diagnosis for the prevention of serious genetic diseases is illegal in some countries (Pavone, 2012).

This shows that intelligence is not the only form of human capital that is essential for social and economic development. It is an instrument for the pursuit of personal gain and thereby indirectly for the attainment of society-wide prosperity. Sustainable progress, however, requires more than intelligence. It requires a level of ethical development, and a kind of value system, that human societies may not be able to attain during the current bout of civilization. But since the ethical advancement of human societies has tracked cognitive advancement in the past (Flynn, 2014; Oesterdiekhoff, 2014; see also variables C1-C3 in Table 4), it is likely to do so in the future. High intelligence is a necessary but not sufficient condition for the attainment of an ethical consensus that would make modern societies sustainable.

REFERENCES

Aiyar, S., Dalgaard, C.-J., and Moav, O. (2008). Technological progress and regress in pre-industrial times. *Journal of Economic Growth*, 13, 125-144.

Archibugi, D., and Coco, A. (2004). A new indicator of technological capabilities for developed and developing countries (ArCo). *World Development*, 32, 629-654.

Bakhiet, S. E. F. A., and Ahmed, K. Y. (2014). Factor structure of the Wechsler Intelligence Scale for Children -Third Edition (WISC – III) among gifted students in the Sudan. Mankind Quarterly, in press.

Bartels, M., Rietveld, M. J. H., Van Baal, G. C. M., and Boomsma, D. I. (2002). Heritability of educational achievement in 12-year-olds and the overlap with cognitive ability. *Twin Research*, 5, 544-553.

Baten, J., and van Zanden, J. L. (2008). Book production and the onset of modern economic growth. Working Paper JEL: O14, O40, N10, available at http://repositori.upf.edu/bitstream/handle/10230/757/1030.pdf?sequence=1

Batterjee, A. (2011). Intelligence and education: the Saudi case. *Mankind Quarterly*, 52, 133-190.

Beaujean, A. A., and Osterlind, S. J. (2008). Using item response theory to assess the Flynn effect in the National Longitudinal Study of Youth 79 children and young adults data. *Intelligence*, 36, 455-463.

Behrman, J. R., Hoddinott, J., Maluccio, J. A., Soler-Hampejsek, E., Behrman, E. L., Martorell, R., Ramírez-Zea, M., and Stein, A. D. (2014). What determines adult cognitive skills? Influences of pre-school, school, and post-school experiences in Guatemala. *Latin American Economic Review*, 23, 4.

Benavot, A., and Riddle, P. (1988). The expansion of primary education, 1870-1940: Trends and issues. *Sociology of Education*, 61, 191-210.

Beraldo, S., Montolio, D., and Turati, G. (2009). Healthy, educated and wealthy: a primer on the impact of public and private welfare expenditures on economic growth. *Journal of Socio-Economics*, 38, 946-956.

Bloom, N., Mahajan, A., McKenzie, D., and Roberts, J. (2010). Why do firms in developing countries have low productivity? *American Economic Review Papers and Proceedings*, 100, 619-623.

Boberg-Fazlic, N., Sharp, P., and Weisdorf, J. (2011). Survival of the richest? Social status, fertility and social mobility in England 1541-1824. *European Review of Economic History*, 15, 365-392.

Bradmetz, J., and Mathy, F. (2006). An estimate of the Flynn effect: changes in IQ and subtest gains of 10-yr-old French children between 1965 and 1988. *Psychological Reports*, 99, 743-746.

Brinch, C. N., and Galloway, T. A. (2012). Schooling in adolescence raises IQ scores. *Proceedings of the National Academy of Sciences USA*, 109, 425-430.

Bruhn, M., Karlan, D., and Schoar, A. (2010). What capital is missing in developing countries? *American Economic Review Papers and Proceedings*, 100, 629-633.

Burks, S. V., Carpenter, J. P., Goette, L., and Rustichini, A. (2009). Cognitive skills affect economic preferences, strategic behavior, and job attachment. *Proceedings of the National Academy of Sciences USA*, 106, 7745-7750.

Calvin, C. M., Deary, I. J., Webbink, D., Smith, P., Fernandes, C., Lee, S. H., Luciano, M., and Visscher, P. M. (2012). Multivariate genetic analyses of cognition and academic achievement from two population samples of 174,000 and 166,000 school children. *Behavior Genetics*, 42, 699-710.

Carabaña, J. (2011). Why do the results of immigrant students depend so much on their country of origin and so little on their country of destination? In: M. A. Pereyra, H.-G. Kotthoff and R. Cowen (eds.): PISA under examination: changing knowledge, changing tests, and changing schools, pp. 207-221. Rotterdam: Sense Publishers.

Carter, T. F. (1955). The invention of printing in China and its spread westward, 2nd edition. New York: Ronald Press Co.

Christainsen, G. B. (2013). IQ and the wealth of nations: how much reverse causality? *Intelligence*, 41, 688-698.

Clark, G. (2007). A farewell to alms. A brief economic history of the world. Princeton, NJ: Princeton University Press.

Clark, G., and Hamilton, G. (2006). Survival of the richest: the Malthusian mechanism in pre-industrial England. *Journal of Economic History*, 66, 707-736.

Coleman, D. A. (2002). Replacement migration, or why everyone is going to have to live in Korea: a fable for our times from the United Nations.

Philosophical Transactions of the Royal Society of London B, 357, 583-598.

Cummins, N. (2013). Marital fertility and wealth during the fertility transition: rural France, 1750-1850. *Economic History Review*, 66, 449-476.

Deary, I. J., Strand, S., Smith, P., and Fernandes, C. (2007). Intelligence and educational achievement. *Intelligence*, 35, 13-21.

Doucouliagos, H., and Ulubaşoğlu, M. A. (2008). Democracy and economic growth: a meta-analysis. *American Journal of Political Science*, 52, 61-83.

Dutton, E., and Lynn, R. (2013). A negative Flynn effect in Finland, 1997-2009. *Intelligence*, 41, 817-820.

Ehrlich, P. (1968). *The population bomb.* New York: Ballantine Books.

Eisner, M. (2003). Long-term historical trends in violent crime. *Crime and Justice*, 30, 83-142.

Elley, W. B. (1969). Changes in mental ability in New Zealand school children, 1936-1968. *New Zealand Journal of Educational Studies*, 4, 140-155.

Falch, T., and Massih, S. S. (2011). The effect of education on cognitive ability. *Economic Inquiry*, 49, 838-856.

Fernando, S. D., Rodrigo, C., and Rajapakse, S. (2010). The 'hidden' burden of malaria: cognitive impairment following infection. *Malaria Journal,* 9, 366.

Ferrie, J. P., Rolf, K., and Troesken, W. (2011). Cognitive disparities, lead plumbing, and water chemistry: intelligence test scores and exposure to water-borne lead among World War II army enlistees. NBER Working Papers, no. 17161.

Fisher, R. A. (1918). The correlation between relatives on the supposition of Mendelian inheritance. *Transactions of the Royal Society of Edinburgh*, 52, 399-433.

Fitzpatrick, T. M., and Spohn, K. (2009). A 25th anniversary redux of the Simon and Ehrlich global sustainability wager. *Journal of International Business and Cultural Studies*, 1, 1-7.

Flynn, J. R. (1984). IQ gains and the Binet decrements. *Journal of Educational Measurement*, 21, 283-290.

Flynn, J. R. (1987). Massive IQ gains in 14 nations: what IQ tests really measure. *Psychological Bulletin*, 101, 171-191.

Flynn, J. R. (2009). Requiem for nutrition as the cause of IQ gains: Raven's gains in Britain 1938-2008. *Economics and Human Biology*, 7, 18-27.

Flynn, J. R. (2012). Are we getting smarter? Rising IQ in the twenty-first century. Cambridge: Cambridge University Press.

Flynn, J. R. (2014). The folly of writing history without a cognitive dimension. *Mankind Quarterly*, 54, 313-321.

Flynn, J. R., and Rossi-Casé, L. (2012). IQ gains in Argentina between 1964 and 1998. *Intelligence*, 40, 145-150.

Forbes, K. J. (2000). A reassessment of the relationship between inequality and growth. *American Economic Review*, 90, 869-887.

Franzoni, C., Scellato, G., and Stephan, P. (2012). Foreign born scientists: mobility patterns for sixteen countries. NBER Working Papers, 18067.

Gaj, T., Gersbach, C. A., and Barbas, C. F. III (2013). ZFN, TALEN, and CRISPR/Cas-based methods for genome engineering. *Trends in Biotechnology*, 31, 397-405.

Gelade, G. A. (2008). IQ, cultural values, and the technological achievement of nations. Intelligence, 36, 711-718.

Goldin, C. (1998). America's graduation from high school: the evolution and spread of secondary schooling in the twentieth century. Journal of Economic History, 58, 345-374.

Greenfield, P. M. (1997). You can't take it with you: why ability assessments don't cross cultures. American Psychologist, 52, 1115-1124.

Hansen, K. T., Heckman, J. J., and Mullen, K. J. (2004). The effect of schooling and ability on achievement test scores. *Journal of Econometrics*, 121, 39-98.

Haworth, C. M. A., Wright, M. J., Luciano, M., Martin, N. G., de Geus, E. J. C., van Beijsterveldt, C. E. M., Bartels, M., Posthuma, D. et al. (2010). The heritability of general cognitive ability increases linearly from childhood to young adulthood. *Molecular Psychiatry,* 15, 1112-1120.

Headey, D. D., and Hodge, A. 2009. The effect of population growth on economic growth: a meta-regression analysis of the macroeconomic literature. *Population and Development Review*, 35, 221-248.

Hens, K., Dondorp, W., Handyside, A. H., Harper, J., Newson, A. J., Pennings, G., Rehmann-Sutter, C., and de Wert, G. (2013). Dynamics and ethics of comprehensive preimplantation genetic testing: a review of the challenges. *Human Reproduction Update*, 19, 366-375.

Heston, A., Summers, R., and Aten, B. (2011). Penn World Tables, version 7.0. Center for International Comparisons of Production, Income and Prices at the University of Pennsylvania.

Hu, L., and Bentler, P. M. (1999). Cutoff criteria for fit indexes in covariance structure analysis: conventional criteria versus new alternatives. *Structural Equation Modeling*, 6, 1-55.

Huff, T. E. (1993). The rise of early modern science. Islam, China, and the West. Cambridge, New York: Cambridge University Press.

Hunter, R. S., Oswald, A. J., and Charlton, B. G. (2009). The elite brain drain. *Economic Journal*, 119, F231-F251.

Jensen, A. R. (1998). The g factor. Westport CT: Praeger.

Jones, G. (2008). Are smarter groups more cooperative? Evidence from prisoner's dilemma experiments, 1959-2003. *Journal of Economic Behavior and Organization*, 68, 489-497.

Jones, G., and Schneider, W. J. (2010). IQ in the production function: evidence from immigrant earnings. Economic Inquiry, 48, 743-755.

Justesen, M. K. (2008). The effect of economic freedom on growth revisited: New evidence on causality from a panel of countries 1970-1999. European Journal of Political Economy, 24, 642-660.

Kalonda Kanyama, I. (2014). Quality of institutions: does intelligence matter? Intelligence, 42, 44-52.

Kan, K.-J., Wicherts, J. M., Dolan, C. V., & van der Maas, H. L. J. (2013). On the nature and nurture of intelligence and specific cognitive abilities: The more heritable, the more culture dependent. Psychological Science, 24, 2420-2428.

Kaplan, J. S. (2012). The effects of shared environment on adult intelligence: A critical review of adoption, twin, and MZA studies. Developmental Psychology, 48, 1292-1298.

Kaufman, S. B., Reynolds, M. R., Liu, X., Kaufman, A. S., and McGrew, K. S. (2012). Are cognitive *g* and academic achievement *g* one and the same *g*? An exploration on the Woodcock-Johnson and Kaufman tests. *Intelligence*, 40, 123-138.

Kenny, C. (2010). Is anywhere stuck in a Malthusian trap? *Kyklos*, 63, 192-205.

Khaleefa, O., Sulman, A., and Lynn, R. (2009). An increase of intelligence in Sudan, 1987-2007. *Journal of Biosocial Science*, 41, 279-283.

Khaleefa, O., Amer, Z., and Lynn, R. (2014). IQ differences between arts and science students at the University of Khartoum. Mankind Quarterly, in press.

Kirkegaard, E. O. W. (2013). Predicting immigrant IQ from their countries of origin, and Lynn's national IQs: a case study from Denmark. *Mankind Quarterly*, 54, 151-166.

Kremer, M., Brannen, C., and Glennerster, R. (2013). The challenge of education and learning in the developing world. *Science*, 340, 297-300.

Kuncel, N. R., and Hezlett, S. A. (2010). Fact and fiction in cognitive ability testing for admissions and hiring decisions. *Current Directions in Psychological Science*, 19, 339-345.

Lamson, H. D. (1935). Differential reproduction in China. *Quarterly Review of Biology*, 10, 308-321.

Levels, M., and Dronkers, J. (2008). Educational performance of native and immigrant children from various countries of origin. *Ethnic and Racial Studies*, 31, 1404-1425.

LeWinn, K. Z., Stroud, L. R., Molnar, B. E., Ware, J. H., Koenen, K. C., and Buka, S. L. (2009). Elevated maternal cortisol levels during pregnancy are associated with reduced childhood IQ. *International Journal of Epidemiology*, 38, 1700-1710.

Livi-Bacci, M. (1986). Social-group forerunners of fertility control in Europe. In: A. J. Coale and S. C. Watkins (eds): The decline of fertility in Europe. Princeton NJ: Princeton University Press.

Luria, A. (1976). Cognitive development. Its cultural and social foundations. Cambridge Mass., London: Harvard University Press.

Lutz, W. (2009). Sola schola et sanitate: human capital as the root cause and priority for international development? *Philosophical Transactions of the Royal Society B*, 364, 3031-3047.

Lynn, R. (1990). The role of nutrition in secular increases in intelligence. *Personality and Individual Differences*, 11, 273-275.

Lynn, R. (2008). The global bell curve. Race, IQ and inequality worldwide. Augusta GA: Washington Summit.

Lynn, R. (2011). Dysgenics. Genetic deterioration in modern populations, 2nd revised edition. London: Ulster Institute for Social Research.

Lynn, R., and Hampson, S. (1986). The rise of national intelligence: evidence from Britain, Japan and the U.S.A. *Personality and Individual Differences*, 7, 23-32.

Lynn, R., and Vanhanen, T. (2001). National IQ and economic development: a study of eighty-one nations. *Mankind Quarterly*, 41, 415-435.

Lynn, R., and Vanhanen, T. (2002). IQ and the wealth of nations. Westport CN: Praeger.

Lynn, R., and Vanhanen, T. (2006). IQ and global inequality. Augusta GA: Washington Summit.

Lynn, R., and Harvey, J. (2008). The decline of the world's IQ. *Intelligence*, 36, 112-120.

Lynn, R., and Vanhanen, T. (2012). Intelligence: A unifying construct for the social sciences. London UK: Ulster Institute for Social Research.

Matte, T. D., Bresnahan, M., Begg, M. D., and Susser, E. (2001). Influence of variation in birth weight within normal range and within sibships on IQ at age 7 years: cohort study. *British Medical Journal*, 323, 310-314.

McLaren, A. (1990). A history of contraception. From antiquity to the present day. Oxford: Basil Blackwell.

Meisenberg, G. (2007a). Does multiculturalism promote income inequality? *Mankind Quarterly*, 47, 3-39.

Meisenberg, G. (2007b). In God's image. The natural history of intelligence and ethics. Brighton: Book Guild.

Meisenberg, G. (2008a). How does racial diversity promote income inequality? *Journal of Social Political and Economic Studies*, 33, 3-26.

Meisenberg, G. (2008b). How universal is the negative correlation between education and fertility? Journal of Social Political and Economic Studies, 33, 205-227.

Meisenberg, G. (2008c). On the time scale of human evolution: evidence for recent adaptive evolution. Mankind Quarterly, 48, 407-443.

Meisenberg, G. (2009). Wealth, intelligence, politics and global fertility differentials. *Journal of Biosocial Science*, 41, 519-535.

Meisenberg, G. (2014). What are the causes of cognitive evolution? A critique and extension of psychogenetic theory. *Mankind Quarterly*, 54, 326-338.

Meisenberg, G, Lawless, E., Lambert, E., and Newton, A. (2005). The Flynn effect in the Caribbean: generational change of cognitive test performance in Dominica. *Mankind Quarterly*, 46, 29-69.

Meisenberg, G., and Lynn, R. (2011). Intelligence: a measure of human capital in nations." *Journal of Social Political and Economic Studies*, 36, 421-454.

Meisenberg, G., and Woodley, M. A. (2013). Are cognitive differences between countries diminishing? Evidence from TIMSS and PISA. *Intelligence*, 41, 808-816.

Mill, J. S. (1976) [1848]. Principles of political economy, edited by P. Appleman. New York: Norton.

Miller, A. K. H., and Corsellis, J. A. N. (1977). Evidence for a secular increase in human brain weight during the past century. *Annals of Human Biology*, 4, 253-257.

Mitch, D. (1992). The rise of popular literacy in Europe. In: The political construction of education. The state, school expansion, and economic change (B. Fuller and R. Rubinson, eds.), pp. 31-46. New York: Praeger.

Moise, E. E. (1977). Downward social mobility in pre-revolutionary China. *Modern China*, 3, 3-31.

Mokyr, J. (1990). The lever of riches. Technological creativity and economic progress. Oxford: Oxford University Press.

Mokyr, J. (2005). The intellectual origins of modern economic growth. *Journal of Economic History*, 65, 285-351.

Mokyr, J. (2009). Intellectual property rights, the Industrial Revolution, and the beginnings of modern economic growth. *American Economic Review* Papers and Proceedings, 99, 349-355.

Musallam, B. F. (1983). Sex and society in Islam. Birth control before the 19th century. Cambridge: Cambridge University Press.

Myrskylä, M., Goldstein, J. R., & Cheng, Y.-H. A. (2013). New cohort fertility forecasts for the developed world: rises, falls, and reversals. Population and Development Review, 39, 31-56.

Nagoshi, C. T., and Johnson, R. C. (2005). Socioeconomic status does not moderate the familiality of cognitive abilities in the Hawaii family study of cognition. *Journal of Biosocial Science*, 37, 773-781.

Noonan, J. T. (1986). Contraception. A history of its treatment by the Catholic theologians and canonists, enlarged edition. Cambridge (Mass.): Belknap Press.

Notestein, F. W. (1938). A demographic study of 38,256 rural families in China. *Milbank Memorial Fund Quarterly*, 16, 57-79.

Oesterdiekhoff, G. (2014). The rise of modern industrial society. The cognitive-developmental approach as a new key to solve the most fascinating riddle in world history. *Mankind Quarterly*, 54, 262-312.

Pavone, I. R. (2012). The legal implications of preimplantation genetic diagnosis. In: Bin, R., Lorenzon, S., and Lucchi, N. (Eds.): Biotech. innovations and fundamental rights, pp. 155-169. Milan: Springer.

Persson, I., and Savulescu, J. (2013). Getting moral enhancement right: the desirability of moral bioenhancement. *Bioethics*, 27, 124-131.

Pietschnig, J., Voracek, M., and Formann, A. K. (2011). Female Flynn effects: no sex differences in generational IQ gains. *Personality and Individual Differences*, 50, 759-762.

Piff, P. K., Stancato, D. M., Côté, S., Mendoza-Denton, R., and Keltner, D. (2012). Higher social class predicts increased unethical behavior. *Proceedings of the National Academy of Sciences USA*, 109, 4086-4091.

Piffer, D. (2013a). Statistical associations between genetic polymorphisms modulating executive function and intelligence suggest recent selective pressure on cognitive abilities. *Mankind Quarterly*, 54, 3-25.

Piffer, D. (2013b). Factor analysis of population allele frequencies as a simple, novel method of detecting signals of recent polygenic selection: the example of educational attainment and IQ. Mankind Quarterly, 54, 168-200.

Plomin, R., De Fries, J. C., Knopik, V. S., & Neiderhiser, J. M. (2012). Behavioral Genetics, 6th edition. New York: Worth Publishers.

Pomeranz, K. (2000). The great divergence. Europe, China, and the making of the modern world economy. Princeton: Princeton University Press.

Ram, R. (2007). IQ and economic growth: further augmentation of the Mankiw-Romer-Weil model. *Economics Letters*, 94, 7-11.

Raven, J. Raven, J. C., and Court, J. H. (1998). Standard Progressive Matrices, 2998 edition. Oxford: Oxford Psychologists Press.

Razi, Z. (1980). Life, marriage and death in a medieval parish. Economy, society and demography in Halesowen, 1270-1400. Cambridge: Cambridge University Press.

Riddle, J. M. (1992). Contraception and abortion from the ancient world to the Renaissance. Cambridge (Mass.): Harvard University Press.

Rietveld, C. A., Medland, S. E., Derringer, J., Yang, K., Esko, T. et al. (2013). GWAS of 126,559 individuals identifies genetic variants associated with educational attainment. *Science*, 340, 1467-1471.

Rindermann, H. (2013). African cognitive ability: Research, results, divergences and recommendations. *Personality and Individual Differences*, 55, 229-233.

Rindermann, H., Sailer, M., and Thompson, J. (2009). The impact of smart fractions, cognitive ability of politicians and average competence of peoples on social development. *Talent Development and Excellence*, 1, 3-25.

Rindermann, H., and Thompson, J. (2013). Ability rise in NAEP and narrowing ethnic gaps? *Intelligence*, 41, 821-831.

Rönnlund, M. and Nilsson, L.-G. (2008). The magnitude, generality, and determinants of Flynn effects on forms of declarative memory and visuospatial ability: time-sequential analyses of data from a Swedish cohort study. *Intelligence*, 36, 192-209.

Rushton, J. P., and Ankney, C. D. (2009). Whole brain size and general mental ability: a review. *International Journal of Neuroscience*, 119, 692-732.

Schallberger, U. (1991). Das Ausmass des "IQ-Gewinns" im deutschen Sprachraum von ca. 1956 bis ca. 1983. *Berichte aus der Abteilung Angewandte Psychologie Universität Zürich*, 27.

Schmidt, F. L., and Hunter, J. (2004). General mental ability in the world of work: Occupational attainment and job performance. *Journal of Personality and Social Psychology*, 86, 162-173.

Schofer, E., and Meyer, J. W. (2005). The worldwide expansion of higher education in the twentieth century. *American Sociological Review*, 70, 898-920.

Shamosh, N. A., and Gray, J. R. (2008). Delay discounting and intelligence: a meta-analysis. *Intelligence*, 36, 289-305.

Shayer, M., and Ginsburg, D. (2009). Thirty years on – a large anti-Flynn effect? (II): 13- and 14-year-olds. Piagetian tests of formal operations norms 1976-2006/7. *British Journal of Educational Psychology*, 79, 409-418.

Simon, Julian L. (1996). The ultimate resource, 2nd revised edition. Princeton NJ: Princeton University Press.

Simon, J. L. (2000). The great breakthrough and its cause. Ann Arbor: University of Michigan Press.

Skirbekk, V. (2008). Fertility trends by social status. Demographic Research, 18(5), 145-180.

Solow, R. M. (1956). A contribution to the theory of economic growth. Quarterly Journal of Economics, 70, 65-94.

Sorjonen, K., Hemmingsson, T., Lundin, A., Falkstedt, D., and Melin, B. (2012). Intelligence, socioeconomic background, emotional capacity, and level of education as predictors of attained socioeconomic position in a cohort of Swedish men. *Intelligence*, 40, 269-277.

Spearman, C. (1904). "General intelligence," objectively determined and measured. *American Journal of Psychology*, 15, 201-293.

Stone, L. (1969). Literacy and education in England 1640-1900. *Past and Present*, 42, 69-139.

Strenze, T. (2007). Intelligence and socioeconomic success: A meta-analytic review of longitudinal research. *Intelligence*, 35, 401-426.

Sundet, J. M., Barlaug, D. G., and Torjussen, T. M. (2004). The end of the Flynn effect? A study of secular trends in mean intelligence test scores of Norwegian conscripts during half a century. *Intelligence*, 32, 349-362.

te Nijenhuis, J., Cho, S. H., Murphy, R., and Lee, K. H. (2012). The Flynn effect in Korea: large gains. *Personality and Individual Differences*, 53, 147-151.

Teasdale, T. W. and Owen, D. R. (2005). A long-term rise and recent decline in intelligence test performance: the Flynn effect in reverse. *Personality and Individual Differences*, 39, 837-843.

Teasdale, T. W. and Owen, D. R. (2008). Secular declines in cognitive test scores: a reversal of the Flynn effect. *Intelligence*, 36, 121-126.

Tuddenham, R. D. (1948). Soldier intelligence in World Wars I and II. *American Psychologist*, 3, 54-56.

Turkheimer, E., Haley, A., Waldron, M., D'Onofrio, B., and Gottesman, I. I. (2003). Socioeconomic status modifies heritability of IQ in young children. *Psychological Science*, 14, 623-628.

Van der Sluis, S., Willemsen, G., de Geus, E. J. C., Boomsma, D. I., and Posthuma, D. (2008). Gene-environment interaction in adults' IQ scores: Measures of past and present environment. *Behavior Genetics*, 38, 348-360.

Van Zanden, J. L. (2009). The skill premium and the 'Great Divergence.' *European Review of Economic History*, 13, 121-153.

Weede, E., and Kämpf, S. (2002). The impact of intelligence and institutional improvements on economic growth. *Kyklos*, 55, 361-380.

Wicherts, J. M., Dolan, C. V., Carlson, J. S., and van der Maas, H. L. J. (2010). Raven's test performance of sub-Saharan Africans: average performance, psychometric properties, and the Flynn effect. *Learning and Individual Differences*, 20, 135-151.

Wilkinson, D. (1995). Decline phases in civilizations, regions and oikumenes. *Comparative Civilizations Review*, 33, 33-68.

Wilkinson, R., and Pickett, K. (2009). The spirit level. Why greater equality makes societies stronger. New York: Bloomsbury Press.

Wolf, A. P. (1984). Fertility in prerevolutionary rural China. *Population and Development Review*, 10, 443-470.

Woodley, M. A. (2012). The social and scientific temporal correlates of genotypic intelligence and the Flynn effect. *Intelligence*, 40, 189-204.

Woodley, M. A., te Nijenhuis, J., and Murphy, R. (2013). Were the Victorians cleverer than us? The decline of general intelligence estimated from a meta-analysis of the slowing of simple reaction time. *Intelligence*, 41, 843-850.

Wrulich, M., Brunner, M., Stadler, G., Schalke, D., Keller, U., Chmiel, M., and Martin, R. (2013). Childhood intelligence and adult health: the mediating roles of education and socioeconomic status. *Intelligence*, 41, 490-500.

In: Economic Growth in the 21st Century
Editor: Tara Abrahams
ISBN: 978-1-63321-623-5

Chapter 5

THE STRATEGIC GROWTH APPROACH AS A RELEVANT ECONOMIC GROWTH MODELLING FOR THE 21ST CENTURY

Juan M. C. Larrosa [*]
Department of Economics, Universidad Nacional del Sur and Instituto de Investigaciones Económicas y Sociales del Sur (IIESS), Argentina

ABSTRACT

Globalization has highly increased the interconnection among the economies of the 21st century. A consequence is that local production plans may depend now on many international partners and providers. This, in turn, has led to the prevalence of production and complementation agreements among multinational firms acting on different countries. This mutual interdependence makes economic growth dependent of other economies' performances. For instance, a considerable part of the car production in a given economy requires importing spare parts and non-locally produced components. In this way, manufacturing processes in diverse economic sectors become internationally complemented through the interaction of local production with foreign raw and intermediate inputs. Many contributions in the literature conclude that the most of international trade is composed of intermediate and raw goods, which require local processing before reaching the final consumer. Trade agreements have fostered this process

[*] Email: jlarrosa@criba.edu.ar.

and helped firms in different economies to ground their production plans on free tariff inputs. In fact, local production and foreign inputs usually compete in the domestic market. In these highly integrated economies, the production of intermediate inputs in one economy becomes crucial for production of final or intermediate goods in associated economies. How we can model optimal economic growth in this context of interdependence?

Strategic growth models capture the mutual interdependence in economic growth assuming that the process can be conceived as a differential game. Players with conflicting interests must decide how to respond with contingency plans. The model presented here analyzes economic growth in the light of the theory of differential games to reveal new aspects of macroeconomic interrelations. This contribution presents a brief survey of the relevant literature, postulates a generic model and concludes by working out two examples in which the main features are interdependence of inputs and arms race.

1. INTRODUCTION

Economic growth has been modeled mostly considering an economy in isolation. However interactions are the most prominent feature of the 21st century. From individual agents to aggregate organizations, interacting and responding to others' actions has been a great challenge to take into account in modeling. The strategic growth approach deals with interaction in a simple and powerful way. Based on the Dockner and Nishimura (2004) paper, it is based in an application of differential game theory to a classical optimal growth model. We begin this chapter by introducing and solving two examples of modern macroeconomic interaction.

During the past century the theory of economic growth has based its fundamental in an isolated economy that accumulates diverse stocks of capitals and by combining them with technological progress obtains an increasing output. However, countries do not remain isolated and interact. Economies compete to each other as firms in the goods and services market or individuals in the job market. Just as the mercantilism proposes as good economic policy to increase the strength of the state in each aspect of the economy, the final goal was on compete with other economies. Diverse goals are pursuing when interacting with other economies and this chapter will deal with two of these aspects.

Consider this first scenario. Countries compete to foster growth. Many reasons back this statement. First, the results of competition in the goods and services provided to consumers at a lower price and thus consume more and produce. Most producers are also consumers. To the extent that they pay higher prices for inputs than their foreign competitors, due to the lack of competition or anti-competitive practices in these markets, companies will be less competitive. Second, competition policy, properly implemented, promotes efficiency and productivity. Companies face vigorous competition are continuously pressed to become more efficient and productive internal. Competition forces manage to reduce waste, improve the technical efficiency of production, abandon outdated production techniques and operations and invest in new technologies. Third, competition fosters innovation - Companies that do not innovate are left behind.

Since Ramsey's seminal paper the optimal economic growth has been represented by a single agent that maximizes an intertemporal welfare function. His basic construction has remained as the fundamental building block of models of optimal growth. The welfare function consists of the discounted sum of instantaneous utilities. In most models the rates of time preference were assumed to be constant and therefore independent over time. Instead, some researchers considered a variable rate of time preference: (Uzawa, 1968; Beals and Koopmans, 1969; Iwai, 1972; Blanchard and Fischer, 1989) and in the last decade, (Mantel, 1993, 1995, 1997). The key difference among these approaches lies on the particular characteristics of the preference rate. Uzawa, for example, assumes that it increases with the income level, making the optimal growth paths independent of the initial conditions. On the contrary, following a suggestion of (Fisher, 1930), (Mantel, 1997) postulates that the degree of impatience (the rate of time preference) should be a decreasing function of consumption and thus, indirectly, of the income level. The lower the income, the higher the sacrifice of postponing present consumption in exchange for future consumption. I study a simple model of optimal economic growth in which two countries maintain an interdependence relation in intermediate goods production. Each economy produces a final good and an intermediate good that exports to its trading partner. Producing one unit of its own capital requires a non-domestically produced input (intermediate good) that is imported from another economy. Both economies have liberated their middle product trade and intermediate goods and services are available to both economies free of any commercial restriction. The reasons for this trade liberalization can be associated to comparative advantages in production or extraction cost or maybe the result of a political trade agreement previously signed. We assume that both economies acknowledge this mutual interdependence and plan its long-run growth paths assuming this interdependence.

Consider now a second scenario. Investment in defense without affecting social welfare has been a concern of most economies. It implies a sacrifice of private consumption and would represent a benefit in cases of preventing an attack or providing a decisive winning position when following an aggressive policy. Several modeling approaches have been used in attempting to capture the interaction between competing economies, synthesized mostly in reaction functions (Brito and Intriligator, 1995). On the other hand, political science literature like the contribution of Glaser (2000) has identified two causes for defense expenditure. First, driven by internal factors, defense investment can be pursued for providing basic protection for the socioeconomic infrastructure and other related issues such as internal security or national prestige. Here, defense industry is embedded in the economic infrastructure and produces for accomplishing an agenda set internally in the country. Secondly, and driven by external factors, defense investment can be pursued for matching the capabilities of another country considered as an actual or potential threat. While very similar in nature to the former, this second cause however requires the observation and response to another economies' behavior. They end up "living a parallel life", paraphrasing Bester and Konrad (2005:199).

How could be analyze these interactions? I propose a modeling way, following Dockner and Nishimura (2004) seminal paper, called strategic growth approach. This is a difference game applied to an optimal growth basic structure. We work with a two-economy model, where each economy is represented by an agent that maximizes consumption by producing two types of goods: productive capital and an intermediate good. The production of intermediate goods has strategic considerations: each economy requires intermediate goods from another economy to produce its own intermediate goods. In the second scenario, I try to capture a dynamic dimension of the external and internal causes for defense expenditure and each cause affects growth. I model a two-country difference game, where each country is represented by an agent that maximizes consumption by producing two types of capital: productive and defense capital. The production of the second type of capital is the strategic variable: each country observes its counterpart for deciding how much to produce.

The chapter follows with section 2 where strategic growth models are presented. Section 3 will derive equilibria for these models and section 4 will assess the equilibria. Finally, section 5 will conclude with discussions.

2. The Models

Now I present two modeling approaches for the scenarios presented in section 1. Both share many modeling and solving issues. At the end of the chapter we will find many insights for each model.

2.1. Intermediate Input Interdependence Model

Consider two economies, each of which is represented by a single agent indexed by $i \neq j$, that accumulates productive capital and produces intermediate goods through capital investment and input imports and derives utility from consumption[1]. Each country tries to maximize economic growth observing this mutual interdependence. Output of one country's middle products not only depends on its capital stock and labor but also on the use of intermediate goods from the other country. Thus, each country faces an externality in its production depending of the adopted behavior of the other economy.

The structure of the model is as follows. Let K_t^i, Z_t^i, Y_t^i, and C_t^i be the productive capital stock, intermediate-goods stock, output, and consumption of agent i in period t, respectively. For simplicity, we assume that total labor used in each country is constant and given by L^i. The production function of agent i is $Y_t^i = \pi_i (\theta K_t^i)^{\alpha_i} (Z_t^i)^{\beta_i} (L^i)^{1-\alpha_i-\beta_i}$ where $\pi_i > 0$ is a total factor productivity index and θ is the proportion of capital allocated in producing the final good[2]. We assume that the level of $Z_t^i = f(K_t^i, Z_t^j)$, with $j \neq i$, in a formulation of the type:

$$Z_t^i = \left(\frac{(1-\theta)K_t^i}{L^i} \right)^{\frac{\varsigma_i}{\beta_i}} \left(\frac{Z_t^j}{L^j} \right)^{\frac{\varphi_j}{\beta_i}} L^i \tag{1}$$

[1] The model could also be interpreted as a two-region one, with different agents in each region.

[2] I thank to an anonymous referee for this suggestion.

where $\varsigma_i + \varphi_j = \beta_i < 1$. This function expresses that intermediate goods Z_t^i are produced as a combination of the stock of productive capital of economy i, K_t^i, and intermediate inputs from the economy j, Z_t^j.

Assuming a constant rate of depreciation for the stock of capital, δ , and applying the income identity, i.e., output in the current period is used for consumption and investment, results in the following accumulation equation

$$K_{t+1}^i = \pi_i \left(\theta K_t^i\right)^{\alpha_i} \left(Z_t^i\right)^{\beta_i} \left(L^i\right)^{1-\alpha_i-\beta_i} - C_t^i + (1-\delta) K_t^i$$

If we redefine variables in terms of units per labor employed, i.e., $k_t^i \equiv K_t^i / L^i$, $z_t^i \equiv Z_t^i / L^i$, $c_t^i \equiv C_t^i / L^i$, and assume that there is full depreciation[3], $\delta = 1$, we obtain the following

$$k_{t+1}^i = \pi_i \left(\theta k_t^i\right)^{\alpha_i} \left(z_t^i\right)^{\beta_i} - c_t^i \tag{2}$$

The initial state dynamics is represented by (2). But for (1) we have that $z_t^i \equiv Z^i / L^i \equiv \left((1-\theta) k_t^i\right)^{\frac{\varsigma_i}{\beta_i}} \left(z_t^j\right)^{\frac{\varphi_j}{\beta_i}}$, and then replacing we obtain $k_{t+1}^i = \pi_i \left(\theta k_t^i\right)^{\alpha_i} \left((1-\theta) k_t^i\right)^{\varsigma_i} \left(z_t^j\right)^{\varphi_i} - c_t^i$ this way, in case the interaction is fully internalized by the two agents the state dynamics becomes

$$k_{t+1}^i = \pi_i \left(\xi k_t^i\right)^{\alpha_i + \varsigma_i} \left(z_t^j\right)^{\varphi_j} - c_t^i \tag{3}$$

where $\xi = \theta)^{\alpha_i} (1-\theta))^{\varsigma_i}$. The accumulation equation (3) gives rise to a model of strategic growth in which agents recognize that their respective productions do influence each others so this is internalized and emerges as a strategic externality resulting in a model that can be either formulated as an open-loop (precommitment) or a Markov game without commitment[4]. In case agents play a game in which they have access to Markov strategies they design their current actions as decision rules that depend on the current stocks of both countries, while in the case of an open-loop game agents choose their

[3] While unrealistic this assumption is made for the sake of simplicity.

[4] Readers interested in this concept of solutions should consult Dockner et al. (2000) for the differential games case and Zeeuw and van der Ploeg (1991) for the difference games case.

strategies as simple time paths that do not depend on the current level of the capital stocks.

We assume that the production function, $y_t^i = \pi_i \left(\xi k_t^i\right)^{\alpha_i + \varsigma_i} \left(z_t^j\right)^{\varphi_j}$, satisfies the following parameter restrictions: π_i is strictly positive and constant and $0 < \alpha_i, \varsigma_i, \varphi_j < 1$ and $\alpha_i + \varsigma_i + \varphi_j \leqslant 1$. Each agent derives utility in period t only from current consumption and the utility function, $u^i\left(c_t^i\right)$ is logarithmic, i.e. $u^i\left(c_i^t\right) = \ln c_t^i$. Each agent lives forever, i.e. $T = \infty$, and maximizes the discounted stream of utility with the discount rate given by $\rho = \left(1/(1+r)\right)$, where r is the rate of interest satisfying $r > 0$. We consider only domestic consumption in this model. Intermediate importing and exporting is fully liberalized between countries. Finally, we assume that trade balance is always in equilibrium and does not require any capital flows compensation.

Each agent maximizes the discounted stream of utility given by

$$J^i = \sum_{i=0}^{\infty} \rho^t \ln c_t^i,$$

subject to

$$k_{t+1}^i = \pi_i \left(\xi k_t^i\right)^{\alpha_i + \varsigma_i} \left(z_t^j\right)^{\varphi_j} - c_t^i$$

and given initial conditions $\left(k_0^i, z_0^j\right)$.

Specifically, this strategic growth game in reduced form looks as follows:

$$\max_{\left\{k_{t+1}^i\right\}_{t=0}^{\infty}} \left\{ J^i = \sum_{t=0}^{\infty} \rho^t \ln\left(\pi_i \left(\xi k_t^i\right)^{\alpha_i + \varsigma_i} \left(z_t^j\right)^{\varphi_j} - k_{t+1}^i\right) \right\} \tag{4}$$

subject to the initial conditions $\left(k_0^i, z_0^j\right)$.

Before solving the model, we introduce in the following section the arms race model.

2.2. Arms Race Model

Consider two countries, each of which is represented by a single agent indexed by $i \neq j$. Each economy produces two goods: a private consumption good and a defense good. The private consumption good adopts a traditional normal good of the economic growth theory that derives utility from its consumption. The defense good, on the other hand, is produced with the capital stock of the economy but its level of production strategically determined by the level of production of its analogous in the other economy. I follow Lichbach (1990: 33) and assume the interaction between these two economies as represented by a type of Richardson (Intriligator and Brito (2000)) arms rivalry model where two economies' defense investment is partially dependent upon what the other economy does. A typical Richardson reaction function of military expenditure of country *i*, Z^i , on the expenditure of country *j*, Z^j, follows the form of a differential equation $dZ^i / dt = aZ^j - bZ^i + g$, where *j* is the other country, *a* is a threat coefficient, *b* is a fatigue coefficient and *g* is a grievance term. This equation postulates a relationship between the own investment in weapons affected by a fatigue coefficient (producing more non-productive assets affect total productivity in the economy), a threat coefficient (indicating the relative intensity in the utility of the representative agent of one economy to the variations in the military expenditure of the other economy) and a term representing an autonomous effect. One interpretation for the fatigue coefficient involves the affectation of the utility trough reduction in consumption of private goods. This is the interpretation adopted for this contribution. In broader terms, a Richardson reaction function describes military expenditure as positively related to other economies' military expenditure, and negatively related (in terms of sacrificing levels of consumption) to its own level of military expenditure. I will make the assumption that the grievance term becomes null in the long run[5].

Each country tries to maximize economic growth but observing some constant relationship in the production of the defense capital. Output of one country's defensive capital not only depends on its capital stock and labor but also in the defense capital stock of the another country. Thus, each country faces an externality in its capital stock depending of the adopted behavior of the other country.

[5] van der Ploeg and de Zeeuw (1990) modelated this term explicitly.

The structure of the model is as follows. Let K_t^i, Z_t^i, Y_t^i, and C_t^i be the productive capital stock, defense (or military) goods/services, output, and consumption of agent *i* in period *t*, respectively. For simplicity, I assume that total labor used in each country is constant and given by L^i. The production function of agent *i* is $Y_t^i = \pi_i \left(K_t^i\right)^{\alpha_i} \left(Z_t^i\right)^{\beta_i} \left(L^i\right)^{1-\alpha_i-\beta_i}$ where $\pi_i > 0$ is a total factor productivity index. I also assume that the level of defense goods or services depends on the current capital stock and on the production of the other economy, $Z_t^i = f\left(K_t^i, Z_t^j\right)$, with $j \neq i$.

The production of the defense goods/services is an embedded production function in the economy with (strictly) decreasing returns. It is represented by a piecewise function that responds drastically to a cooperative behavior of the counterpart: if the other country invests zero in defense goods (cooperate), the answer is to responds with zero investment in defense goods too (cooperate). In case of non-negative investment (noncooperative), the answer is to match the threat (noncooperative). This part of the modeling approach resembles the threat coefficient of the Richardson reaction function and represents a tit-for-tat strategy (Axelrod (1984)). The formulation is then:

$$Z_t^i = \begin{cases} \theta \left(\dfrac{K_t^i}{L^i}\right)^{\frac{\vartheta_i}{\beta_i}} \left(\dfrac{Z_t^j}{L^j}\right)^{\frac{\nu_j}{\beta_i}} L^i & \text{if } Z_t^j > 0 \\ \theta \left(\dfrac{K_t^i}{L^i}\right)^{\frac{\vartheta_i+\nu_j}{\beta_i}} L^i & \text{if } Z_t^j = 0 \end{cases} \tag{5}$$

where θ is a constant and it is assumed that $\vartheta_i + \nu_j = \beta_i < 1$ and I will consider that $Z_t^j > 0$ for the rest of the analysis. I assume that θ is a proportion that signals some (historically and conventionally accepted) power parity in weapons stock or threat threshold. ν_j is a parameter of intensity[6]. Observe, as stated earlier, that if $Z_t^j \to 0 \Rightarrow Z_t^i \to 0$, i.e., if there is no threat, there is no military expenditure; if $K_t^i \to 0 \Rightarrow Z_t^i \to 0$, meaning that if the economy *i* does not produce weapons, it is optimum for the economy *j* not to

[6] This formulation is inspired in the index of defense by Brito (1972). It only adds the direct dependence of the level of defense production with the actual state of the capital stock.

produce weapons at all, and vice versa. It is also noted that if the economy i does not use any of the local stock of capital, the production of defense also becomes null.

I will not model any specific process of conflict triggering (as Bester and Konrad (2005)). Both countries could never end up in a war even if they departed from their equilibrium paths. The "threat" it is assumed to be exogenous to the model (historical rivalry, common resources disputes, and geopolitical strategy, among others.) The model also accepts low intensity conflict (skirmishes and other threats that not initiate a full scale war) that barely affects capital stock. In this sense this model represents a large number of developing countries (Deger and Sen (1995)) that invest in defense but that hardly ever have faced a real conflict even if they create a considerable structure of defense with force projection capabilities.

Each agent derives utility in period t only from current consumption[7] and the utility function, $u^i\left(c_t^i\right)$ is logarithmic, i.e. $u^i\left(c_i^t\right)=\ln c_t^i$. Each agent lives forever, i.e. $T=\infty$, and maximizes the discounted stream of utility with the discount rate given by $\rho=\left(1/(1+r)\right)$, where r is the rate of interest satisfying $r>0$. I consider only domestic consumption. In the state dynamics of the model it will be considered that investment in defense goods and services will harm consumption. Specifically, I will consider a variable ϕ_i (with $0\leq\phi_i\leq 1$) that is positively (and highly) correlated[8] with the intensity in defense goods and services production β_i that will affect consumption in a proportion $\left(1-\phi_i\right)$. This will reflects the fatigue coefficient of the Richardson reaction function.

Assuming a constant rate of depreciation of the stock of capital, δ, and applying the income identity, i.e., output in the current period is used for consumption and investment, results in the following accumulation equation

$$K_{t+1}^i=\pi_i\left(K_t^i\right)^{\alpha_i}\left(Z_t^i\right)^{\beta_i}\left(L^i\right)^{1-\alpha_i-\beta_i}-\left(1-\phi_i\right)C_t^i+\left(1-\delta\right)K_t^i$$

[7] I assume that consumption includes private and defensive goods as assumed by many other models like Brito (1972), Intriligator and Brito (2000) and Shieh et al. (2002).

[8] In fact, I could use β_i directly but I avoid this oversimplification for the sake of clarity.

If we redefine variables in terms of units per labor employed, i.e., $k_t^i \equiv K_t^i / L^i$, $z_t^i \equiv Z_t^i / L^i$, $c_t^i \equiv C_t^i / L^i$, and assume that there is full depreciation, $\delta = 1$, we obtain the following dynamic equation:

$$k_{t+1}^i = \pi_i \left(k_t^i\right)^{\alpha_i} \left(z_t^i\right)^{\beta_i} - \left(1-\phi_i\right) c_t^i \tag{6}$$

The initial state dynamics is represented by (2). But for (1) we have that $z_t^i \equiv Z_t^i / L^i = \theta\left(k_t^i\right)^{\frac{\vartheta_i}{\beta_i}} \left(z_t^j\right)^{\frac{\nu_j}{\beta_i}}$, and then we obtain $k_{t+1}^i = \pi_i \theta \left(k_t^i\right)^{\alpha_i} \left(k_t^i\right)^{\vartheta_i} \left(z_t^j\right)^{\nu_j} - \left(1-\phi_i\right) c_t^i$ in case the interaction is fully internalized by the two agents the state dynamics becomes

$$k_{t+1}^i = \xi_i \left(k_t^i\right)^{\alpha_i + \vartheta_i} \left(z_t^j\right)^{\nu_j} - \left(1-\phi_i\right) c_t^i \tag{7}$$

where $\xi_i = \pi_i \theta^{\vartheta_i}$. I assume that the production function satisfies the following parameter restrictions: ξ_i is strictly positive and constant and $0 < \alpha_i, \vartheta_i, \nu_j < 1$ and $\alpha_i + \vartheta_i + \nu_j \leq 1$, for $i \neq j$. Again, the accumulation equation (6) delineates a model of strategic growth in which agents recognize that their respective capital stocks and defense investment do influence each other in a way that allows to be internalized as a strategic externality. The resulting model can either be formulated as a difference game with potential open-loop (precommitment) or Markov game without commitment (closed-loop) equilibrium. In case agents play a game in which they have access to Markov strategies they design their current actions as decision rules that depend on the current stocks of capital and defense capital of both countries, while in the case of an open-loop game agents choose their strategies as simple time paths that do not depend on the current level of the capital stocks. I am going to assume that the Markov equilibrium represents more adequately an "arms race" scenario while the open-loop equilibrium will more closely approach to an "arms build-up" scenario.

Each agent maximizes the discounted stream of utility given by

$$J^i = \sum_{i=0}^{\infty} \rho^i \ln c_t^i,$$

subject to

$$k_{t+1}^{i} = \xi_i \left(k_t^i\right)^{\alpha_i + \vartheta_i} \left(z_t^j\right)^{\nu_j} - \left(1 - \phi_i\right) c_t^i$$

and given initial conditions $\left(k_0^i, z_0^j\right)$.

Specifically, defining $\varpi_i = 1/\left(1-\phi_i\right)$, the strategic growth game in reduced form looks as follows:

$$\max_{\left\{k_{t+1}^i\right\}_{t=0}^{\infty}} \left\{ J^i = \sum_{t=0}^{\infty} \rho^t \ln\left(\varpi_i \left(\xi_i \left(k_t^i\right)^{\alpha_i + \vartheta_i} \left(z_t^j\right)^{\nu_j} - k_{t+1}^i \right)\right)\right\} \tag{8}$$

subject to the initial conditions $\left(k_0^i, z_0^j\right)$.

I follow with the derivation of equilibria of the two postulated models.

3. Equilibria in Both Models

We have two possible equilibrium strategies for the agents. The first one that we are going to analyze is the open-loop solution that requires that agents commit to some initial strategy of capital augmentation during the complete period of analysis. In the second, agents used Markov strategies that reconsider in each period of time their strategy during the complete period of analysis.

In both open-loop and Markov perfect equilibria, countries understand that a change in their actions (e.g., a deviation from the equilibrium production value) causes a change in the state variable. In open-loop equilibrium, an economy believes that the interdependent economy will not respond to such changes. This equilibrium will be interpreted as an arms buildup according to Glaser (2000)'s definition. In Markov Perfect Equilibrium (MPE), on the contrary, an economy realizes that the interdependent country will respond to change in the state variable. That way, MPE assumption attributes greater rationality to policy makers in charge of conducting these production decisions. This equilibrium best represent an arms races process as suggested also by Glaser (2000).

3.1. The Open-Loop Equilibrium

To characterize the open-loop equilibrium we apply the first order conditions, which are also sufficient given strict concavity, and get

$$\frac{-1}{\pi_i\left(\xi k_t^i\right)^{\alpha_i+\varsigma_i}\left(z_t^j\right)^{\varphi_j}-k_{t+1}^i}+\rho\frac{\pi_i\left(\alpha_i+\varsigma_i\right)\left(\xi k_{t+1}^i\right)^{\alpha_i+\varsigma_i-1}\left(z_{t+1}^j\right)^{\varphi_j}}{\pi_i\left(\xi k_{t+1}^i\right)^{\alpha_i+\varsigma_i}\left(z_{t+1}^j\right)^{\varphi_j}-k_{t+2}^i}=0 \tag{9}$$

Rearranging terms and dividing (5) by $\left(\xi k_{t+1}^i\right)^{\alpha_i+\varsigma_i}\left(z_{t+1}^j\right)^{\varphi_j}$ we obtain

$$\pi_i+\rho\alpha_i\pi_i-\rho\alpha_i\pi_i^2\frac{\left(\xi k_t^i\right)^{\alpha_i+\varsigma_i}\left(z_t^j\right)^{\varphi_j}}{k_{t+1}}-\frac{k_{t+2}^i}{\left(\xi k_{t+1}^i\right)^{\alpha_i+\varsigma_i}\left(z_{t+1}^j\right)^{\varphi_j}}=0$$

Now we create a variable $x_{t+1}^i=\dfrac{k_{t+1}^i}{\left(\xi k_t^i\right)^{\alpha_i+\varsigma_i}\left(z_t^j\right)^{\varphi_j}}$ and we replace in the FOC and we get the dynamic equation:

$$\pi_i+\rho\alpha_i\pi_i-\rho\alpha_i\pi_i^2\frac{1}{x_{t+1}}-x_{t+2}^i=0 \tag{10}$$

Any growth process is governed by the dynamical system (6).

Proposition 1. *The followings results hold: There exists an open-loop equilibrium of the strategic growth model that results in consumption rules given by*

$$c^i\left(k_t^i,z_t^j\right)=\left(1-\alpha_i\rho\right)\pi_i\left(\xi k_t^i\right)^{\alpha_i+\varsigma_i}\left(z_t^j\right)^{\varphi_j} \tag{11}$$

Departing from initial stocks $\left(k_0^i,z_0^j\right)$, equilibrium dynamics is governed by

$$k_{t+1}^i=\omega_i\left(\xi k_t^i\right)^{\alpha_i+\varsigma_i}\left(z_t^j\right)^{\varphi_j} \tag{12}$$

$$k_{t+1}^{j} = \omega_{j}\left(\xi k_{t}^{j}\right)^{\alpha_{j}+\varsigma_{j}}\left(z_{t}^{i}\right)^{\varphi_{i}} \tag{13}$$

where $\omega_i = (\alpha_i + \varsigma_i)\rho\pi_i$ and $\omega_j = (\alpha_j + \varsigma_j)\rho\pi_j$.

Proof: See Appendix.

The system develops governed by (12) and (13). For characterizing the system we propose the following theorem.

Proposition 2. *In case there are decreasing returns to scale, i.e.* $\alpha_i + \varsigma_i + \varphi_j < 1$, *equilibrium dynamics admit a unique and stable steady state given by*

$$\left(\bar{k}_{0}^{i}, \bar{z}_{0}^{j}\right) = \left([(\omega_i)]^{\frac{1-\alpha_j-\varsigma_j}{\Phi}} \left[\omega_j\right]^{\frac{\varphi_j}{\Phi}}, \left[\omega_i\right]^{\frac{1-\alpha_i-\varsigma_i}{\Phi}} \left[\omega_j\right]^{\frac{\varphi_j}{\Phi}} \right) \tag{14}$$

where $\Phi = (1-\alpha_i-\varsigma_i)(1-\alpha_j-\varsigma_j) - \varphi_i\varphi_j$

Proof: See Appendix.

The case of decreasing returns of scale leads results directly interpretable. The case of constant returns to scale follows as another interesting case for analysis.

Proposition 3 *Assume that the technologies exhibit constant returns to scale, that is,* $\alpha_i + \varsigma_i + \varphi_j = 1$ *and that* π_i *is chosen in a way that* $\pi_i(\alpha_i + \varsigma_i)\rho > 1$ *and* $\pi_j(\alpha_j + \varsigma_j)\rho > 1$ *is verified. Then it verifies that there exists a balanced growth path factor given by*

$$\iota = \left[\omega_i\right]^{\frac{\varphi_j}{\varphi_i+\varphi_j}} \left[\omega_j\right]^{\frac{\varphi_i}{\varphi_i+\varphi_j}} \tag{15}$$

where $\omega_i = \pi_i(\alpha_i + \varsigma_i)\rho$, $\forall i, j$.

Proof: See Appendix.

Notice that these results also resemble the AK-model. For instance, if both countries begin with the same initial capital stocks, then the equilibrium dynamics is represented by:

$$k_{t+1} = \omega(\xi k_t)^{\alpha+\varsigma+\varphi}$$

but if the available technology shows constant returns to scale we derive that the dynamics of balanced-growth path is represented by

$$k_{t+1} = \omega\xi k_t = Ak_t,$$

known as a type of AK-growth model.

Now the very same modeling approach can be articulated into the model of arms race. This is modeled as an open-loop game where agents choose their consumption as simple time paths and commit themselves to stick to these time profiles during the entire game. It is clear that such a game cannot capture all the strategic interactions present in the dynamic game. It resembles many features of a one shot game and the equilibrium optimum could be analyzed as the Nash equilibrium of this game. This leads to a static view of the interaction analysis.

The best-response function in static game determines, in this case, how a country would want to respond to an arbitrary action by its interdependent country if it were able to response indeed. However, the assumption of simultaneous moves prevents this actual response to happen. In a static setting what a best-response function shows is the direction of the desired contemporaneous response to the linked country's actions. Notice that there is not updating of the strategic variable at each period of time. An economy does not observe how much the other economy is spending in defense for deciding how much to invest itself. One interpretation of this is that the economy follows other goals for deciding military budgeting and that goals may be of internal nature.

To characterize the open-loop equilibrium we apply the first order conditions, which are also sufficient given strict concavity, and get

$$\frac{-1}{\varpi_i\left(\xi_i\left(k_t^i\right)^{\alpha_i+\vartheta_i}\left(z_t^j\right)^{v_j}-k_{t+1}^i\right)}+\rho\frac{\xi_i\left(\alpha_i+\vartheta_i\right)\left(k_{t+1}^i\right)^{\alpha_i+\vartheta_i-1}\left(z_{t+1}^j\right)^{v_j}}{\left(\xi_i\left(k_{t+1}^i\right)^{\alpha_i+\vartheta_i}\left(z_{t+1}^j\right)^{v_j}-k_{t+2}^i\right)}=0 \quad (16)$$

Rearranging terms and dividing (5) by $\xi_i\left(k_{t+1}^i\right)^{\alpha_i+\vartheta_i}\left(z_{t+1}^j\right)^{\nu_j}$ and creating a new variable $h_{t+1}=\frac{k_{t+1}}{\xi k_t^{\alpha_i+\vartheta_i}z_t^{\nu_j}}$ and replacing in the first order condition and we get the dynamic equation:

$$\left(1+(\alpha_i+\vartheta_i)\rho\varpi_i\right)-(\alpha_i+\vartheta_i)\rho\varpi_i\frac{1}{h_{t+1}}-h_{t+2}=0 \tag{17}$$

The dynamical system (10) is a key to any growth process in this system.

Proposition 4. The followings results hold:

a) There exists an open-loop equilibrium of the strategic growth model that results in consumption rules given by

$$c^i\left(k_t^i,z_t^j\right)=\left(1-(\alpha_i+\vartheta_i)\rho\varpi_i\right)\xi_i\left(k_t^i\right)^{\alpha_i+\vartheta_i}\left(z_t^j\right)^{\nu_j} \tag{18}$$

b) Departing from initial stocks $\left(k_0^i,z_0^j\right)$, equilibrium dynamics is governed by

$$k_{t+1}^i=\eta_i\left(k_t^i\right)^{\alpha_i+\vartheta_i}\left(z_t^j\right)^{\nu_j} \tag{19}$$

$$k_{t+1}^j=\eta_j\left(k_t^j\right)^{\alpha_j+\vartheta_j}\left(z_t^i\right)^{\nu_i} \tag{20}$$

With $\eta_i=\left(\alpha_i+\vartheta_i\right)\rho\varpi_i\xi_i$ and $\eta_j=\left(\alpha_j+\vartheta_j\right)\rho\varpi_j\xi_j$.

Proof: See Proof of Proposition 1.

The system develops governed by (8) and (9). For characterizing the system I propose the following theorem.

Proposition 5. *In case there is decreasing returns to scale, i.e.* $\alpha_i+\vartheta_i+\nu_j<1$, *equilibrium dynamics admits a unique and stable steady state given by*

$$\left(\bar{k}_0^i,\bar{z}_0^j\right)=\left(\left[(\eta_i)\right]^{\frac{1-\alpha_j-\vartheta_j}{\Phi}}\left[\eta_j\right]^{\frac{\nu_j}{\Phi}},\left[\eta_i\right]^{\frac{1-\alpha_i-\vartheta_i}{\Phi}}\left[\eta_j\right]^{\frac{\nu_i}{\Phi}}\right) \tag{21}$$

where $\Phi = (1-\alpha_i - \vartheta_i)(1-\alpha_j - \vartheta_j) - \left(\nu_j\right)\left(\nu_i\right)$

Proof: See Proof of Proposition 2.

Proposition 6. *Assume that the technologies exhibit constant returns to scale, that is,* $\alpha_i + \vartheta_i + \nu_j = 1$ *and that* ξ_i *and* ξ_j *are chosen in a way that* $\xi_i \alpha_i \rho \varpi_i > 1$ *and* $\xi_j \alpha_j \rho \varpi_j > 1$ *are verified. Then it verifies that there exists a balanced growth path factor given by*

$$\upsilon = [\eta_i]^{\frac{\nu_i}{\nu_j + \nu_i}} \left[\eta_j\right]^{\frac{\nu_j}{\nu_j + \nu_i}} \tag{22}$$

Proof: See Proof of Proposition 3.

At this point, Propositions 1 to 3 and 4 to 6 remark that both economies can obtain nonnegative rates of growth only by internalizing their mutual interdependence. Two issues have to be remarked. First, in this case, the internalization is made on the very first period of the process of optimization and it remains constant to the end. One interpretation of this position is that economies do recognize an initial interdependence but they do not utterly update in further periods with newer information. Some other priorities (perhaps an internal agenda) are pursued. Secondly, as mentioned in the definitions of the model, β and ϕ are correlated. The effect of these two terms, embedded in the transformations ν and ϖ, are present in the final rates of growth. At the end, if ϕ is higher, ϖ will be higher too, which is unusual given that a harm in consumption will end up increasing the rate of growth.

3.2. The Markovian Perfect Equilibrium

We follow with the derivation of a Markov Perfect Equilibrium of the strategic growth model. A MPE is a Markov Nash Equilibrium that is at the same time a subgame perfect equilibrium (SPE). The issue of existence of MPE for difference games is not an easy test. The approach resembles many features of a repeated game where agents can revise their strategies and the equilibrium optimum could be analyzed as the subgame perfect equilibrium of this game. This leads to a dynamic setting of the interaction. When countries use Markov strategies in a dynamic setting they are able to respond to their rivals' actions, although they respond after they observe rivals' movements. In a dynamic setting a best-response function shows the actual future response to a interdependent country's actions.

We begin with the following lemma:

Proposition 7. *The following results hold: A MPE equilibrium exists to the strategic growth game that results in consumption rules given by*

$$c^i\left(k_t^i, z_t^j\right) = \left(1 - \rho\left(\left(\alpha_i + \varsigma_i\right) + \frac{\rho\varphi_i\varphi_j}{1 - \left(\alpha_i + \varsigma_i\right)\rho}\right)\right)\pi_i\left(\xi k_t^i\right)^{\alpha_i + \varsigma_i}\left(z_t^j\right)^{\varphi_j} \tag{23}$$

Departing from initial stocks $\left(k_0^i, z_0^j\right)$, equilibrium dynamics is governed by

$$k_{t+1}^i = \psi_i\left(\xi k_t^i\right)^{\alpha_i + \varsigma_i}\left(z_t^j\right)^{\varphi_j} \tag{24}$$

$$k_{t+1}^j = \psi_j\left(\xi k_t^j\right)^{\alpha_j + \varsigma_j}\left(z_t^i\right)^{\varphi_i} \tag{25}$$

for $i \neq j$, where

$$\psi_i = \pi_i\left(\left(\alpha_i + \varsigma_i\right)\rho + \rho^2\frac{\varphi_i\varphi_j}{1 - \left(\alpha_i + \varsigma_i\right)\rho}\right) \text{ and}$$

$$\psi_j = \pi_j\left(\left(\alpha_j + \varsigma_j\right)\rho + \rho^2\frac{\varphi_i\varphi_j}{1 - \left(\alpha_j + \varsigma_j\right)\rho}\right).$$

In case there are decreasing returns to scale, i.e. $\alpha_i + \varsigma_i + \varphi_j < 1$, equilibrium dynamics admit a unique steady state given by

$$\left(\bar{k}_0^i, \bar{z}_0^j\right) = \left(\left[\psi_i\right]^{\frac{1-\alpha_j-\varsigma_j}{\Phi}}\left[\psi_j\right]^{\frac{\varphi_i}{\Phi}}, \left[\psi_j\right]^{\frac{1-\alpha_i-\varsigma_i}{\Phi}}\left[\psi_i\right]^{\frac{\varphi_j}{\Phi}}\right) \tag{26}$$

where $\Phi = \left(1 - \alpha_i - \varsigma_i\right)\left(1 - \alpha_j - \varsigma_j\right) - \varphi_i\varphi_j$

In case of constant returns to scale, i.e. $\alpha_i + \beta_i + \nu_j = 1$, there exists a balanced growth path with the growth factor given by

$$\vartheta = \psi_i^{\frac{\varphi_j}{\varphi_i+\varphi_j}} \psi_j^{\frac{\varphi_i}{\varphi_i+\varphi_j}} \tag{27}$$

Proof: See Appendix.

Now again we can apply the same procedures to solve the arms race case. I follow with the derivation of a Markov Perfect Equilibrium of the strategic growth model. A MPE is a Markov Nash Equilibrium that is at the same time a subgame perfect equilibrium (SPE) and resembles many features of a repeated game where agents can revise their strategies and the equilibrium optimum could be analyzed as the subgame perfect equilibrium of this game, i.e., it is a dynamic interaction setting. When an economy uses Markov strategies in a dynamic setting it is able to respond to its rival' actions, although it responds after they observe rival's movements. In a dynamic setting a best-response function shows the actual future response to an interdependent country's actions.

Proposition 8. The following results hold:

a) A MPE equilibrium exists to the strategic growth game that results in consumption rules given by

$$c^i\left(k_t^i, z_t^j\right) = \left(1 - \rho\varpi_i\left(\alpha_i + \frac{\rho\nu_i\nu_j}{1-(\alpha_i+\vartheta_i)\rho\varpi_i}\right)\right)\xi_i\left(k_t^i\right)^{\alpha_i+\vartheta_i}\left(z_t^j\right)^{\nu_j} \tag{28}$$

b) Departing from initial stocks $\left(k_0^i, z_0^j\right)$, equilibrium dynamics is governed by

$$k_{t+1}^i = \psi_i\left(k_t^i\right)^{\alpha_i+\vartheta_i}\left(z_t^j\right)^{\nu_j}, \text{ for } i \neq j \tag{29}$$

$$k_{t+1}^j = \psi_j\left(k_t^j\right)^{\alpha_j+\vartheta_j}\left(z_t^i\right)^{\nu_i}, \text{ for } i \neq j \tag{30}$$

where

$$\psi_i = \xi_i\left((\alpha_i+\vartheta_i)\rho\varpi_i + \rho^2\frac{\nu_i\nu_j}{1-(\alpha_i+\vartheta_i)\rho\varpi_i}\right) \text{ and}$$

$$\psi_j = \xi_j\left(\left(\alpha_j+\vartheta_j\right)\rho\varpi_j + \rho^2\frac{\nu_i\nu_j}{1-(\alpha_j+\vartheta_j)\rho\varpi_j}\right).$$

In case there are decreasing returns to scale, i.e. $\alpha_i + \beta_i + \nu_j < 1$, equilibrium dynamics admit a unique steady state given by

$$\left(\overline{k}_0^i, \overline{z}_0^j\right) = \left([\psi_i]^{\frac{1-\alpha_j-\vartheta_j}{\Phi}} [\psi_j]^{\frac{\nu_j}{\Phi}}, [\psi_j]^{\frac{1-\alpha_i-\vartheta_i}{\Phi}} [\psi_i]^{\frac{\nu_i}{\Phi}} \right) \tag{31}$$

where $\Phi = \left(1-(\alpha_i+\vartheta_i)\varpi_i\right)\left(1-(\alpha_j+\vartheta_j)\varpi_j\right) - \left(\nu_j\right)\left(\nu_i\right)$

c) In case of constant returns to scale, i.e. $\alpha_i + \vartheta_i + \nu_j = 1$, there exists a balanced growth path with the growth factor given by

$$\tau = \psi_i^{\frac{\nu_i}{\nu_i+\nu_j}} \psi_j^{\frac{\nu_j}{\nu_i+\nu_j}} \tag{32}$$

Proof: See Proof of Proposition 7.
Next section is dedicated to analyze the results of both games.

4. Effects

In both models, equilibria share a common component but MPE adds a new one. The common part of the equilibrium is the open-loop equilibrium. This is presented in Proposition 1 and 4. These results explain growth as a combination of the intensity in the production of private goods and defense goods. As the production of defense is part of the production of the economy, its increment derives in higher GDP.

The MPE is closer to an expected rational behavior in equilibrium for the policy maker. That is to say, it shows the actions taken by one economy in response to the actions taken by the other economy in the recent past. At this respect, the MPE shows the equilibrium at each step of the time. In our case, MPE steady state rate of growth is higher than the open-loop case. This is because $\psi > \omega$ for i, j given that always $\rho^2 \frac{\varphi_i \varphi_j}{1-(\alpha_j + \varsigma_j)\rho} > 0$.

The difference is directed explained by the intensity in the use of intermediate good production in each economy. This added part in the MPE explains how each economy is reacting to changes in the intermediate goods production. Whenever both economies increased the allocation of capital in producing both intermediate goods that would result in an increase in the rate of growth.

In open-loop strategies, policy makers estimate an initial optimal allocation in intermediate input production and they believe that any changes they may make won't generate any response in the partner behavior. It is a plan that has to be followed in a rigid way. So, the rate of growth using open-loop strategies makes no use of the information in the composition of capital allocated in the middle products. On the other hand, in Markovian strategies, economies consider that if they make changes in the intensity of using capital in the middle products market, they will have a response in the counterpart.

In the empirics of international trade, the static game outcome resembles some aspects of the commercial agreements signed under political interest rather than economic interest. For instance, the trade arrangements signed by many countries of the COMECON with the former Soviet Union were rather stiff deals where the absence of conjunctural adjustments or at least with highly bureaucratized procedures for adapting the production process were common practice. International trade under this framework was focused to meet the planned objectives for a five-year master plan (Pelzman (1978)). The model's open-loop equilibrium can be understood as an equilibrium where production decisions are taken not analyzing all the relevant economic information available to the economy at every step of the time but focusing in a long run objective that has to be accomplished. That objective may include political or development justifications[9].

In terms of policy implications, the result expresses that agreements of inter-industrial cooperation require constant updating for a continuous and smooth adaptation to changes in the production process. By doing this it is granted a more efficient use of capital in both economies and that ensures the joint production efficiency providing greater growth rates.

It is interesting to note that an economy could enjoy at the same time of international transactions that reflect both types of equilibria. A part of the international trade could reflect programs that allow for small or null adaption to shocks while another part of the commerce could reflect open exchange fully adaptable to conjunctural variations. It is foreseeable that the larger the composition of the international trade based on the first, the effect on growth would be in the direction of lower growth rates.

As mentioned, the MPE adds a new part observed in Proposition 4(b). This new addition depends directly on the relative intensity of the defense investment of both countries. Interestingly, this very same addition, under

[9] Another reason can be national defense objectives. Independently of the political system, several international defense programs are continued and concluded even if intermediate goods prices rise sensitively.

specific circumstances, can compensate the effect of the former. Observe that if $1/(\alpha_i+\vartheta_i)\rho<\varpi_i$ or, by construction, $\phi_i>1-(\alpha_i+\vartheta_i)\rho$ the second component becomes negative, subtracting growth from the first component in the MPE. This happens when the intensity in the opportunity cost of augmenting defense investment surpasses the intensity of the discounted production of private goods. Here we have the cost in terms of welfare that an arms race provokes on an economy and is related with the fatigue effect in the Richardson equation. This fact can be observed when the economy involves itself in allocating resources in defense goods but fails to provide the adequate quantities of private goods that enhance the utility of their consumers.

It is worth noting that under open-loop strategies, policy makers estimate an initial optimal allocation in the production of defense goods and they believe that any changes they may make won't generate any response in the neighbor behavior. In more colloquial terms, there is no necessity for observing what the other country is doing at every time step. It is a plan that has to be followed in a rigid way, perhaps following internal objectives of expenditure. This way, the rate of growth using open-loop strategies makes no use of the information in the composition of capital allocated in military goods. On the other hand, in Markovian strategies, economies consider that if they make changes in the intensity of using capital in defensive goods, they will have a response in the counterpart.

Historically, the case for the MPE can be observed in the fall of the Soviet Union associated to the end of a long arms race against USA where mainly the USSR was trying to catch up with USA (Michael Ward, 1984). This is an example where an excess in military spending affects the total productivity of the economy. The case for the open-loop equilibrium can be associated with most countries that have a defense sector as a part of their defense strategy and their industrial complex.

In terms of policy implications, the result expresses that producing weapons with the same common stock of capital of the rest of the economy can induce a higher level of general economic activity up to certain threshold. This would be a positive channel of connecting military expenditure with economic growth. Increasing arms production from that point on, the effect in the rate of growth will be negative. The statement goes that policies that conjoint both sectors (military and non-military) will induce higher growth but the military sector imposes a limit to growth if not restricted. As modeled in this contribution, arms build-up could enhance economic activity but arms races could be counterproductive to economic growth.

5. Discussions on Strategic Growth

Strategic growth models deal with interacting macroeconomics. This is something novel in many aspects. First, it allows tackling interdependence in a more direct, tractable way compared to more aggregate models (traditional open economy's economic growth model). Second, this strategic interdependence allows for modeling diverse situations historically (and currently) observed when international politics combine or collide with economic goals. Many times in history economic objectives have been deviated or halted because other objectives (usually political ones) are affected. This other objectives, exogenous to the economic agenda, can be treated as externalities one country imposes to other/s.

Technically, the model represents two economies that strategically interact in the process of growth. This interaction, when taken into account dynamically, enhances the growth rate of both economies compared to the open-loop equilibrium. By applying Markovian strategies, strategically connected economies recognize the role of increasing capital stock in favoring increasing rates of growth. This equilibrium presupposes that agents are fully rational in terms of economic behavior. It seems that not only by internalizing but for dynamically reviewing the optimality of the investment decision at each time step requires a higher rate of economic growth. The open-loop equilibrium, on the other hand, implies agents that are not focused in pursuing only economic goals in the exchange.

According to this setting, if both countries look for greater rates of growth they should enhance trade between them in a way intermediate input provision never affect the production process. Again, a simple model like this strongly suggests that trade coordination policies should be essential part of the international exchange.

Inputs and domestic capital produce the exportable intermediate good under decreasing scale returns. While this is consistent with the structure of the model, empirical evidence shows that international intermediate goods usually embody increasing scale returns associated with technological improvements (Ciccone (2002)). This is an issue that deserves further improvements.

In the model that represents a defensive capital, the chapter presents a formal framework for a variant of the arms-race vs. arms-build-up dilemma. Arms race is a better choice for obtaining higher growth rates, associated with optimality in resource utilization, only if its opportunity cost, in terms of consumption sacrifice, is low. On the other hand, arms build-up is associated with constant and nonnegative rate of growth.

This way, interactions are at the core of the strategic growth models. We live in an interconnected world, as never before seeing in History. It is a valid conjecture to postulate that this approach will play an increasing role in explaining problems in an interconnected global macroeconomics.

APPENDIX

Following demonstrations are adapted from Dockner and Nishimura (2004) and refers only to the case of the arms race.

Proof of Proposition 1

The dynamical system (6) has two negative steady states given by

$$\hat{h}^i = (\alpha_i + \vartheta_i)\rho\varpi,$$
$$\hat{h}^i = 1$$

$\hat{h}^i = 1$ implies zero consumption so it is not an interesting equilibrium. Even more, it is easy to show that $\hat{h}^i = (\alpha_i + \vartheta_i)\rho\varpi$, is unstable. Now, we employ the transversality condition to derive an equilibrium.

$$\lim_{t\to\infty} \rho^{t+1} \frac{\partial \ln\left(\varpi\left(\xi_i \left(k_t^i\right)^{\alpha_i+\vartheta_i} \left(z_t^j\right)^{\nu_j} - k_{t+1}^i\right)\right)}{\partial k_{t+1}^i} k_{t+1}^i = 0$$

Where we follow that

$$\rho^{t+1} \frac{\partial \ln\left(\varpi\left(\xi_i \left(k_t^i\right)^{\alpha_i+\vartheta_i} \left(z_t^j\right)^{\nu_j} - k_{t+1}^i\right)\right)}{\partial k_{t+1}^i} k_{t+1}^i = \frac{-\rho^{t+1} k_{t+1}^i}{\xi_i \left(k_t^i\right)^{\alpha_i+\vartheta_i} \left(z_t^j\right)^{\nu_j} - k_{t+1}^i}$$

and the transversality condition becomes

$$\lim_{t\to\infty}\rho^{t+1}\frac{h_{t+1}^{i}}{\xi_i - h_{t+1}^{i}} = 0,$$

and it is satisfied if h_{t+1}^{i} is bounded away from ξ_i. However, since $\hat{h}^i$ is unstable, the path which does not start from $\hat{h}^i$ converges to zero or to ξ_i. Since this last result makes consumption goes to zero, we look forward for the path converging to zero. From (6) any path $\{h_t^i\}$ converging to ξ_i is monotone and satisfies

$$\frac{h_{t+1}^{i}}{\xi_i - h_{t+1}^{i}} = \frac{h_{t+1}^{i}}{\xi_i}\left(\frac{h_t^i}{\xi_i\rho\alpha_i - h_t^i}\right)$$

Iterating we obtain

$$\rho^{t+1}\frac{h_{t+1}^{i}}{\xi_i - h_{t+1}^{i}} = \frac{h_{t+1}^{i}h_t^i\cdots h_1^i}{\left((\alpha_i+\vartheta_i)\xi_i\right)^{t+1}}\left(\frac{h_0^i}{\xi_i - h_0^i}\right)$$

As $h_{t+1}^{i}\to\xi_i$ the right hand side goes to infinity. Therefore, a path violates the transversality condition. The other possible solution, the steady state $\hat{h}^i = (\alpha_i+\vartheta_i)\rho\xi_i$ does not violate the transversality condition and hence it corresponds to an equilibrium path. This steady state results in the following optimum dynamics

$$k_{t+1}^{i} = (\alpha_i+\vartheta_i)\rho\xi_i\left(k_t^i\right)^{\alpha_i+\vartheta_i}\left(z_t^j\right)^{\nu_j}$$

which implies, by (2), a consumption function equal to

$$c^i\left(k_t^i, z_t^j\right) = \xi_i\left(k_t^i\right)^{\alpha_i+\vartheta_i}\left(z_t^j\right)^{\nu_j} - (\alpha_i+\vartheta_i)\rho\xi_i\left(k_t^i\right)^{\alpha_i+\vartheta_i}\left(z_t^j\right)^{\nu_j}$$

$$c^i\left(k_t^i, z_t^j\right) = \left(1-(\alpha_i+\vartheta_i)\rho\right)\xi_i\left(k_t^i\right)^{\alpha_i+\vartheta_i}\left(z_t^j\right)^{\nu_j}$$

Proof of Proposition 2

I begin for defining the Jacobian of the dynamical system for analyzing the characteristic equation. This would be the first step for dealing with the existence of a steady state in this system.

$$\begin{bmatrix} \alpha_i + \vartheta_i & \nu_i \pi_i (\alpha_i + \vartheta_i) \rho^{\frac{1-\alpha_i-\vartheta_i-\nu_i}{\Phi}} \pi_j (\alpha_j + \vartheta_j) \rho^{\frac{\alpha_i+\vartheta_i+\nu_i-1}{\Phi}} \\ \nu_j \pi_i (\alpha_i + \vartheta_i) \rho^{\frac{\alpha_i+\vartheta_i+\nu_i}{\Phi}} \pi_j (\alpha_j + \vartheta_j) \rho^{\frac{1-\alpha_i-\vartheta_i-\nu_i}{\Phi}} & \alpha_j + \vartheta_j \end{bmatrix}$$

where $\Phi = (1-\alpha_i-\vartheta_i)(1-\alpha_j-\vartheta_j) - \nu_i \nu_j$.

By getting the characteristic equation of this system we obtain

$$f(\lambda) = \lambda^2 - (\alpha_i + \vartheta_i + \alpha_j + \vartheta_j)\lambda + ((\alpha_i + \vartheta_i)(\alpha_j + \vartheta_j)) - \nu_i \nu_j$$

Roots are real and we have that

$$f(1) = (1-\alpha_i-\vartheta_i)(1-\alpha_j-\vartheta_j) - \nu_i \nu_j > \nu_i \nu_j - \nu_i \nu_j = 0$$

and

$$f(-1) = (1-\alpha_i-\vartheta_i)(1-\alpha_j-\vartheta_j) - \nu_i \nu_j > 0$$

The function is strictly convex since $f'' = 2 > 0$ and its minimum is at $(\alpha_i + \vartheta_i + \alpha_j + \vartheta_j)/2 < 1$ existing two roots, $\lambda_i, i = 1,2$, such that $|\lambda_i| < 1$. Both roots are positive if $(\alpha_i + \vartheta_i)(\alpha_j + \vartheta_j) > \nu_i \nu_j$; one is positive and the other is negative if $(\alpha_i + \vartheta_i)(\alpha_j + \vartheta_j) < \nu_i \nu_j$.

Proof of Proposition 3

Assume that the technologies exhibit constant returns to scale, that is, $\alpha_i + \vartheta_i + \nu_j = 1$ and that ξ_i and ξ_j is chosen in a way that $(\alpha_i + \vartheta_i)\rho\varpi_i\xi_i > 1$ and $(\alpha_j + \vartheta_j)\rho\varpi_j\xi_j > 1$ is verified.

We get the following result:

The rate of growth for the economy in the open-loop case is giving by

$$\upsilon = [\eta_i]^{\frac{\nu_j}{\nu_i+\nu_j}} [\eta_j]^{\frac{\nu_i}{\nu_i+\nu_j}}$$

where $\eta_i = (\alpha_i + \vartheta_i)\rho\varpi_i\xi_i$ and $\eta_j = (\alpha_j + \vartheta_j)\rho\varpi_j\xi_j$.

Proof

Assuming that

$$k_t^i = \upsilon^t k_0^i \text{ and } k_t^j = \upsilon^t k_0^j \tag{33}$$

is verified. Then we get that $k_t^j / k_t^i = k_t^i / k_t^j$. Substituting (33) in (8) we get that

$$\upsilon^{t+1} k_0^i = ((\alpha_i + \vartheta_i)\rho\varpi_i\pi_i)\upsilon^{t\nu_i}\upsilon^{t(\alpha_i+\vartheta_i)}(k_0^i)^{\alpha_i+\vartheta_i}(k_0^j)^{\varphi_i}$$

$$\upsilon^{t+1} k_0^i = ((\alpha_i + \vartheta_i)\rho\varpi_i\pi_i)(k_0^i)^{\alpha_i+\vartheta_i-1}(k_0^j)^{\nu_i}$$

$$\upsilon = ((\alpha_i + \vartheta_i)\rho\varpi_i\pi_i)\left(\frac{k_0^j}{k_0^i}\right)^{\nu_i}$$

An identical argument states that

$$\upsilon = ((\alpha_j + \vartheta_j)\rho\varpi_j\pi_j)\left(\frac{k_0^i}{k_0^j}\right)^{\nu_j}$$

By joining both results we obtain

$$\upsilon=\left[\pi_i\left(\left(\alpha_i+\vartheta_i\right)\rho\varpi_i\pi_i\right)\right]^{\frac{v_j}{v_i+v_j}}\left[\pi_j\left(\left(\alpha_j+\vartheta_j\right)\rho\varpi_i\pi_j\right)\right]^{\frac{v_i}{v_i+v_j}}$$

Proof of Proposition 4

Employing Markovian decision rules means that representative agents choose strategies of the type $c_t^i=c^i\left(k_t^i,z_t^j\right)$ when designing their actions. In order to derive a Markovian Perfect Equilibrium I therefore make use of dynamic programming techniques. Let me define the value function for agent i as

$$V^i\left(k_t^i,z_t^j\right)\equiv\max\sum_{s=t}^{\infty}\rho^s\ln c_s^i \tag{34}$$

These value functions must satisfy the Bellman equations

$$V^i\left(k_t^i,z_t^j\right)\equiv\max_{c^i}\left\{\ln c^i+\rho V^i\left(\pi_i\left(k_t^i\right)^{\alpha_i+\vartheta_i}\left(z_t^j\right)^{v_j}-c^i,\pi_j\left(k_t^j\right)^{\alpha_j+\vartheta_j}\left(z_t^i\right)^{v_i}-c^j\right)\right\} \tag{35}$$

By following Dockner and Nishimura (2004) and Ronald Fischer and Leonard Mirman (1996), I guess a candidate solution for the value function of the type:

$$V^i\left(k_t^i,z_t^j\right)\equiv A_{ii}\ln\left(\pi_i\left(k_t^i\right)^{\alpha_i+\vartheta_i}\left(z_t^j\right)^{v_j}\right)+B_{ij}\ln\left(\pi_j\left(k_t^j\right)^{\alpha_j+\vartheta_j}\left(z_t^i\right)^{v_i}\right)+D_i \tag{36}$$

where A_{ii},B_{ij}, and D_i are appropriately chosen constants. Based on these value functions I can guess a policy function for the consumption strategy of agent i by

$$c^i\left(k_t^i,z_t^j\right)=a_i\left(k_t^i\right)^{\alpha_i+\vartheta_i}\left(z_t^j\right)^{v_j} \tag{37}$$

where a_i, in the same way, needs to be determined from the equilibrium conditions. Taking under consideration these specifications of the policy functions the corresponding dynamical system of the capital stock becomes

$$k_{t+1}^i = (\pi_i - a_i)(k_t^i)^{\alpha_i+\vartheta_i}(z_t^j)^{v_j} \tag{38}$$

If we now substitute the policy functions (20) and the proposed value functions (19) into the Bellman equation (18) we get

$$\begin{aligned} &A_{ii}\ln\left((k_t^i)^{\alpha_i+\vartheta_i}(z_t^j)^{v_j}\right)+B_{ij}\ln\left((k_t^j)^{\alpha_j+\vartheta_j}(z_t^i)^{v_i}\right)+D_i=\ln\left(a_i(k_t^i)^{\alpha_i+\vartheta_i}(z_t^j)^{v_j}\right)+\\ &+\rho\left[A_{ii}\ln\left(\pi_i(k_t^i)^{\alpha_i+\vartheta_i}(z_t^j)^{v_j}-a_i(k_t^i)^{\alpha_i+\vartheta_i}(z_t^j)^{v_j}\right)\right]\\ &+\rho\left[B_{ij}\ln\left(\pi_j(k_t^j)^{\alpha_i+\vartheta_i}(z_t^i)^{v_i}-a_i(k_t^j)^{\alpha_j+\vartheta_j}(z_t^i)^{v_i}\right)+D_i\right]\end{aligned}$$

where we see that if the constants A_{ii} and B_{ij} satisfy the equations

$$A_{ii} = 1+\rho\left[(\alpha_i+\vartheta_i)A_{ii}+\varphi_j B_{ij}\right] \tag{39}$$

$$B_{ij} = \rho\left[\varphi_i A_{ii}+(\alpha_j+\vartheta_j)B_{ij}\right] \tag{40}$$

Then (19) and (20) solve (18). A solution to system (22) and (23) is easily found and given by

$$A_{ii} = \frac{1-(\alpha_i+\vartheta_i)\rho}{(1-(\alpha_i+\vartheta_i)\rho)(1-\rho)-\rho^2 v_j v_i}, \text{ for } i \neq j \tag{41}$$

$$B_{ij} = \frac{v_j\rho}{(1-(\alpha_i+\vartheta_i)\rho)(1-\rho)-\rho^2 v_i v_j}, \text{ for } i \neq j \tag{42}$$

Proving that the policy function (21) is in fact an equilibrium I need to show that the maximum of the right hand side of (19) given the specification (20)

The maximization gives:

$$\frac{1}{c^i} = \frac{\rho\left(\left(\alpha_i + \vartheta_i\right) A_{ii} + \nu_i B_{ij}\right)}{\pi_i \left(k_t^j\right)^{\alpha_j + \vartheta_j} \left(z_t^i\right)^{\nu_i} - c^i}$$

Solving for the optimal policy rule shows that the functional form given by (20) is attended, by using A_{ii} and B_{ij} as obtained earlier, i.e.,

$$c^i\left(k^i, z_t^j\right) = \frac{\pi_i \left(k_t^j\right)^{\alpha_j + \vartheta_j} \left(z_t^i\right)^{\nu_i}}{1 + \rho\left(\left(\alpha_i + \vartheta_i\right) A_{ii} + \nu_i B_j\right)} = a_i \left(k_t^j\right)^{\alpha_j + \vartheta_j} \left(z_t^i\right)^{\nu_i}$$

where $a_i = \pi_i / 1 + \rho\left(\left(\alpha_i + \vartheta_i\right) A_{ii} + \nu_i B_j\right)$. Hence, the equilibrium dynamics becomes

$$k_{t+1}^i = \psi_i \left(k_t^i\right)^{\alpha_i + \vartheta_i} \left(z_t^j\right)^{\nu_j}, \text{ for } i \neq j \tag{43}$$

$$k_{t+1}^j = \psi_j \left(k_t^j\right)^{\alpha_j + \vartheta_j} \left(z_t^i\right)^{\nu_i}, \text{ for } i \neq j \tag{44}$$

where

$$\psi_i = \pi_i \left(\left(\alpha_i + \vartheta_i\right) \rho \varpi_i + \rho^2 \frac{\nu_i \nu_j}{1 - \left(\alpha_i + \vartheta_i\right) \rho \varpi_i} \right) \text{ and}$$

$$\psi_j = \pi_j \left(\left(\alpha_j + \vartheta_j\right) \rho \varpi_i + \rho^2 \frac{\nu_i \nu_j}{1 - \left(\alpha_j + \vartheta_j\right) \rho \varpi_i} \right)$$

In case of constant returns to scale, the balanced growth path with the growth factor given by

$$\tau = \psi_i^{\frac{\nu_i}{\nu_i + \nu_j}} \psi_j^{\frac{\nu_j}{\nu_i + \nu_j}}$$

Propositions 5 to 8 can be derived analogously as Propositions 1 to 4.

REFERENCES

Axelrod, R. (1984), *The Evolution of Cooperation.* New York: Basic Books.

Azariadis C. (2004). The theory of poverty traps: What have we learned? In D.S. Bowles S. and K. Hoff, editors, *Poverty Traps,* chapter 1. Princeton NJ: Princeton University Press, City, State of Publication.

Azariadis C. and J. Stachurski (2006). *Poverty traps.* In P. Aghion and S. Durlauf, editors, *Handbook of Economic Growth,* chapter 5. Amsterdam: North-Holland, City, State of Publication.

Beals R. and Koopmans T. (1969). Maximizing stationary utility in a constant technology. *SIAM Journal of Applied Mathematics,* 17:1009–1015.

Benoit, E. (1973), *Defense and Economic Growth in Developing Countries.* Lexington (Massachussets): Lexington Books.

Bester, H. and K.A. Konrad (2005), "Easy Targets and the Timing of Conflict." *Journal of Theoretical Politics* 17 (2): 199-215.

Bethmann, D. (2002), *"Notes on an Endogenous Growth Model with two Capital Stocks I. The Deterministic Case".* Humboldt University Working Paper 65.

Blanchard O. and Fischer S. (1989). Lectures on Macroeconomics. Cambridge MA: MIT Press.

Border K. (1985). Fixed Point Theorems with Applications to Economics and Game Theory. Cambridge, UK: Cambridge University Press.

Brito, D.L. (1972), "A Dynamic Model of an Armaments Race." International Economic Review 13: 359-375.

Brito, D.L., and M. Intriligator (1995), "Arms races and proliferation", in K. Hartley, and T. Sandler, (Eds.), Handbook of Defense Economics, Elsevier, Volume 1; 109-164.

Buzan, B. and E. Herring (1998), The Arms Dynamic in World Politics. Boulder, CO: Lynne Rienner Publishers.

Chen Y., J. Ishikawa, and Z. Yu, (2004) "Trade liberalization and strategic outsourcing", *Journal of International Economics* 63: 419-436.

Ciccone A. (2002), "Input chains and industrialization", *Review of Economic Studies*, 69: 565–587.

Deger, S. and S. Sen (1995). "Military Expenditure and Developing Countries" In K. Hartley and T. Sandler (Eds) *Handbook of Defense Economics, Elsevier* Vol 1: 275-307.

Dockner E. and K. Nishimura (2004) "Strategic growth." *Journal of Difference Equations and Applications*, 10:515–527.

Dockner E., S. Jorgersen, N. Long, and G. Sorger (2000), *Differential games in economics and management science*, Cambridge MA: Cambridge University Press.

Dunne, J., D. Willenbockel and R. Smith (2005), "Models of Military Expenditure and Growth: A Critical Review." Defence and Peace Economics 16 (6): 449-461.

Easterly W. (2001). The Elusive Quest for Growth: Economists Adventures and Misadventures in the Tropics. Cambridge MA: MIT Press.

Evanson, R., (1985), "Soviet Political Uses of Trade with Latin America", *Journal of Interamerican Studies and World Affairs*, 27: 99—126.

Fischer, R. and L. Mirman (1996), "The complete fish war: biological and dynamic interactions". *Journal of Environmental Economics and Management* 30: 34-42.

Fisher I. (1930). *The Theory of Interest.* New York: Macmillan.

Gillespie, J.V., D.A. Zinnes, G.S. Tahim, P.A. Schrodt and R.M. Rubison (1977), "An Optimal Control Model of Arms Races." *American Political Science Review* 71: 226-244.

Glaser, Charles L. (2000), "The Causes and Consequences of Arms Races," in N.W. Polsby (ed.) *Annual Review of Political Science* 3: 251–276.

Harris C. (1985). Existence and characterization of perfect equilibrium in games of perfect information. *Econometrica,* 53:613–628.

Hellwig M. and Leininger W. (1987). On the existence of subgame-perfect equilibrium in infinite-action games of perfect information. *Journal of Economic Theory,* 43:55–75.

Hoff K. (2000). Beyond Rosenstein-Rodan: The modern theory of coordination problems in development. In *Proceedings of the Annual World Bank Conference on Development Economics.* The World Bank, Washington DC.

Ihori, T. (2004). "Arms race and economic growth". *Defence and Peace Economics* 15 (1): 27-38.

Intriligator, M.D. and D. Brito (2000). "Arms Races". *Defence and Peace Economics* 11 (1): 45-54.

Iwai K. (1972). "Optimal economic growth and stationary ordinal utility". *Journal of Economic Theory* 5:121–151.

John, A. A., R.A. Pecchenino, and S.L. Schreft (1993), "The Macroeconomics of Dr. Strangelove." *American Economic Review* 83 (1): 43-62.

Jones R. (2000), *Globalization and the Theory of Input Trade*, Cambridge MA: MIT Press.

Kollias, C., G. Manolas, and S-M. Paleologou (2004), "Defence expenditure and economic growth in the European Union: a causality analysis." *Journal of Policy Modeling* 26: 553-569.

Laibson D. (1997). Golden eggs and hyperbolic discounting. *Quarterly Journal of Economics,* 112:443–477.

Larrosa, J.M.C. (2012) "Strategic Equilibria in a Model of Economic Growth with Input Interdependence". *Bulletin of Economic Research* 64 (4): 537-548.

Lichbach, M.I. (1990), "When Is and Arms Rivalry a Prisoner's Dilemma?" *Journal of Conflict Resolution* 34 (1): 29-56.

Mantel R. (1967) *"Maximization of utility over time with a variable rate of time preference".* CF 70525, Cowles Foundation for Research in Economics.

Mantel R. (1993) "Grandma's dress, or what's new for optimal growth". *Revista de Análisis Económico,* 8: 61–81.

Mantel, R. (1995) "Why the rich get richer and the poor get poorer". *Estudios de Economía, 22:177–205, 1995.*

Mantel, R. (1997) "Optimal economic growth with recursive preferences: Decreasing rate of time preference". *Económica (La Plata),* 45:331–348.

McDonald, B.D. and R.J. Eger (2010), "The Defense-Growth Relationship: An Economic Investigation into Post-Soviet States". *Peace Economics, Peace Science and Public Policy* 16 (1).

Mintz, A. and R. Stevenson (1995), "Defense Expenditures, Economic Growth and the 'Peace Dividend': A Longitudinal Analysis of 103 Countries." *Journal of Conflict Resolution* 39 (2): 283-305.

Peng S.K., J. Thisse, and P. Wang (2006) "Economic integration and agglomeration in a middle product economy", *Journal of Economic Theory*, 131: 1—25.

Pelzman, J., (1978) "Soviet-COMECON trade: The question of intra-industry specialization", *WeltWirschaftliches Archiv* 114: 297—304.

Ploeg, F. van der and A.J. de Zeeuw (1990), "Perfect Equilibrium in a Model of Competitive Arms Accumulation." *International Economic Review* 31: 131-146.

Richardson, L.F. (1960). *Arms and Insecurity: A Mathematical Study of the Causes and Origins of War*. Chicago: The Boxwood Press.

Sanyal K. and R. Jones (1982), "The theory of trade in middle products", *American Economic Review*, 72: 16—31.

Shieh, J., C. Lai and W. Chang (2002), "The impact of military burden on long-run growth and welfare." *Journal of Development Economics* 68: 443-454.

Simaan, M. and J.B. Cruz (1975), "Formulation of Richardson's Model of Arms Race from a Differential Game Viewpoint." *Review of Economic Studies* 42 (1): 67-77.

Tohmé F. and Dabús C. (2000). Optimal economic growth with decreasing rate of time preference in a two-agent economy. In Proceedings of the XXVIIIth Meeting of the Brazilian Econometric Society. Brazilian Econometric Society, Sao Paulo,.

Tohmé, F.A. and J.M.C. Larrosa (2007). "Strategic Economic Growth with Decreasing Rates of Time Preference in a Two-Agent Economy". *Mecánica Computacional* 26: 513-522.

Tsokhas, K. (1980), 'The political economy of Cuban dependence on the Soviet Union', *Theory and Society*, 9: 319–362.

Uzawa H. (1968) "Time preference, the consumption function and optimum assets holdings". In J. Wolfe, editor, Value, Capital, and Growth : Papers in Honour of Sir John Hicks. Aldine, Chicago.

Ventura J., (1997) "Growth and interdependence", *Quarterly Journal of Economics*, 112: 57–84.

Ward, M.D. (1984), "Differential Paths to Parity: A Study of the Contemporary Arms Race". *The American Political Science Review* 78 (2): 297-317.

Williams, J.T. and M.D. McGinnis (1988), "Sophisticated reaction in the U.S.-Soviet arms race: Evidence of rational expectations." *American Journal of Political Science* 32: 968-995.

Zeeuw, de A.J. and F. van der Ploeg (1991), "Difference Games and Policy Evaluation: A Conceptual Framework." *Oxford Economic Papers* 43: 612-636.

In: Economic Growth in the 21st Century
Editor: Tara Abrahams
ISBN: 978-1-63321-623-5

Chapter 6

ECONOMIC GROWTH, INTEGRATION AND RESEARCH-DEVELOPMENT IN THE EUROPEAN UNION: AN EMPIRICAL ESSAY IN PANEL DATA

***Bassem Kahouli*[1,*] *and Mounir Smida*[2,†]**
[1]Faculty of Economics and Management,
University of Sousse, Sousse, Tunisia
[2]Faculty of Economics and Management,
University of Sousse, Sousse, Tunisia

ABSTRACT

In recent decades, there has been an unprecedented number of regional agreements constitute one of the crucial characteristics of international economic relations. Many developing countries and / or developed countries have begun to explore and participate in RIAs. The necessitated of regional integration has been emphasized by a combination of external and internal factors, such as the acceleration of the globalization process. In this study it is assumed that economic integration is very important, especially in strengthening and accelerating

* Email: kahoulibassem@yahoo.fr.
† Email: Mounir.Smida2003@yahoo.fr.

economic growth and promotes Research and Development (R&D). This work is based on two samples, the EU10 and the EU15 for the period (1981-2007) and (1995-2007) respectively.

Keywords: Integration, Growth, R&D, Panel

JEL Classification: F13, F15, F43, C23

1. INTRODUCTION

In recent decades, there have been an unprecedented number of regional agreements which constitutes a main characteristic of the international economic relations. Many developing countries and / or developed countries have begun to explore and participate in RTAs. The necessitated of the regional integration was highlighted by a combination of external and internal factors, such as the acceleration of the globalization process. Thus, the risk of marginalization in a multipolar world dominated by commercial blocks makes economic integration a necessity. The challenge is to take the necessary mechanisms to ensure the success of this process. Generally, more countries are integrated, the more he wills synergy of economic development. Economic integration is generally defined as the elimination of discrimination and the removal of trade barriers between groups of countries and enables integrated countries to achieve a number of economic objectives. Several trade agreements have been established in most parts of the world: Europe (EU and its successive enlargements) , North America (NAFTA), Latin America (MERCOSUR), Asia Pacific (APEC, ASEAN, CER), Caribbean (CARICOM), Africa (UEMOA, SADC, AMU), among others.

Although most regional integration agreements are in the geographical sense, some of them involve very geographically distant countries; see located on different continents (e.g., EU-ACP, EUROMED). Indeed, the developing countries seeking to join the major developed countries to provide access to their markets. Among the experiences of integration, the EU is the model most successful economic integration. Economic integration aims to accelerate the development of partner countries through several factors: the expanding the size of the domestic market and the achievement of economies of scale, the allocation of resources, the development of trade between member countries, the FDI, the technology transfer and the increased competition (Silaghi, 2009; Singh, 2010). It seems that economic integration is beneficial because it allows you to enjoy the technology transfer to confront competition, improve productivity and the reallocation of resources, etc. The successful integration must be interpreted by an amplification of the economic growth, development of the industrial base, increased intra-regional trade and lower development gaps (Pradhan, 2011; Dreger and Herzer, 2013). At this level, regional integration is a mechanism that contributes to higher rates of growth, economic stability and focus on improving the living conditions of citizens. It is evident that the effects of economic integration on growth are unevenly distributed among member countries.

This work focuses on the economic aspects of regional integration, and their importance for the various parties. In this study it is assumed that economic integration is very important for different countries, especially in strengthening and accelerating economic growth and development of members. We examine how this process can help to accelerate economic growth in member countries. Theoretical studies have not been able to decide whether or not trade liberalization contributes to economic growth, however, various empirical studies have led to similar results as the effect of the opening is generally favorable to growth. We try in this paper to present an empirical study on the relationship - growth economic integration. Our work is based on two samples, the EU-10 and EU-15, respectively, for the period (1981-2007) and (1995-2007). This paper is composed of four parts. Following the introduction, in the second part we try to summarize the theoretical and empirical studies that have investigated the effects of economic integration on growth. The third part seeks to determine the empirical methodology. The fourth part presents the estimates of our model and the interpretation of results. It concludes with implications and recommendations in the conclusion (part 5).

2. Openness and Economic Growth: Theoretical and Empirical Literature

2.1. Theoretical Literature

The international trade theory teaches that the opening has positive effects likely to support growth. The expansion of the market to achieve economies of scale improves the efficiency of producers. The effects of economic integration can be called from two perspectives, namely static effects and dynamic effects (Carbaugh, 2004). Static effects of economic integration are related to production efficiency and well- being of consumers. One can observe the static effects on well-being, when the tariff barriers of the member countries in trade bloc are decreased. The effects creation and trade diversion are often referred to as welfare effects (Viner, 1950). The overall effects of economic integration on the well-being of its members will depend on the sum of these two opposite effects (Zu and Corpus, 2000). To determine the net effect of integration on well-being, we must compare the effects of creation and diversion trade. There are several factors used to determine the relative size of these two effects of welfare. An important factor is the difference between the cost of production in the country, other members and the outside world. The formation of a customs union also creates an effect of production, which will result in a more efficient use of resources. Where imports of a country with low costs are replaced by imports from a country of the customs union with high costs, this suggests that production is reorganized less efficiently. In this case, the production has been diverted from a low-cost producer to a producer with a high cost in another country. Lipsey (1957) argues that the analysis of Viner is incomplete, since it only considered the effects of the customs union on production. According to Lipsey, it must be taken into account the impact of integration on consumption.

The dynamic effects influence the growth rate of members at long-term. Carbaugh (2004) argues that the dynamic gains from economic integration are primarily the creation of a larger market by the movement of trade liberalization under the customs union. The principle of economic integration is to combine the market, which reduces the power of monopoly. In addition, companies from different member countries are being in intense competition with each other. So the benefits of dynamic gains from a customs union can further offset any adverse effects static. In general, economies of scale imply an increase in production due to lower average costs. The gains from economies of scale can improve the productivity of the economy, competitiveness and consequently leads to the triggering mechanisms multipliers for economic growth. While the exploitation of economies of scale can be the center of the cumulative process enhancing competitiveness and dynamism of the economy. At this level, Venables (2000) considers that the mechanisms of economic integration are beneficial, especially for smaller countries because they generate economies of scale. Indeed, in smaller markets, the number and size of businesses or development projects are reduced, eliminating the competition between companies and therefore obtain economies of scale.

In the same context, Maillet and Rollet (1988) distinguish two main and complementary reasons that allow economic integration to enjoy a better exploitation of economies of scale. First, expanding the market directly and positively affects the most efficient producers and motivates them to develop their production to improve their competitiveness. Second, integration reveals phenomena of specialization include replacing the less efficient producers to more efficient producers which leads to lower costs of these. Competition is an important feature of modern economies to ensure the vitality of enterprises and accelerate the innovation phenomenon. The technological transformations of all kinds promote the economic growth. Maillet and Rollet (1988) put forward two additional arguments justifying the experience of integration and implementation of the single market. First, we need to reconcile both the requirement to exploit economies of scale (which limits the number of producers) and the requirement of competition. Then, open borders, trade liberalization and increased FDI flows by adopting the integration process to enable local businesses to compete. Increasing FDI flows, leading to competitive which ensures the domestic producers adopting strategies for increasing productivity and efficiency by streamlining capabilities of firms (Andraz and Rodrigues, 2010; Forte and Moura, 2013). Also, it will encourage the acceleration of the phenomenon of innovation that is to say; technological transformation herself will have an effect on economic growth by improving productivity in member countries. Integration is a way to increase the competitiveness of companies in the global market and therefore their ability to be successful. In addition, foreign firms who move will be more competitive (Li and Liu, 2005). Therefore, local firms face competition will become increasingly acute.

The success of economic integration will not happen by chance, but it will be as a result of sustained efforts and enthusiasm to improve the conditions and economic relations of these areas. It is clear that trade liberalization is likely to benefit various integrated countries. However, these countries should be cautious against some challenges if he wants to get to persuade them to participate actively in the RTA. In addition to their concerns about the disturbances that may affect farmers and workers, these countries fear the consequences that trade liberalization will have on the balance of payments, fiscal accounts and the terms of trade. Concerns mainly the following points: First, the collateral effects of trade liberalization on the economies result of the misallocation of resources (Schiff and Winters, 2003). Second, the possible drop in export receipts if the erosion of preferences makes them in competition with the products exported by the lowest-cost producers (Baunsgaard and

Keen, 2010). Third, the loss of public revenues as a result of elimination of tariffs on imports (Alexandraki and Lankes, 2004). Finally, the rise in world prices of imported food if agricultural subsidies are removed (Tokarick, 2003).

2.2. Review of the Empirical Literature

The purpose of this part is to summarize some empirical studies that investigated the effects of economic integration on growth. At this level, it is divided into two periods. Over the 70 years, empirical work explaining the relationship between openness and growth typically uses the cross-sectional regressions on a set of countries. This is mainly due to the unavailability of data over a long period and the lack of econometric techniques (estimation technique software). These studies have focused mainly on static gains from opening. These studies focus on the relationship between exports and economic growth and the relationship between growth and openness and trade policy some indicators. The majority of these studies have confirmed the existence of a positive correlation between openness and growth. The second period is characterized by the appearance of the new trade theory and the theory of endogenous growth. Both theories have allowed the researchers to focus on richer ways in terms of analysis. Generally, the impact of openness on growth takes place in three ways, namely: the formation of physical capital (import goods), human capital and knowledge (diffusion). In recent years, the relationship between economic growth and the volume of international trade has been the subject of numerous empirical studies.

Siliverstovs and Herzer (2005) presented a study that examines the hypothesis of export-led growth. They used annual data for Chile to explain how manufactured and primary exports affect economic growth via increases in productivity. The estimation results support the hypothesis that growth is driven from the Export and specify the same time the positive and significant impact of manufactured primary and exports on economic growth. In the same way, Rodrik and Rodriguez (2000) have uncertainty suggested a causal relationship between openness and growth. Their studies focus on a sample of 57 countries during the period 1970-1989. They assess the channels linking trade policy and growth empiric model. They stressed that openness to trade is only one aspect of a comprehensive economic organization. The countries that are the choice of aperture are generally those who are better organized internally (political and macroeconomic stability, rule of law, good governance). The results suggest a positive effect of trade openness on growth policy, accelerated accumulation of physical capital accounting for more than half of the impact. To summarize, the estimated model shows a positive total effect of trade openness on growth.

In the same direction, Dollar and Kraay (2004) are based on a sample of 100 countries for the years 1980 and 1990. To study the effects of openness on economic growth, Dollar and Kraay are estimated equations in first differences. To eliminate the fixed effects, the explanatory variables are the lagged changes of the same income in the previous decade and the rate of opening. The authors estimated that a doubling of the share of trade in GDP would result in an additional 25 % of income after 10 years. In addition, Jin (2004) proposed a model based on a function of usual production, introducing technological change, which itself depends on the degree of openness of the country. He used the technique of co-integration for the time series. Jin analyzed the co-movement between the opening and growth in China's 17 provinces and three municipalities. The author wanted to examine whether the correlation between opening and growth was also valid at the provincial level, and if we could detect a difference between the coastal provinces and those enclaves. The results indicate a positive relationship between trade openness and growth rates for four of the seven coastal provinces and a negative relationship for the majority of landlocked provinces (three of them have a negative and significant effect). The interpretation that emerges is that the non-coastal provinces do not have a strong enough economy to face foreign competition. While coastal provinces are directed outwards, and consequently, they are more competitive. The study of Galinberti (2009) is a re-evaluation of the hypothesis of export-led growth. The variables used by Galinberti are GDP per capita, the stock of human capital and the share of exports in GDP. In this context, the author uses a technique introduced by Hansen to estimate the threshold effect. This technique is applied in the cross-country regression studies covering a large sample of 72 countries and two sub-samples during the period 1974-2003. In general, the author considers that a situation of free trade as a result of increased exports will foster growth. From the estimated results, the author concludes that the critical growth variables are statistically significant. Similarly, countries that have reached an advanced level of development are those that have a significant stock of human capital. However, for underdeveloped countries, the growth of skilled labor is a major constraint to growth. In summary, a wide range of very different from other empirical studies in the relationship between opening-growth economic often come to the same basic conclusion, that is to say, to demonstrate a positive impact of openness on growth. At this level, so that the productive forces of the economy can spread without hindrance, it is necessary that the other elements of economic policy are appropriate. However, if the results of this work are able to demonstrate a positive impact of openness on growth, robustness is questionable, for two main reasons. The first is related to the choice of the indicator of openness. The second refers to the econometric methods that do not control rigorously the bias related to unobserved individual heterogeneity of countries.

3. Empirical Methodology

The objective is to estimate the effects of openness, R&D stocks and economic integration of the countries of the EU growth and the impact of EU enlargement on the success of the integration process. To do this, panel data on two samples of European countries are used. The first contains 10 countries, while the second consists of 15 countries. The estimates periods are 1981-2007 and 1995-2007. The choice of the EU is explained by the fact that this area is experiencing the most successful integration. In addition, the data for this area are relatively more available and reliable. To account for the effects of openness and R&D stocks on economic growth, I test for two samples, respectively, the model of the general form following:

$$ln GDP_{it} = \alpha_1 ln\, FDI_{it} + \alpha_2 HK_{it} + \alpha_3 OP_{it} + \alpha_4 \ln GFCF_{it} + \alpha_5 ln\, \mathrm{R\,\&\,}D_{it} + \alpha_6 ln\, \mathrm{POP}_{it} + U_{it} \quad (1)$$

where, GDP is the gross domestic product (in constant dollars), a variable that reflects the level of development of a country which is an indicator of growth. FDI determines the stocks of foreign direct investment (inward) expressed at constant prices (base year 2000). HK is human capital is proxied by secondary school enrollment. OP indicates the intra-European open rates. GFCG is the Gross Fixed Capital Formation (in constant dollars). R&D represents the stocks of Researches and Development (in constant dollars). POP is the labor force. U_{it} is the error term. For each country, the calculations have yielded the following annual growth rates means for investment in R&D for (1981-2007) and (1995-2007), respectively.

Table 1. the average annual growth rate of investment in R & D (1981-2007)

Pays	Taux en %	Pays	Taux en %
UEBL	2,664	Irlande	8,053
France	2,398	UK	1,472
Allemagne	2,202	Danemark	5,638
Italie	2,835	Grèce	7,468
Pays-Bas	2,450		

Table 2. the average annual growth rate of investment in R & D (1995-2007)

Pays	Taux en %	Pays	Taux en %
UEBL	2,754	Danemark	4,664
France	1,206	Grèce	5,902
Allemagne	2,531	Portugal	8,457
Italie	2,680	Espagne	7,065
Pays-Bas	1,492	Autriche	6,215
Irlande	7,252	Finlande	6,976
UK	1,906	Suède	3,640

The stock of domestic R&D is calculated using the perpetual inventory method. This method is often used to convert flows into stocks. Thus, the stock of R&D in year t is equal to its value t-1, adjusted by depreciation rate which is added the internal expenditure on R&D in year t. Internal R&D expenditure (IRDE) at constant prices are calculated by multiplying the IRDE / GDP ratio by GDP at constant 2000 prices in U.S. dollars. Then we use this series to calculate the stock of R&D.

$$R\&D_t = I_t + (1-\delta) R\&D_{t-1} \tag{2}$$

where I_t is the investment in R&D of the year t et δ the rate of depreciation. The depreciation rate is estimated at 5% as in some empirical work. The initial stock of R&D is calculated by taking into account three elements: investment in R&D in the first available year, the depreciation (δ) and the growth rate of investment in R&D: (g). Otherwise, the initial stock of R & D ($R\&D_0$) is equal to the initial investment divided by the sum of the rate of R&D.

$$R\&D_0 = \frac{I_0}{(g+\delta)} \tag{3}$$

The use of panel estimation techniques allow to take into account the temporal and cross-specificity of these samples. The panel estimation with fixed effects introduced various advantages, especially related to the inclusion of time characteristics unobservable and stable. First, this technique creates more variability, more degrees of freedom, more efficient and minimizes the risk of multi-collinearity between the explanatory variables. Second, it can deal with the problem of the potential correlation between some explanatory variables and the error term that does not vary over time. Third, the fixed effects model uses the temporal dimension of data and can take into account the dynamic adjustment. Fourth, it controls the heterogeneity by including invariant characteristics over time and / or space.

Table 3. The results of the estimated model for Europe 10

Dependent variable GDP period 1981-2007: Sample 1: EU-10							
Independent variables	(1)	(2)	(3)	(4)	(5)	(6)	(7)
Constant	14.780 (18.60)	15.951 (18.73)	14.089 (22.61)	16.417 (20.61)	13.729 (20.74)	15.920 (18.37)	13.658 (20.28)
OP	0.406 (6.52) **	0.224 (3.41) **	0.170 (3.48) **	0.238 (3.65) **	0.157 (3.17) **	0.224 (3.41) **	0.158 (3.19) **
GFCF	0.462 (14.06) **	0.317 (8.12) **	0.146 (4.53) **	0.322 (8.25) **	0.142 (4.43) **	0.316 (8.07) **	0.141 (4.37) **
FDI		0.082 (6.20) **	0.045 (4.38) **	0.082 (5.77) **	0.045 (4.33) **	0.083 (5.89) **	0.047 (4.29) **
POP		0.038 (1.47)			0.030 (1.57)	0.040 (1.44)	0.035 (1.68)
R&D Stock			0.308 (13.33) **		0.307 (13.32) **		0.308 (13.31) **
HK	0.001 (2.26) **			0.000 (0.37)		-0.000 (-0.20)	-0.000 (-0.60)
Observations	243	243	243	243	243	243	243
Hausman Test	227.73	210.51	-116.22	400.20	1021.14	221.22	175.53
F test	41.21	38.84	64.49	50.53	47.87	38.64	34.48
R^2	0.73	0.77	0.87	0.77	0.87	0.77	0.87

Notes: Values in parentheses are t-statistics.

** Significant at 5%.

For the Hausman test, the probabilities are reported.

Table 4. The results of the estimated model for Europe 15

Dependent variable GDP period 1995-2007: Sample 2: EU-15					
Independent variables	(1)	(2)	(3)	(4)	(5)
Constant	19.633	14.096	26.403	13.268	19.634
	(23.62)	(25.06)	(198.2)	(22.08)	(23.11)
OP	0.294	0.038	0.397	0.037	0.294
	(5.49) **	(1.09)	(5.99) **	(1.10)	(5.09) **
GFCF	0.271			0.074	0.271
	(8.08) **			(3.31) **	(8.04) **
FDI					
POP					
R&D Stock		0.500		0.459	
		(21.78) **		(17.96) **	
HK			-0.000		-1.06e-06
			(-0.44)		(0.00)
Observations	182	182	182	182	182
Hausman Test	-1.60	5.69	2.28	25.09	-3674.11
F test	1077.55	648.24	1067.51	96.33	54.31
R^2	0.21	0.79	0.21	0.80	0.43

Notes: Values in parentheses are t-statistics.
** Significant at 5%.
For the Hausman test, the probabilities are reported.

4. Estimates Results and Interpretations

The following development presents our econometric results and their statistical and economic interpretations. The results of the estimated model are shown in Tables (3) and (4) for two samples of the EU-10 and EU-15. All estimates are performed with fixed effects.

For the EU-10, the empirical estimates show a positive effect of openness on growth in member countries. All coefficients of the explanatory variables are positive and significant in all columns of Table (3). This implies that economic integration has a positive and significant effect on growth. However, this positive effect is relatively diminished by introducing GFCF, stocks of FDI and R&D in the estimate. The same is also observed for the second sample, most of the coefficients of the explanatory variables are positive and significant, especially in the first, second and third column of Table (4). In this context, several empirical studies have been able to show the positive effect of openness on economic growth. At this level, our results confirm those of other studies that have confirmed the positive effect of openness on growth (Dollar and Kraay, 2004; Andraz and Rodrigues, 2010; Afshari et al., 2013). On GFCF, for both samples, the coefficients of this variable are highly significant and positive. The first and third column of the first table shows a strong significance of GFCF. Generally, the opening and / or economic integration increases and motivate GFCF. The entry of other variables in the regression has no effect on the significance of GFCF. The introduction of FDI and R&D in the regression reduces the coefficient of GFCF while it remains important with other variables.

The economic integration can increase investment in the development of SMEs and the micro-credit. In addition, it generates the widespread simplification of procedures, accelerated privatization of infrastructure, including telecommunications, and improving the business environment, in particular the Labor Code, the Competition Law, the Code Customs and the Law on industrial Property. The positive effect of openness and economic integration on domestic investment occurs through multiple channels. Among these channels, increased competition and efficiency, transmission techniques and quality control contractors and the introduction of a new skill. The MNCs can also push local firms to improve their management or adopt some of the marketing techniques employed by multinationals, either on the local market or internationally. Markusen and Venables (1999) consider that there are possible effects of complementarity between openness and domestic investment although this effect is indirect. The openness and economic integration can increase the number of foreign companies which boosts domestic investment conditions necessary due to spillover effects created (Agosin and Mayer, 2000). Introducing FDI in the regression, we find that the coefficients of FDI and openness are positive and significant for the first sample. This means that both variables affect economic growth. This result supports the idea that integration by openness and abolition of trade barriers as a source of FDI attractiveness. The entry of other variables in the regression has no effect on the significance of FDI. The introduction of these variables slightly reduces the significance of FDI. Several empirical studies have investigated the effects of FDI have affirmed the existence of a positive effect of FDI on growth (Darrat et al., 2005; Agrawal and Khan, 2011).

Generally, openness and economic integration positively affect the workforce by creating jobs after increasing the number of MNCs. It makes sense that openness boosts FDI and it would create jobs. In the long run, openness and economic integration contributes to the improvement of the situation of the labor force in the creation of new employment opportunities, increasing wages and improving the quality of workforce training force. Usually, openness and economic integration have led to increased demand for skilled workers in the labor market. In this case, a skilled workforce is an asset to any country. The European labor market provides the necessary skills that ensure a number of essential to the development of competitive ability of the company functions. In the EU-10, the coefficients of R&D stocks are positive and significant implying that this variable promotes growth. The same is also observed for the second sample. At this level, our results are consistent with other studies that have reported empirically the importance of the R&D growth (Evenson and Sing, 1997; Hudea and Stancu, 2012). Some work, such as Coe et al. (1997), Edwards (1998) suggest that to take advantage of the opening, the country must have a skilled workforce , that is to say, human capital capable of assimilating the foreign technology. On the effects of human capital, estimates show the EU-10 as the coefficient of the latter is positive and significant in the first column. Following the introduction of other variables (FDI, labor force and the stock of R&D) in the regression there is a loss of significance and positive sign of HK. This cannot neglect the role of human capital as an important factor in growth and development. The presence of a skilled workforce can participate and / or to advance economic integration between the different parts (Gould and Ruffin, 1995). For the EU-15, unfortunately, the estimates do not show positive and significant coefficients of human capital. But this cannot neglect the importance of human capital in these European countries.

In conclusion, in this work, we empirically tested the impact of openness and integration on economic growth in the EU. Our work is based on two samples are respectively 10 and 15 countries for the period (1981-2007) and (1995-2007). It was built in our estimates several indicators that can represent more fully the various dimensions of the opening: the degree of opening intra-EU, stocks R&D and FDI. As a result, we presented the econometric methodology adopted to estimate our model. The main results are the following: the coefficients attached to the variables representing the opening are in the most positive and significant for the EU-10 cases and the EU-15. Similarly, there is a positive and significant effect of FDI stocks and R&D on economic growth of the member countries of the two samples. These results confirm the hypothesis that economic integration allows different parties to access to knowledge and foreign knowledge.

CONCLUSION

The economic integration is not simply a matter of potential earnings and balance between benefits and costs. It involves national economic strategies that have ramifications. It cannot be achieved by simply setting up frameworks and signing treaties and it cannot solve all economic problems. It must be backed by political will and commitment of countries to implement the programs agreed, and allows some form of sovereignty to supranational bodies. Thus, it must be seen as part of a broader strategy to accelerate growth and equitable prosperity. However, the benefits of economic integration make it imperative that it remains the central pillar of development. The different countries have understood that it is an essential instrument to create more viable economic market that can facilitate the production capacity in industry and agriculture. This can be done through collective exploitation of human and natural resources. Empirically, the objective of this work was to investigate how and to what extent the openness and economic integration generally affect growth. For this, we used panel data on two samples: EU-10 during the period 1981-2007 and the EU-15 during the period 1995-2007.

In what follows, we present the recommendations to help advance economic integration and strengthen the pace of this process, given the challenges, opportunities and progress. The consistency of trade policies and integration is important to allow member countries to benefit more. Similarly, trade reforms must be accompanied by other economic measures as a good macroeconomic environment, appropriate laws, infrastructure and well-developed institutions, etc. Thus, in terms of economic integration it is important in guiding this process. It should be reviewed, taking into account the levels of development and current realities in different regions. In addition, the diversification of the economy is necessary to minimize the impact of economic shocks, and increase the benefits of trade reforms. The members of an RIA should develop industrial policies that would expand the industrial base in different countries and to improve the capacity to enhance competitiveness. Private investment in industry, agriculture and infrastructure should be encouraged by favorable investment policies. It is important to be consistent with the communities on issues such as the reduction of tariff and non-tariff schedules and the achievement of the most difficult objectives (macroeconomic stabilization and harmonization of economic policies). In consideration of the above recommendation, trade reforms must not only focus on imports. They need to promote exports to have a positive impact on the economy. However, the most important in this regard is to ensure that intra-community and intra-regional trade will be encouraged.

The economic integration of countries is only possible when there is a number of economic and non-economic prerequisites (social or cultural geographical political) conditions. These conditions play an important role in the success of any integration project. First, the success of integration depends on the nature of the input of the country integrated. Generally, economic synchronism and integration agreements or cooperation are easier between countries with additional structures between countries that have competitive structures of specialization. Second, the ability of the area to obtain most significant foreign investment flows, facilitating consequently the process of technological diffusion and catching up. Indeed, the increase in foreign investment flows is considered an important driver of economic cooperation and a means of strengthening the interdependence of the economies of the region. Third, a high level of stock of infrastructure such as railway, highway, and electric power generated and the number of telephone line is always a catalyst for development as a process of economic integration. The inadequate infrastructure or geographic misdistribution prevents rapid movement of people, goods and services. Fourth, the political elements are necessary conditions which play a key role in the success of economic integration. The degree of coordination and communication network between the member countries of the integration plays a very important role for the success of integration agreements especially when it includes countries assigns structures and policies different.

ANNEXES

Annex 1. Samples of countries

Samples	Countries
EU10	BLEU (Belgium and Luxembourg Economic Union), France, Germany, Italy, Netherlands, United Kingdom, Ireland, Denmark and Greece.
EU15	EU10 + Spain, Portugal, Finland, Austria and Sweden.

Annex 2. Names and sources of the of the variables used

	Variable	Definition	Source
Dependent variables	GDP	The Gross Domestic Product (constant dollars).	World Development Indicators (2009)
Explanatory variables	FDI	The stock of foreign direct investment (inward) expressed at constant prices (base year 2000).	Global Development Finance (2009)
	HK	Gross enrollment ratio at the secondary level.	WDI (2004), UNESCO Statistical Yearbooks
	OP	The intra-European Open Rates: (Exports + Imports) / GDP	World Development Indicators (2009)
	GFCF	The Gross Fixed Capital Formation (constant dollars).	World Development Indicators (2009)
	R&D	Stocks of Research and Development.	World Development Indicators (2009)
	POP	Labor force.	World Development Indicators (2009)

REFERENCES

Afshari, Z., Shirinbakhsh, S., Saberi, M. (2013). The impact of globalization. *Advances in Environmental Biology*. 7, 1597-1604.

Agosin M., Mayer, R. (2000). Foreign Direct Investment in Developing Countries: Does it Crowd in Domestic Investment?, UNCTAD Discussion paper (2), N°146.

Agrawal, G., Khan, M. A. (2011). Impact of FDI. *European Journal of Scientific Research*. 57, 257-264.

Alexandraki, K., Lankes, H. P. (2004). Estimating the Impact of Preference Erosion on Middle-Income Countries. IMF Working Paper, International Monetary Fund, Washington, DC.

Andraz, J. M., Rodrigues, P. M. M (2010). What causes economic growth in Portugal: Exports or inward FDI? *Journal of Economic Studies*. 37, 267-287.

Baunsgaard. T., Keen, M. (2010). Tax revenue and (or?) trade liberalization. *Journal of Public Economics*. 94, 563–577.

Carbaugh. R. J (2004). International Economics, 9th edition. Australia. Thomas South-Western.

Coe David T., Helpman E., Hoffmaister A. (1997). North South R&D Spillovers. *The Economic Journal*. 107, 134-149.

Darrat, A., Kherfi, S., Soliman, M. (2005). FDI and Economic Growth in CEE and MENA Countries : A Tale of Two Regions " ERF, 12th Annual Conference 19th – 21st December, 2005, Egypt.

Dollar, D., Kraay, A. (2004). Trade, Growth and Poverty. *The Economic Journal*. 114, 22-49.

Dreger, C., Herzer, D. (2013). A further examination of the export-led growth. *Empirical Economics* 45, 39-60.

Edwards, S. (1998). Openness, Productivity and Growth : What do we Really Know? *Economic Journal*. 18, 383-398.

Evenson, R. E., Singh, L. (1997). Economic Growth, International Technological Spillovers and Public Policy: Theory and Empirical Evidence from Asia. Yale University Economic Growth Center Discussion Papers 777, Yale University: New Haven CT.

Forte, R., Moura, R. (2013). The effects of foreign direct investment on the host country's economic growth: Theory and empirical evidence. *Singapore*. 58, 25-54.

Galimberti, J. K (2009). Conditioned Export-Led Growth Hypothesis: A Panel Threshold Regressions Approach, Federal University of Santa Catarina, Munich Personal RePEc Archive. Paper No. 13417, posted 15.

Gould, D. M., Ruffin, R. J. (1995). Human capital, trade. *Weltwirtschaftliches Archiv*, 131, 425-445.

Hudea, O. S., Stancu, S. S. (2012). Foreign direct investment*Romanian Journal of Economic Forecasting*. 15, 85-102.

Jin, C. J (2004). On the Relationship Between Openness and Growth in China: Evidence from Provincial Time Series Data. *The World Economy*. 27, 1571-1582.

Li, X., Liu, X. (2005). Foreign Direct Investment and economic growth*World Development*. 33, 393-407.

Lipsey, R. G. (1957). The Theory of Custorns Unions: A general Survey. *Economica Journal*. 60, 496-513.

Maillet, P. et Rollet, P. (1988). L'insertion de l'Europe dans la division internationale du travail : appréciations et suggestions. Revue du marché commun, n° 299, pp. 371-386.

Markusen J. and Venables A. (1999). Foreign Direct Investment as a Catalyst for Industrial Development. *European Economic Review*. 43, 335-356.

Pradhan, R. P. (2011). The effect of FDI *International Journal of Green Economics*. 5, 306-320.

Rodrik, D., Rodriguez, F. (2000). Trade Policy and Economic Growth: A Skeptic's guide to the Cross-National Evidence. *Macroeconomics Annual* 2000, MIT Press, Boston.

Schiff M. and Winters A. L. (2003). Regional Integration and Development. Washington D.C. The International Bank for Reconstruction and Development/ World Bank and Oxford University Press.

Silaghi, M. I. (2009). Exports-economic growth. *Romanian Journal of Economic Forecasting*. 10, 105-117.

Siliverstovs. B., Herzer. D, (2005). Manufacturing exports, mining exports and growth: cointegration and causality analysis for Chile (1960-2001). Ibero America Institute for Econ. Research (IAI) Discussion Papers 104, Ibero-America Institute for Economic Research.

Singh, T. (2010). Does international trade. *World Economy* 33, 1517-1564.

Tokarick, S. (2003). Measuring the impact of distortions in agricultural trade in partial and general equilibrium, IMF Working Paper, WP/03/110.

Venables, A. J (2000). International trade; regional economic integration. Prepared for the 'International encyclopedia of social and Behavioral Sciences'; LSE and CEPR.

Viner, J. (1950). The Customs Union Issue. Carnegie Endowment for International Peace. New York.

Zu, K. K., Corpus, C. (2000). The effects of International Economic Integration on FDI Determinants: Japanese and US FDI in Europe. Texas, USA.

In: Economic Growth in the 21st Century
Editor: Tara Abrahams
ISBN: 978-1-63321-623-5

Chapter 7

THE INCLUSIVE GROWTH IMPACTS OF FISCAL POLICIES IN DEVELOPING ASIA

***Almas Heshmati*[1,2,*] *and Jungsuk Kim*[3,†]**
[1]Jönköping University, Jönköping, Sweden
[2]Department of Economics, Sogang University,
Mapo-gu, Seoul, Korea
[3]Institute of International and Area Studies, Sogang University,
Mapo-gu, Seoul, Korea

June 18, 2014

ABSTRACT

A growing concern on widening income gap between the rich and the poor have resulted in an increasing volumes of research focusing on the nexus between equity and efficient growth. Developed countries have experienced the critical challenges and trade-off between their generous welfare provisions and economic growth. Developing countries in Asia are in the process of shifting their policy direction toward more inclusive growth. This has stimulated the need to better formulate policies of fostering inclusive growth. Asian governments used many forms of fiscal policy to mitigate income gaps because they will substantially undermine the economic growth if left unchecked. The objective of this study is to

---

* E-mail: heshmati@sogang.ac.kr.
† E-mail: jungsuk@sogang.ac.kr.

review the previous studies, particularly literatures related with inclusive growth of advanced economies, and to offer efficient policy options for Asian countries. In this study, policy measures are initiated which are based on experiences of advanced welfare economies. Lessons derived from them will be a meaningful guideline for Asian countries to achieve inclusive growth.

Keywords: Income inequality, inclusive growth, fiscal policy, developing Asia, advanced welfare Economies

1. INTRODUCTION

One of the nucleus macroeconomic objectives in recent decades has been the economic growth with promoting equity. The widening income gap between the rich and the poor has stimulated the need to understand the roots of inequality and poverty, and to construct policies that trim down poverty levels and narrow the income gaps. A series of fiscal policy designed to tackle the growing income inequality and poverty has been competitively introduced from countries at all stages of development and income. (ADB, 2014) These factors, without proper supervision, will eventually undermine the strength of the economies and cause an economic instability and possibly even social unrest (Stiglitz, 2012a). Depending on their economic growth pattern and fiscal constraints, each government can intervene and promote equity with a range of economic measures, mainly related to tax and benefit system. Unemployment plays a critical role in creating higher levels of inequality and poverty. In an attempt to overcome the threat that unemployment poses, governments have used remedies that foster employability such as stimulating aggregate demand through policies of monetary, fiscal and labor market intervention. Provision of re-training schemes and welfare-to-work schemes are the first-rate examples that would encourage active labor market participation.

The research on inequality, poverty and their link with economic growth is voluminous. Many suggests that economic growth itself reduces poverty while amplifies inequality in the initial developing stage. The negative or a rather slow economic growth in recent years has deteriorated the equity. This has called an increased interest in fiscal policy and its impact on the progressivity and distributive effects. Succeeding volumes of research on the issue of inclusive growth has been dynamically released especially issues of widened income gap between the high and low skilled. It does reflect a high demands from the public for equitable distribution of economic growth. In order to bridge the needs of economic growth, which is still the top priority of policy agenda in Asian economy and equitable sharing the fruits of economic growth, countries in this region need to learn from the previous experiences of advanced welfare economies, where our main focus and objective of this literature study are anchored with.

The rest of this study is organized as follows. In Section 2 we review the literature on income inequality, it determinants, inequality trend and fiscal policy instruments. Fiscal policy in both advanced and developing Asian countries are discussed in Sections 3 and 4. Section 5 is on poverty reduction, its relationship with economic growth, reductions trend, measurements and policy effects. The final section summarizes and provides policy implications of the results for developing Asia.

2. Income Inequality and its Determinants

A growing concern on widening income gap between the rich and the poor, the policy mismatch in tackling the relative poverty, and income inequality have invited volumes of studies from researchers, international and national organizations.

Estimation of income inequality is dependent on the indicators used for the estimation as well as the inclusion of other control variables to the model. Some studies present an alternative way to improve the analysis. Knight and Sabot (1983) proposed a way to quantify the effects between education and income gap. The effect of a rise in the number of highly educated workers on income inequality was attributed to the pure composition effect and the relative returns to education. Gottschalk and Huynh (2010) measured inequality and mobility based on self-reported earnings. They found clear links between measurement error and various measures of inequality and mobility. In order to figure out the primary cause of income inequality, one must not only be concerned with economic development over time but also changes in means and distribution of income (Gordon and Becker, 2008). Atkinson et al. (2011) asserts that the aggregate economic growth per capita and Gini indexes can be very sensitive to the inclusion of top incomes. According to the study of Wade (2004) who used China's income statistics, income inequality has been falling when measured with PPP, weighted by population and averaging Gini index. Nolan et al. (2011) found key issues of how best to approach the measurement of income and wage inequality. The estimated results of income inequality are varied by the selection of data and indicators.

According to Stiglitz (2012a), "Inequality undermines the strength of the economy and contributes to economic instability". In recent times its importance, especially after witnessing the Wall Street movement, inequality issue has fired countries to pay an immediate attention on addressing the problems and to prioritize it as an urgent policy agenda. In analysis of the determinant factors of income inequality, a larger part of the literature centered at earning inequality related to: skill-biased technical change (SBTC) and polarization, returns to education, globalization and financial market, labor market institutions, and inequality trend. Recently other factors have been added to this list, including immigration and finances. These measurements and the role of selected determinants are explained below.

The question if productivity determines the workers' pay has long been an important research subject in inequality literature. One of the predominant views on identifying the main causes of growing inequality are increased demand for high skilled workers. Technological progress will disproportionately benefit richer and better-educated population groups (ADB, 2014). Such argument has been challenged by several authors (Card and DiNardo, 2002: Piketty and Saez, 2001). Simultaneously, attention has sharply increased on the issue of the top income group's share on total income. (Bastagli et al., 2012). Gordon and Becker (2008) provide a survey of aspects of rising inequality by arguing that SBTC accounts for the major part of increased skewness of labor incomes at the top. Worker's jobs at the top and bottom income level are hardly outsourced while the works of middle income group can easier be substituted. Antonczyk et al. (2010) compare trends in wage inequality in the U.S. and Germany, find the two countries showed a high increase of wage inequality between 1979 and 2004. The interaction effect between the SBTC and institutional factors explains the dissimilar inequality trends across two countries. Atkinson (2007) suggests a new approach which can supplement evaluation of the race between technology and education. Overall, most of the studies suggest SBTC can explicate some portion of recent trends in growing income inequality.

Gregorio and Lee (2002) empirically test the relationship between education and income distribution. Findings revealed that educational factors have contributed to the equalization of income distribution. Chiswick (2003) reviews Jacob Mincer's (1974) contributions to the analyses of human capital, earnings and the distribution of incomes. For instance, Belzil (2007) performs estimation of a reduced-form dynamic model of the transition from one grade level to the next. Martins and Pereira (2004) propose possible education related explanations for the higher returns among high-income workers. Peñalosa (2010) found that growth reduce inequality of relative wages through the opportunity of education; whilst faster technology-driven growth results in greater earning inequality when technical change is skill-biased. The Lemieux (2006) study shows that for the U.S., returns to post-secondary education have increased over time, with sharp leap for higher-income workers than those of lower incomes. On the other hand, sstudies by Checchi (2000) Sylwester (2000), Willen et al. (2005) and Kenworthy and Smeeding (2013) provided a different perspective by showing that expenditure on education does not affect economic growth nor does it improve income inequality. Overall, a high fraction of literatures find that education is one of the crucial determinants of an individual's earning potential as well as an income-equalizing tool.

According to Gordon and Becker (2008), the economic growth from expansion of international trade is negative or less distributive because low-paid foreign workers do compete with domestic workers, and that greater import penetration has pushed wages downwards. Wade (2004) tested whether the neoliberal argument about the benign effects of globalization on growth, poverty and income distribution, can be empirically valid and the answer was no. Stockhammer (2013) studied the source of the substantial fall of wage shares. Globalization in production has showed extensive negative effects, even in developing economies. In a more recent study, Asteriou et al. (2014) show that financial globalization through FDI, has expanded inequality in the EU-27 since 1995. The Rada and Kiefle (2013) study confirmed that globalization has a negative effect on wage share. On the other hand, Agnello and Sousa (2012) showed that an increase in the degree of trade openness endorse greater equality. Stiglitz (2012b) argues that "uneven income distribution undermined U.S. household's consumption" and "the financial market failure was the main cause of the economic downturn". While Milanovic (2009) and Stockhammer (2013) claim that the roots of the recent crisis are due to the long-run structural changes in income distribution. Atkinson and Morelli (2011) found no clear links between increases in income inequality and systemic banking crises. Freeman (2010) advocated institutions and experts had failed to detect rising risk levels in the deregulated financial sector.

Willen et al. (2005) specifically focused on which type of labor market institutions affect inequality. The labor market components affect relative wages, however the overall impact remains equivocal. Lemieux (2007) discuss studies on labor market institutions whereby workers are paid for performance.

Checchi and Peñalosa (2008) using a panel data of OECD countries for the period 1960-2000 found the high degree of wage bargaining coordination under strong unionization increase income inequality. According to surveys conducted by Gordon and Becker (2008), quantitative evidence in the studies exhibits a rather small role for the decline in unionization. Sologon and O'Donoghue (2009) estimated the impact of labor market policies and institutional factors on earnings mobility. The relative high unemployment benefits would imply a relative low willingness to accept a lower paid job. Peñalosa (2010) found that strong labor market institutions not only reduce inequality but also increase employment and economic growth. Lee and Saez (2012) made a theoretical analysis of optimal minimum wage policy. Rada and Kiefle (2013) by examining the long run dynamics in income distribution in OECD found unionization to have a pro-labor effect. Kenworthy and Smeeding (2013) found that the minimum wage was allowed to fall in real terms. Several studies show that the high degree of wage bargaining coordination under strong unionization negatively affects inequality.

The evolution of income inequality over recent decades has been explored in several studies. Jäntti (1997) uses data from Luxembourg Income Study. Increases in labor earnings inequality has primarily caused an increase in household income inequality in some countries. Bowlus and Robin (2012) compared earnings inequality and mobility across several industrialized economies during the late 1990s. They found that earnings mobility and employment risk are positively correlated with base-year inequality. However, Gordon and Becker (2008) found no distinctive changes in labor's share of national income over the last two decades. Rada and Kiefle (2013) find that the long-run equilibrium has been deviating towards a lower wage share. Gottschalk et al. (2008) estimate the trend in the transitory variance of male earnings in the U.S. and find that changes over time are transitory variances. Antonczyk et al. (2010) compares trends in wage inequality in the U.S. and results showed a high degree of wage inequality increases. Peñalosa (2010) studied whether growth is in tandem with income inequality. Output growth is achieved as a consequence of increases in physical capital, human capital, employment or the level of technology, shaping the relationship between growth and inequality. Smeeding and Thompson (2010) using surveys of consumer finances data found that the impact of the great recession on inequality is ambiguous. Atkinson et al. (2011) found that most countries experienced plunge in top income shares in the first part of the 20th century. Osberg (2013) shows that that, increasing economic instability in Canada and the U.S. is an implication of increasing inequality. Stockhammer (2013) found that wage shares have fallen substantially over the past 25 years. Overall, the impact of the financial crisis on inequality is imprecise.

3. FISCAL POLICY IN ADVANCED ECONOMIES

Fiscal policy, i.e. direct income tax and transfers, exercised by advanced economies in general, have been proved to be distributive and progressive. Some studies have uncovered the fact that there is a positive relationship between fiscal consolidations and an increase in the income gap, which includes the European Monetary Union effect on income inequality. There are mixed views on the effect of fiscal policy on income inequality. This section reviews the various topics of income inequality, improved growth, financial consolidation and other effects of fiscal policies implemented by advanced economies.

Wolf and Zacharias (2007) assess the effects of U.S. government expenditures and taxation on household. They find that the overall income inequality declined significantly in line with net government expenditures. Alesina and Ardagna (2009) examined the cases of fiscal stimuli and fiscal adjustments in OECD countries. It concludes that fiscal adjustments based on spending cuts accompanied by tax cuts is the most successful form of policy adaption. Kitao (2010) tested whether temporary fiscal policy, tax-cut and rebate transfer, to stimulate economic activities can enhance an economic recovery. A reduction in income taxation stipulates an immediate incentive to work and save more, which in turn raises aggregate output and consumption. Peñalosa (2010) argues that fiscal policy can affect both economic growth and income distribution. Muinelo-Gallo and Roca-Sagalés (2011) examine the impact of different fiscal policy instruments on economic growth and income inequality of the 43 upper-middle and high-income countries. Increase in public investment is proved to reduce inequality without harming output while larger current expenditures and direct taxes diminish economic growth and reduce inequality. Muinelo-Gallo and Roca-Sagalés (2013) using high income OECD countries data found that distributive expenditures and direct taxes deteriorate GDP growth and net income inequality.

Bargain (2012) applied micro-simulations to quantify the relative effects of fiscal policy and checking the sensitivity of the policy effect. Silva et al. (2013) studied how large fiscal multipliers in Europe are for spending and revenue. The effectiveness of the tax multiplier is shown to be greater in recessions. Peñalosa and Orgiazzi (2013) using the Luxembourg Income Study data examine some of the forces that have driven changes in household income inequality. The study found that earnings distribution is one important driving force behind recent trends. As in Jäntti (1997), in some countries the contribution of self-employment income and increases in inequality in capital income account for a substantial fraction of the distributional changes. Thompson and Smeeding (2013) explore trends in inequality and poverty using market and after-tax and transfer income during and after the Great Recession. Using market income, inequality and poverty rose sharply between 2008 and 2010. In sum, government expenditures, when compared to taxes, yield greater inequality-reducing results. Spending cuts accompanied by tax cuts has been successful forms of policy to reducing inequality and facilitating GDP growth simultaneously.

In general, the increases in government revenue that occur as a result of economic growth allow the government to employ policies that promote more jobs and swell benefits in kinds. In this regard, fiscal consolidation can be rather regressive and less distributive. In a comprehensive study, Carre're and De Melo (2012) provided a cross country analysis of the correlation between fiscal policy and growth for 118 developing and 22 high income OECD countries. The study found that a growth event is more likely to occur when there is a fiscal event. The success of a growth-oriented fiscal expenditure plan differ across the population and depends on the country's institutional environment. Mertens and Ravn (2013) estimate the dynamic effects of changes in taxes in the U.S. by distinguishing between the effects of changes in personal and corporate income taxes. The result suggests different types of taxes should be distinguished when estimating their growth impacts. European Commission (2013) reported that fiscal devaluation has only a limited and short-lived expansionary effect on employment and GDP. Kuttner and Posen (2002) investigated the effectiveness of Japanese fiscal policy over the 1976-1999 period by analyzing real GDP, tax revenues and public expenditures. The expansionary fiscal policy, in form of tax cuts or increased public expenditure, does stimulate the economy substantially. Most increases in public debt were associated with declining tax revenues from the recession.

The effects of fiscal policy responses in 118 episodes of banking crisis in advanced and emerging market countries is examined by Baldacci et al. (2009). Timely countercyclical fiscal measures shorten the length of crisis episodes by stimulating aggregate demand. Devereux et al. (2013) studied how Pigouvian levies on bank liabilities associated with systemic risk have affected European banks capital structures. In a related study, Göndör and Nistor (2012) empirically studied the relationship between FDI and fiscal policy and found that fiscal policy affects the competition environment and is a crucial factor affecting FDI. Brzozowski and Gorzelak (2010) provided evidence on the impact of balanced budget and debt rules on the degree of fiscal policy volatility. They concluded that fiscal rules have a significant impact on fiscal policy volatility, but depending on the target, the rules will increase or decrease policy volatility. In sum, a sound fiscal policy stimulates both FDI and economic growth, which in turn indirectly improves income inequality. The increases in government revenues that occur as a result of economic growth allows the government to implement various public policies.

When introducing fiscal policy options, a key challenge is how to fiscal policy generates economy growth which in turn indirectly improves income inequality.

A central concern lies on how to leverage fiscal policy for more inclusive growth while minimizing fiscal constraint. Fiscal consolidation is creation of contraction strategies for minimizing deficits and preventing the accumulation of more public debt. Larch (2012) finds that to run deficits across the cycle, so called deficit bias, is predominantly attributed to the 'common pool' problem of overspending. Failing to address issues of income distribution may lead to unfavorable sustainability outcomes. OECD (2013) reported that fiscal consolidation would make governments' policy goals elsewhere more complicated. The report recommended an implementing of consolidation strategies that minimize these adverse side-effects.

Cottarelli and Jaramillo (2013) discussed the ongoing debate as to trade-off between fiscal policy and economic growth. Stabilizing public debt-to-GDP shows a penalizing effect to potential growth, which in turn would make it harder to sustain high public debt over the longer run. Bouvet (2010) used data from 197 European regions and found that while income inequality has been decreased within richer countries, convergence criteria of the single market exacerbated regional inequality in poorer EU countries. Bertola (2010) argues that Europe's EMU had a relatively petite impact on income inequality. In a recent study, Agnello and Sousa (2012) assess the impact of fiscal consolidation on income inequality. A panel analysis shows significant rises in income inequality during periods of fiscal consolidation. In addition, while fiscal policy driven by spending cuts seems to be detrimental for income distribution, tax hikes have an equalizing effect. The fiscal consolidation program shows quantitative impacts on income inequality. Overall, a number of studies addressed that the relationship between income distribution and fiscal performance is indirect. Income inequality rises during periods of fiscal consolidation.

There are other effects than inequality and growth from fiscal policy and its consolidation. Benetrix (2012) studied the impact of fiscal shocks in a panel of 11 EMU countries and provided empirical evidence on the effects of different types of spending on real wages. Atkinson and Leigh (2010) used taxation data to create the distribution of top incomes covering five Anglo-Saxon countries. They find that a reduction in the marginal tax rate on wage and investment incomes increase the share of the top percentile group. Peñalosa and Turnovsky (2011) examined how changes in tax policies affect the dynamics of distributions of wealth and income. Tax changes that affect working hours will affect wealth and income distributions, which in turn will either reinforce or offset the redistributive impact of taxes. Beetsma et al. (2013) studied budgetary planning and implementation in the Netherlands over the period 1958-2009. Kenworthy and Smeeding (2013) by analyzing U.S. data found that actual changes in tax or transfer policy did not raise inequality, government transfers and economic growth but merely kept up with inflation. Overall, some studies showed that tax changes or transfer based policies had little effect on stemming the rise in inequality. Government transfers only keep up with the level of inflation, rather than making any contribution to economic growth.

4. Fiscal Policies in Asia

Historically in Asia, the role of fiscal policy has been to facilitate economic growth by providing basic infrastructure while safeguarding macroeconomic stability (ADB, 2014). Jomo (2006) argues that both rapid growth and structural change have reduced poverty in a number of East Asian economies. Income inequality has been low in Korea and Taiwan, but has risen in recent years. Contrary to Kuznets' hypothesis, the cases of Korea and Taiwan suggest that lower inequality can be complementary to rapid growth in early stages. In Thailand, Malaysia and Indonesia, despite different policies, poverty has declined, while income inequality trends have varied. With openness and sustained rapid growth, China has experienced increased inequality despite considerable poverty reduction. These suggest that inequality tends to worsen with economic liberalization in the absence of redistribution. Using the Atkinson inequality measure of income distribution, Sato and Fukushige (2010) analyze the impact of China's income inequality on total income inequality among ASEAN countries. They found that China's domestic income inequality worsened income inequality among East Asian countries. The growth of China's per capita GDP had an equalizing effect on income distribution initially, but was reversed around 1997.

The ADB's (2012) research on financing Asian higher education for inclusive growth, have traditionally dominated debates on measures of financing higher education. Privatization of education is a pivotal component of the analysis. The study deliberately links the financing of higher education to questions of equity. Any higher education system that fails to cultivate the breadth of talent in society is sacrificing both quality and efficiency. The failure to make progress on inclusive growth is resulting in lower growth and higher inequalities. This issue is further emphasized in the ADB Outlook (2012) report suggesting that Asia's rapid growth in recent decades has led to a significant reduction in extreme poverty, but it has also been accompanied by rising inequality in many countries. Claus et al. (2012) assesses the impact of fiscal policies on income inequality in Asia. In order to discuss the role and effectiveness of taxation and government expenditure on income distribution, it conducts analysis over the 1970-2009 periods. Even though tax systems tend to be progressive, government expenditures are a more effective tool for redistributing income.

Rodgers and Zveglich (2012) examine gender inequality in labor markets in Asia and the Pacific, with a focus on the structural drivers of women's labor force participation. In Asia's lower-income countries, economic necessity is an important push factor behind women's employment. Kar and Saha (2012) conducted analysis on recent Latin America studies and argued that as the size of the informal economy grows, corruption is less harmful to inequality. They investigated if the Latin American environment applies to cases for developing countries in Asia where corruption, inequality and shadow economies are large. Although corruption increases inequality in the absence of the shadow economy, the income inequality tends to fall as there are larger shadow economies in South Asia. Balakrishnan et al. (2013) assesses how pro-poor and inclusive Asia's recent growth has been, and what factors have been driving these outcomes. It finds that while poverty has fallen across the region over the last two decades, inequality has increased. Compared to other regions and to Asia's own past, the recent period of growth has been both less inclusive and less pro-poor.

Yoshida et al. (2014) reviews different projection methods and estimates the global poverty rate. The study argues that accelerating growth is not enough and that sharing prosperity is essential in order to end extreme poverty in one generation. Cornia and Martorano (2013) focus on the income inequality changes that have taken place in a few representative developing regions during the last 30 years. While inequality rose in the majority of the countries in the 1980s and 1990s, the last decade was characterized by divided inequality trends. Tests conducted confirmed that a reduction in inequality levels is possible if appropriate macroeconomic, labor, fiscal and social policies are adopted by governments. Overall, in many Southeast Asian economies, market liberalization policies and sustained economic growth platforms have led to both declines in poverty levels and variations in inequality trends. For some countries increased inequality levels have been experienced despite considerable poverty reduction. Several studies showed that income inequality tends to worsen with economic liberalization, especially in the absence of effective provisions for redistribution systems.

5. Poverty Reductions Policies

The greater efforts and broad ranges of new policy measures, at the national and international levels, have led to success in lowering the global poverty rate. According to the UNDP (2013), the number of extreme poor has dropped by 650 million in the last three decades. However, human poverty is still prevalent in some parts of the world. During the processes of globalization and national developments, many still suffer extreme poverty. Along with income inequality, one of the major challenges that Asian countries are facing is the issue of poverty. Without properly addressing poverty issues, the region may encounter trouble in achieving its sustainable economic growth and developmental objectives. A large number of studies are reviewed here, which cover issues of ongoing debates on economic growth effects on poverty reduction, the correlation between income distribution and poverty, feasibility of policies implication on poverty reduction, and problems related to measurement and interpretation of the trend. There were neither solid results nor uniform views on the problem and trend while we found each of the studies substantial in their own rights.

Most poverty studies focused on linkage of economic growth and poverty reduction and income distribution. Those giving more weight to economic growth often emphasize the needs to give priority and to exercise the growth oriented policy. Others argued that policy should be designed aiming both economic growth and poverty reduction simultaneously. Each study has addressed its own insight in diagnosing the cause and problems with the reframing of growth patterns. Christiansen and Todo (2013) conducted an empirical on the relationship between economic growth rate and poverty reduction. The results show that migration out of agriculture into non-farm economy and secondary towns yield more inclusive growth patterns and reduce the poverty rate more rapidly than agglomeration in mega cities. In another study, Kurita and Kurosaki (2010) using household expenditure data, conducted an empirical analysis on the relationships among growth, poverty and inequality in Thailand and the Philippines. The result shows that inequality reduced the growth rate of per-capita consumption.

The empirical analysis of Dollar et al. (2013) which used the data from 118 countries over the last four decades, confirms that economic growth significantly reduces poverty. However, the authors are unable to draw a conclusion that any particular policies are more "pro-poor". Using data from nine Asian countries for the period 1985–2009, Perera and Lee (2013) examined the effects of economic growth and institutional quality on poverty reduction and income inequality. Empirical results show that economic growth has no significant effect on income inequality but leads to poverty reduction. Improved government stability, law and order had a positive impact on poverty reduction. The degree of corruption, accountability, and bureaucratic quality matter for reducing poverty and improving income distribution.

Klasen (2009) compared the level of poverty reduction in emerging countries 1980-2005 and found that absolute poverty is immediately reduced by any kind of income redistribution policies. The author argues that low initial inequality promotes subsequent growth. Rising inequality ultimately undermines economic growth. Policy makers should find a way to achieve growth without altering the inequality. Ravallion (2011) found Brazil, China, and India reducing poverty levels during reform periods, but the degrees and causes of such achievement varied across the countries. Montalvo and Ravallion (2010) using Chinese provincial panel data found that the huge reduction in China's poverty levels since 1980 was mainly driven by the rapid economic growth. While debates on how economic growth has effected poverty reduction in developing Asia, the distribution of income has not yet led to a concrete conclusion. Most studies agreed that "the quality of the growth does matter" which requires policy to be designed to accommodate both economic growth and poverty reduction simultaneously to pursue policy initiatives for inclusive growth.

Chandy et al. (2013) studied how future poverty trends may unfold over the coming year. They compared the base line scenario and their alternative scenario on the expected degree of extreme poverty elimination by 2030. Based on the level of progress achieved so far, they viewed that a similar range of progress can be achieved as long as there is equity growth. Sumner

(2010) argued that the global poverty problem has changed because most of the world's poor no longer live in low-income countries (LICs). Previously, poverty was viewed predominantly as an LIC issue; nowadays such simplistic classifications are misleading. According to Chen and Ravillion (2012) who used household survey data from 125 countries for the period of 1979-2011, despite progress has been uneven across the regions, the developing world has achieved a higher degree of decline both in absolute and relative poverty since the 1990s.

The OECD (2008) reported that income inequality of OECD countries has increased over the past two decades. No matter what kinds of measurement are implied, some countries are more unequal in their income distribution. There was also a widespread increase in poverty levels. Income poverty among the elderly has decreased while the contrary result holds for young adults and families with children. The OECD (2013) report compared the living standard of both poor and rich people. Countries with a wide income distribution (U.S.) would have lower living standards than those who live in countries with lower mean incomes but more narrow distributions (Sweden). On the other hand, the opposite trend was shown to be the case of rich people living in countries where mean incomes and distributions vary (Italy and Germany). Education and health are more equally distributed than income.

Alkire and Foster (2009) proposed a new methodology for measurement of multidimensional poverty. It can address various components of poverty, which have multiple domains and vary across people, time, and context. They suggested that each country's different stages of development should be taken into account when setting targets. Ravallion and Chen (2009) found that prevailing measures of relative poverty put an implausibly high weight on relative deprivation, such that measured poverty does not fall when all incomes grow at the same rate. This stems from the assumption that very poor people incur a negligible cost of social inclusion. Ortiz (2007) conducted research on global asymmetric trends in inequality and poverty. Ortiz also reviewed the prevailing debates concerning poverty, inequality and economic growth. Ortiz concludes that without properly addressing the long-term structural problems, neoliberal short-term policies cannot counter the decrease in welfare, low economic growth, unemployment and high public debt.

To gain experience from assessment of poverty reduction policy effects, we review a selection of studies investigating the fiscal and macroeconomic policies at the individual and groups of countries. Barrientos (2013) argued that although the figures of global poverty lines and poverty gaps have shown significant improvements since 1990, the type of poverty during this time has

been uneven across regions and countries. The dominant factor behind the reducing global poverty was mainly due to China effect. Maasoumi et al. (2013) conducted a stochastic dominance analysis to investigate the level of inequality that exists in China, and how relative welfare levels have changed over time and among population subgroups. The results show that continued improvements to the state of the Chinese welfare system during 2000 to 2009 were driven by a strong economic development and growth within the country.

Fasih (2012) researched the factors behind India's rising poverty rates despite of the sound economic growth in the period. New banking policy that allows more citizens to access bank credit was suggested for India. Weiss et al. (2003) argued that although microfinance has positive impact on poverty reduction, it will be source of potential risk for bank's liability and expose bank customers to a great risk. Grassmann (2011) studied both direct and adverse effects of food and fuel price increases in 2007-08 on five poor and five non-poor countries in central Asia. Limited coverage and funding decrease the poverty program effect. Morgan (2012) argues that Asian countries need to seek for new agenda for their economic growth other than export-led growth. The problems related with export driven growth should be rendered to achieve sustainable growth.

According to Cremin and Nakabugo (2012), social development and human development, especially progress towards universal education, made a significant contribution to achieving sustainable economic development. Education efforts for reducing illiteracy, health improvement, lower fertility, improved infant survival, higher labor productivity, and more rapid GDP growth are the major forces behind sustainable development. Tarabini and Jacovkis (2012) analyze the connections between education and poverty and how the poverty reduction has been consolidated and expanded. According to Cremin and Nakabugo (2012), provision of good education is essential to confine poverty. Among policy options of inclusive growth in developing Asia, ADB (2014) finds public spending on health, education, and direct transfers to be particularly successful measures in lessening an inequality.

The Ferreira et al. (2010) using Brazil's GDP data for a twenty-year period found service sector's growth more effective in poverty reduction than growth in the agricultural or industry sectors. Barrientos (2013) suggest providing direct transfers through cash and in kind are proven as the most significant antipoverty policy in developing countries. As for low and middle-income countries, direct transfers to households are most progressive. Caminada and Goudswaard's (2009) provide a descriptive analysis on the efficiency of social transfers for poverty reduction in the EU. A high degree of negative correlation between the level of social expenditure and poverty has been captured. Koch (2012) investigated how the EU development policy can properly accommodate the changes of the development landscape which varies in terms of geography of power, wealth and poverty.

Macroeconomic policy can contribute to rebalancing growth. Agénor (2004) studied the links between macroeconomic adjustment and poverty. Agénor found the relationship between growth rate and poverty to be asymmetric. Hong and Tang (2012) also examined the role of macroeconomic policies during the GDP recessions period and financial downturns of 21 developing Asian economies. When attempting to counteract a GDP recession, Asian economies tend to be more reliant on fiscal than monetary policies. Asian Governments expanded their spending during a recession while OECD economies tried to keep equilibrium between fiscal and monetary policies.

In general, the studies that examined poverty trends, showed evidence of a substantial degree of poverty reduction in terms of absolute poverty levels, but an increasing trend of uneven income distribution. Many studies suggest implementing more even distribution patterns can encourage domestic demand to foster growth through the increased consumption. In Asia, an increase in government spending and a reduction in interest rates during a recession period were progressive. In the case of OECD countries, only monetary policies acted as progressive when they recovered from a credit contraction.

Conclusion and Recommendations

Review of a series of articles on income inequality, poverty reduction and inclusive growth propose remedy measures where most views are centered at seeking the policy options of efficient growth in tandem with equitable distribution of growth. In advanced economies, the setback of high debts and mismatched skills of youth called for a need to integrate professional and academic education system WEF (2014). Both WEF (2014) and IMF (2013) suggest that securing the trust and support from the citizens through the implementation of transparent and reliable fiscal policy is a requisite to have a successful policy effect. A fair and sustainable tax and redistribution system are considered as fairly effective means of achieving economic growth, enhance social protection and alleviates poverty. EC (2013) and IMF (2013) further emphasized that, the political motives of targeting both short term achievements and an immediate public support, would impede the long term economic progress.

In an era of globalization, one country's decision to levy a higher tax rate on the wealth and capital assets, tax evasions, cross border asset transfers will be closely followed. Zucmzn (2013) shows that 8% of the global financial wealth of households is in tax heaven countries. In Göndör and Nistor (2012), the fierce competition amongst nations for inviting more FDI to their country by offering attractive tax packages and benefit schemes is conflicting with countries attempt to alleviate internal income disparity. IMF (2013) report states that, tax policy changes aimed at particular groups has no evident effect on scaling down income inequality, and its distribution effect of wealth is less clear. The effects of changes in personal and corporate income taxes show significant short-term output effects (Mertens and Ravn, 2013). The IMF (2013) report suggests that, personal income tax has larger multipliers effect than that of corporate income tax.

Taxation of the financial sector has attracted attention from academia and international institutions. The marginal tax on capital income is revealed as very progressive because the richer groups are imposed a higher tax rate. Discussion in EC (2013) shows that fiscal devaluation to remedy of economic downturn has a limited effect on structural reform. As evidenced in IMF (2013) and Eurostat (2013) reports, as to the fiscal consolidation effect, the effects of raised property taxes on wealth distribution has been mixed. Provision of direct transfers through cash and in kinds, are demonstrated as the most effective antipoverty policy, particularly in developing countries. Provision of an easy access to the financial market and an expansion of education opportunity to the poor, were recommended as useful poverty reduction measures. Although Caminada and Goudswaard's (2009) show a high degree of negative correlation between the levels of social expenditure and poverty reduction.

Policies adopted by the countries and their experience will be a good lesson for policy makers in achieving inclusive growth of their countries. While the global poverty line and poverty gap have reduced significantly since 1990, the countries' performance rate has been uneven. The studies here discussed economic and social policies toward the poverty reduction and proposed various measures to accomplish a more inclusive growth. Depending on each nation's circumstance, policy would have different effect thus solutions need to be tailored in accordance with individual country's status (ADB, 2014). Policy of quality growth which can smooth out growing unemployment rates and widening income gaps has been recommended by many studies. We find that the evidence-based policy planning and implication required to successfully target the inclusive growth.

REFERENCES

Agénor, P. R. (2004), "Macroeconomic Adjustment and the Poor: Analytical Issues and Cross-Country Evidence", *Journal of Economic Surveys,* 18(3), 351-408.

Agnello, L., Sousa, R. M. (2012), "How Does Fiscal Consolidation Impact on Income inequality?", *Review of Income and Wealth,* DOI: 10.1111/roiw.12004.

Alesina, A. F., Ardagna, S. (2009), "Large Changes in Fiscal Policy: Taxes versus Spending", NBER Working Paper Series 15438.

Alkire, S., Foster, J. (2009), "Counting and multidimensional poverty measurement", Oxford Poverty and Human Development Initiative, Working Paper No. 32.

Antonczyk, D., DeLeire, T., Fitzenberger, B. (2010), "Polarization and Rising Wage Inequality: Comparing the U.S. and Germany", IZA Discussion Paper No. 4842.

Asian Development Bank (ADB, 2012), "Counting the Cost, Financing Asian Higher Education for Inclusive Growth", ISBN 978-92-9092-580-4.

Asian Development Bank outlook (ADB Outlook, 2012), "Confronting Rising Inequality in Asia", ISBN 978-92-9092-607-8.

Asian Development Bank outlook (ADB Outlook, 2014), "fiscal policy for inclusive growth", ISBN 978-92-9254-453-9 (PDF)

Asteriou, D., Dimelis, S., Moudatsou, A. (2014), "Globalization and Income Inequality: A Panel Data Econometric Approach for the EU27 Countries", *Economic Modelling,* 36, 592–599.

Atkinson, A. (2007), "The distribution of earnings in OECD countries", *International Labour Review,* 146(1–2), 41-60.

Atkinson, A., Leigh, A. (2010), "The Distribution of Top Incomes in Five Anglo-Saxon Countries over the Twentieth Century", Australian National University Centre for Economic Policy Research Discussion Paper No. 640.

Atkinson, A., Piketty, T, and Saez, E. (2011), "Top Incomes in the Long Run of history", *Journal of Economic Literature,* 49(1), 3–71.

Atkinson, A., Morelli S. (2011), "Economic Crises and Inequality", UNDP, Research Paper 2011/6.

Balakrishnan,R., Steinberg C., Syed, M. (2013), "The Elusive Quest for Inclusive Growth: Growth, Poverty, and Inequality in Asia, Working Paper/13/152, Asia and Pacific Department of International Monetary Fund.

Baldacci, C., Gupta, S., Granados, C. M. (2009), "How Effective is Fiscal Policy Response in Systemic Banking Crises?" IMF Working Paper 09/160.

Bargain, O. (2012), "The Distributional Effects of Tax-benefit Policies under New Labour: A Decomposition Approach", *Oxford Bulletin of Economics and Statistics,* 74(6), 856-874.

Barrientos, A. (2013), "Inequality, Poverty, and Antipoverty Transfers", Background Research Paper for Post-2015 UN MDG Development Agenda.

Bastagli, F., Coady, D., Gupta1, S. (2012), "Income Inequality and Fiscal Policy", IMF Staff Discussion Note SDN/12/08.

Beetsma, R., Giuliodori, M., Walschot, M., Wierts, P. (2013), "Fifty years of fiscal planning and implementation in the Netherlands", *European Journal of Political Ec*onomy, 31, 119–138.

Belzil, C. (2007), "Testing the Specification of the Mincer Wage Equation", Institute for the Study of Labor (IZA) March 2007 Discussion Paper 2650.

Benetrix, A. S. (2012), "Fiscal Shocks and Real Wages" *International Journal of Finance and Economics,* 17, 203–220.

Bertola, G. (2010), Inequality, integration, and policy: issues and evidence from EMU.

Bouvet, F. (2010), "EMU and the dynamics of regional per capita income inequality in Europe", *Journal of Economic Inequality,* 8,323–344.

Bowlus, A. J., Robin, J.-M. (2012), An International Comparison of Lifetime Inequality: How Continental Europe Resembles North America", *Journal of the European Economic Association,* 10(6), 1236–1262.

Brzozowski M., Gorzelak, J. S. (2010), "The Impact of Fiscal Rules on Fiscal Policy Volatility", *Journal of Applied Economics,* 8(2), 205-231.

Caminada, K, Goudswaard, K. (2009), "Effectiveness of Poverty Reduction in the EU: A Descriptive Analysis", *Poverty and Public Policy,* 1(2), Article 5.

Card, D., DiNardo, J. E. (2002), "Skill-Biased Technological Change and Rising Wage Inequality: Some Problems and Puzzles", *Journal of Labor Economics,* 20(4), 733-783.

Carre`re, C., De Melo, J. (2012), "Fiscal Spending and Economic Growth: Some Stylized Facts", *World Development,* 40(9), 1750–1761.

Chandy, L., Ledlie, N., Penciakova, V. (2013), "The Final Countdown: Prospects for Ending Extreme Poverty by 2030", Policy Paper 2013-04, The Brookings Institution.

Checchi, D. (2000), "Does Educational Achievement Help to Explain Income Inequality? UNU World Institute For Development Economic Research (UNU/WIDER) Working Papers No. 208.

Checchi, D., Peñalosa, C. G. (2008), "Labour Market Institutions and Income Inequality', *Economic Policy,* 23(56), 601–649.

Chen, S., Ravallion, M. (2012). "More Relatively-Poor People in a Less Absolutely-Poor World." Policy Research Working Paper 6114, World Bank.

Chiswick, B. R. (2003), "Jacob Mincer, Experience and the Distribution of Earnings", Institute for the Study of Labor (IZA), DP No. 847.

Christiansen, L., Todo, Y. (2013), "Poverty Reduction during Rural-Urban Transformation-The Role of the Missing Middle", World Development, forthcoming.

Claus, I., Martinez-Vazquez, J., Vulovic, V. (2012), "Government Fiscal Policies and Redistribution in Asian Countries", ADB Working Paper Series No. 310.

Cornia, G. A., Martorano, B. (2013), "Development policies and income inequality in selected developing regions, 1980-2010", Working Paper N. 13/2013, University of Florence and Unicef-IRC.

Cottarelli, C., Jaramillo, L. (2013), "Walking Hand in Hand: Fiscal Policy and Growth in Advanced Economies", *Review of Economics and Institutions,* 4(2), Article 3.

Cremin, P., Nakabugo, M. G. (2012), "Education, development and poverty reduction: A literature critique", *International Journal of Educational Development,* 32, 499–506.

Devereux, M. P., Johannesen, N., Vella, J. (2013), "Can taxes tame the banks? Evidence from European bank levies", Working Paper of 69th Annual Conference of the International Institute of Public Finance (IIPF): 'The Role of the State in Growth and Development', 22/08/2013-25/08/2013, Taormina, Sicily.

Dollar, D., Kleineberg, T., Kraay (2013). "Growth Still is Good for the Poor." *Policy* Research Working Pape*r* 6568. World Bank.

European Commission (2013), "Study on the Impacts of Fiscal Devaluation", Working Paper No. 36.

Eurostat (2013), "Taxation Trends in the European Union: data For the EU Member States, Iceland and Norway Statistical Books.

Fasih, F. (2012), "Inclusive growth in India through Islamic banking", *Procedia - Social and Behavioral Sciences,* 37, 97–110.

Ferreira, F. H. G., Leite, P. G., Ravallion, M. (2010) "Poverty reduction without economic growth? Explaining Brazil's poverty dynamics, 1985–2004", *Journal of Development Economics,* 93, 20–36.

Freeman, R. B. (2010), "its financialization!", *International Labour Review,* 149(2), 163-183.

Grassmann, F. (2011), "Protecting Vulnerable Families in Central Asia: Poverty, Vulnerability and the Impact of the Economic Crisis", UNU-MERIT Working Papers.

Göndör, M. and Nistor, P. (2012), "Fiscal Policy and Foreign Direct Investment: Evidence from some Emerging EU Economies", *Procedia - Social and Behavioral Sciences,* 58, 1256–1266.

Gordon, R. J., Becker, I. D. (2008), "Controversies about the Rise of American Inequality: A Survey", NBER Working Paper Series. 13982.

Gottschalk, P., Huynh, M. (2010), "Are Earnings Inequality and Mobility Overstated? The Impact of Non-Classical Measurement Error". *The Review of Economics and Statistics,* 92(2), 302-315.

Gottschalk, P., McEntarfer, E., Moffitt, R. (2008), "Trends in the Transitory Variance of Male Earnings in the U.S., 1991-2003: Preliminary Evidence from LEHD data" the documents prepared for presentation at the meetings of the American Economic Association, San Francisco, January 2009.

Gregorio, J. D., Lee, J. W. (2002), "Education and income inequality: New evidence from cross-country data", *Review of Income and Wealth,* 48(3), 395-416.

Hong, K. S., Tang, H. C. (2012), "Crises in Asia: Recovery and policy responses", *Journal of Asian Economics,* 23, 654–668.

International Monetary Fund (IMF, 2013), "Fiscal Monitor", October 2013.

Jäntti, M. (1997), "Inequality in five countries in the 1980's: the role of demographic shifts, markets and government policies", London School of Economics and Political Science.

Jomo K. S. (2006), "Growth with Equity in East Asia?", Department of Economic and Social Affairs (DESA) Working Paper No. 33, United Nations.

Kar, S., Saha, S. (2012), "Corruption, Shadow Economy and Income Inequality: Evidence from Asia", IZA Discussion Paper No. 7106.

Kenworthy, L., Smeeding T. (2013), "Growing Inequalities and their Impacts in the United States", GINI Country Report *United States*, January 2013.

Kitao, S. (2010), "Short-run fiscal policy: Welfare, redistribution and aggregate effects in the short and long-run", *Journal of Economic Dynamics and Control,* 34, 2109–2125.

Klasen, K. (2009), "Inequality in Emerging Countries: Trends, Interpretations, and Implications for Development and Poverty Reduction", *Intereconomics,* November/December 2009.

Knight, J. H., Sabot, R. H. (1983), "Education expansion and the Kuznets effect", *The American Economic Review,* 73(5), 1132-1136.

Koch, S. (2012), "From Poverty Reduction to Mutual Interests? The debate on differentiation in EU development policy" Discussion Paper, DIE Research Project, "EU Development Policy to 2020".

Kurita, K., Kurosaki, T. (2010), "Dynamics of Growth, Poverty and Inequality: A Panel Analysis of Regional Data from Thailand and the Philippines", *Asian Economic Journal,* 25(1), 3–33.

Kuttner, K. N., Posen, A. S. (2002), "Fiscal Policy Effectiveness in Japan", *Journal of the Japanese and International Economies,* 16, 536–558.

Larch, M. (2012), "Fiscal Performance and Income Inequality: Are Unequal Societies More Deficit-Prone? Some Cross-Country Evidence", *KYKLOS* 65(1), 53–80.

Lee, D., Saez, E. (2012), "Optimal minimum wage policy in competitive labor markets", *Journal of Public Economics,* 96, 739–749.

Lemieux, T. (2006), "Postsecondary Education and Increasing Wage Inequality", *American Economic Review,* 96(2), 195-199.

Lemieux, T. (2007), "The Changing Nature of Wage Inequality", NBER Working Paper Series, 13523.

Maasoumi, E., S. U., B., Heshmati, A. (2013), "Analysis of Stochastic Dominance ranking of Chinese Income Distributions by Household Attributes", Unpublished, March 20, 2013.

Martins, P. S., Pereira, P. T. (2004), "Does education reduce wage inequality? Quantile regression evidence from 16 countries", *Labour Economics,* 11, 355–371.

Mertens, K., Ravn, M. O. (2013), "The Dynamic Effects of Personal and Corporate Income Taxes in the United States," *American Economic Review,* 103(4), 1212–1247.

Milanovic, B. (2009), "Global Inequality Recalculated the Effect of New 2005 PPP Estimates on Global Inequality", World Bank Development Research Group, Poverty and Inequality Team, September 2009, Policy Research Working Paper No. 5061.

Montalvo, J. G., Ravallion, M. (2010), "The pattern of growth and poverty reduction in China", *Journal of Comparative Economics,* 38, 2–16.

Morgan, P. J. (2012), "The role of macroeconomic policy in rebalancing growth", *Journal of Asian Economics,* 23, 13–25.

Muinelo-Gallo, L., Roca-Sagalés, O. (2011), "Economic Growth and Inequality: The Role of Fiscal Policies", *Australian Economic Papers,* 50(2-3), 74-97.

Muinelo-Gallo, L., Roca-Sagalés, O. (2013),' Joint Determinants of Fiscal Policy, Income Inequality and Economic Growth", *Economic Modelling,* 30, 814–824.

Nolan, B., Marx I., Salverda, W. (2011), "Comparable Indicators of Inequality across Countries", *Growing Inequalities' Impacts,* Gini Discussion Paper 9, March 2011.

Organisation for Economic Co-operation and Development (OECD, 2008), "Growing Unequal? Income Distribution and Poverty in OECD Countries".

Organisation for Economic Co-operation and Development (OECD, 2013), "Choosing Fiscal Consolidation Instruments Compatible with Growth and Equity," Economic Policy Papers No. 07.

Ortiz, I. (2007), "Poverty Reduction", MPRA Paper No. 31961.

Osberg, L. (2013), "Instability implications of increasing inequality: Evidence from North America", *Economic Modelling,* 35, 918–930.

Peñalosa, C. G. (2010), "Income distribution, economic growth and European integration", *Journal of Economic Inequality,* 8, 277–292.

Peñalosa, C. G., Orgiazzi, E. (2013), "Factor Components of Inequality: A Cross-Country Study", *Review of Income and Wealth,* 59(4), 689-728.

Peñalosa, C. G., Turnovsky, S. J. (2011), "Taxation and Income Distribution Dynamics in a Neoclassical Growth Model", *Journal of Money, Credit and Banking,* 43(8), 1543-1577.

Perera, L. D. H., Lee, G. H. Y. (2013), "Have economic growth and institutional quality contributed to poverty and inequality reduction in Asia?", *Journal of Asian Economics,* 27, 71–86.

Piketty, T., Saez, E. (2001), "Income Inequality in the United States, 1913-1998", NBER Working Paper 8467.

Policy brief (2008), "Escaping chronic poverty through economic growth", Policy Brief, No. 8 July 2008, Chronic Poverty Research Centre.

Rada, C., Kiefler, D. (2013), "A note on the wage share in OECD countries: Is there a race to the bottom?", Working Paper 2013-13, Department of Economics, University of Utah.

Ravallion, M., Chen, S. (2009), "Weakly Relative Poverty Policy", Research Working Paper 4844, World Bank, Development Research Group.

Ravallion, M. (2010), "A Comparative Perspective on Poverty Reduction in Brazil, China, and India", *World Bank Research Observer,* 26(1), 71-104.

Rodgers, Y. M., Zveglich, Jr., J.E. (2012), Inclusive Growth and Gender Inequality in Asia's Labor Markets, ADB Economics Working Paper Series, No. 321.

Sato S., Fukushige, M. (2010), "The Chinese Economy and Income Inequality among East Asia," Discussion Papers in Economics and Business 10-06.

Silva, R., Carvalho, V. M., Ribeiro, A. P. (2013), "How Large are Fiscal Multipliers? A Panel-Data VAR Approach for the Euro Area", FEP Working Papers, No. 500 August 2013.

Smeeding. T. M., Thompson, J. P. (2010), "Recent Trends in the Distribution of Income: Labor, Wealth and More Complete Measures of Well Being", Political Economy Research Institute (PERI), University of Massachusetts Amherst.

Sologon, D. M., O'Donoghue, C. (2009), "Equalizing or Disequalizing Lifetime Earnings Differentials? Earnings Mobility in EU: 1994-2001", *SOEP* No 251.

Stiglitz, J. E. (2012a) "The Price of Inequality", Article, 37(11), NEWS and Ideas for the Columbia Community, June 21, 2012.

Stiglitz, J. E. (2012b), The Price of Inequality, W. W. Norton and Company New York, London.

Stockhammer, E. (2013), "Why have wage shares fallen?: "A panel analysis of the determinants of functional income distribution", ILO, Conditions of Work and Employment Series No. 35.

Sumner, A. (2010), "Global Poverty and the New Bottom Billion: What if three-quarters of the World's Poor Live in Middle-income Countries?", Brighton IDS (Institute of Development Studies), Working Paper 349.

Sylwester, K. (2000), "Income inequality, education expenditures, and growth", *Journal of Development Economics,* 63, 379–398.

Tarabini, A., Jacovkis, J. (2012), "The Poverty Reduction Strategy Papers: An analysis of a hegemonic link between education and poverty", *International Journal of Educational Development*, 32, 507–516.

Thompson, J. P., Smeeding, T. M. (2013), "Inequality and Poverty in the United States: the Aftermath of the Great Recession", Finance and Economics Discussion Series Divisions of Research and Statistics and Monetary Affairs Federal Reserve Board, Washington, D.C.

United Nations (UN, 2013), "The Twin Challenges of Reducing Poverty and Creating Employment", United Nations publication, ST/ESA/342.

United Nations Development Programme (UNDP, 2013), "Fast Fact- Poverty Reduction and UNDP" International Policy Centre for Inclusive Growth, Poverty Practice, Bureau for Development Policy.

Wade, R. H. (2004), "Is Globalization Reducing Poverty and Inequality?" *World Development,* 32(4), 567–589.

Weiss, J., Montgomery, H., Elvira, K. (2003), "Micro finance and poverty reduction in Asia: what is the evidence?", ADB Institute Research Paper Series No. 53.

Willen, P., Shapiro, J., Hendel, I. (2005), "Educational opportunity and income Inequality", *Journal of Public Economics,* 89, 841–870.

Wolf, E. N., Zacharias, A. (2007), "The Distributional Consequences of Government Spending and Taxation in the U.S., 1989 and 2000", *Review of Income and Wealth,* 53(4), 692-715.

World Economic Forum (2014), "Global Risks 2014, Ninth Edition".

Yoshida, N., Uematsu, H., Sobrado, C. E. (2014), "Is Extreme Poverty Going to End? An Analytical Framework to Evaluate Progress in Ending Extreme Poverty", Policy Research Working Paper 6740, World Bank Poverty Reduction and Equity Unit.

Zucman, G. (2013), "The Missing Wealth of Nations: Are Europe and the U.S. Net Debtors or Net Creditors?", *Quarterly Journal of Economics,* 128(3), 1321–64.

Index

C

D

E

F

G

H

N

O

N

O

P

Q

R

S

W

Y

Z